Hiller

arthellweg ^verlag

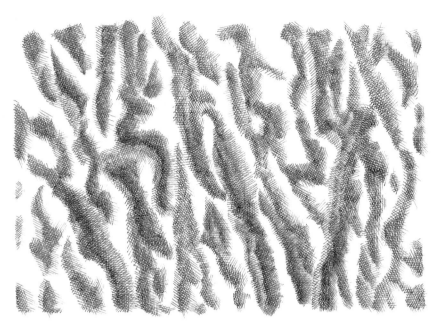

Frühe Studie auf Papier/*Early sketch on paper*

Nicht jeder
Vorwort

ist ein so verrückter Kerl wie Fitzcarraldo. Er lässt ein komplettes Dampfschiff über einen Berg im brasilianischen Urwald schaffen, nur um mit dem lukrativen Kautschukhandel ein Opernhaus errichten zu können. Unvergessen sein unglaubliches Lachen, als endlich die Arie des von ihm vergötterten Enrico Caruso erklingt, obwohl sein Unternehmen letztlich fehlgeschlagen ist. Ein beglückenderes Gesicht als das des Schauspielers Klaus Kinski kennt die Filmgeschichte nicht. Fitzcarraldo ist zwar eine Filmfigur, doch dessen Schöpfer hat tatsächlich ein komplettes Dampfschiff über einen Berg im brasilianischen Urwald schaffen lassen, nur um einen grandiosen Film zu realisieren. Einen verrückten Kerl nennt der eine Generation jüngere amerikanische Fotograf Ryan McGinley den deutschen Filmkünstler Werner Herzog zu Recht, dem es immer wichtig war zu vergegenwärtigen, dass Kunst eine physiologische Sache ist und nicht nur eine Veranstaltung des Als-ob (irgendetwas so wäre, wie es dargestellt wird).

Ein solch verrückter Kerl muss auch der Maler Joachim Hiller sein. Denn als sich das in der westlichen Hemisphäre von allen möglichen Seiten unentwegt erneuerte Versprechen auf ein besseres Leben endlich in der westdeutschen Nachkriegsgesellschaft recht irdisch zu erfüllen schien, stieg er aus. Er gab einen Beruf auf, dessen Aufgabe es war, mit schönen Worten und nicht minder schönen Bildern das anzupreisen, womit das ersehnte Paradies ausgestaltet werden sollte, um es zu möblieren: mit den schillernden Objekten des Konsums, die mehr und mehr verlangen. Ein anscheinend glückliches Leben, das mühelos zu erreichen wäre, wenn die elementaren Ansprüche des Daseins unter den Scheinbefriedigungen des Als-ob verschwänden.

Aus den ihm verfügbaren Inspirationsquellen in Natur und Kultur hat Hiller über Jahrzehnte im bewährten Verfahren von „trial and error" eine eigenständige und prägnante künstlerische Sprache entwickelt.

Ein drei Monate währender Urlaub auf einer dalmatinischen Insel bescherte dem Werbegrafiker Joachim Hiller sein Damaskus. Noch heute, sagt seine Frau Ingetraud, könne sie jeden vor die Felsen führen, die er damals mit unheimlicher Akribie und Intensität zu zeichnen begann. Der Wendepunkt in seinem Leben: Von jetzt an wandte er sich ausschließlich der Malerei zu, einem Metier, das nach Maßgabe der Moderne Erfüllung in sich selbst findet.

Nebenher gemalt hatte der 1933 geborene Hiller, der in Berlin ein kunstgewerbliches Studium absolviert hatte, schon während seiner Zeit als erfolgreicher Artdirector. Aber jetzt erst wurde ihm bewusst, dass Malen keine Nebenbeschäftigung sein konnte, wollte man sich nicht wiederum in den Netzen des Als-ob der Kunst verfangen. Ein glücklicher Umstand kam ihm dabei zupass. Zwischen seiner künstlerischen Inspirationsquelle, der Natur in ihren vielfältigen und sich beständig verändernden Erscheinungsformen, und dem erwählten Medium seiner Kunst, der Malerei, entfaltet sich eine Fülle von Bezügen und Übereinstimmungen. Das Werden und das Machen, das Veränderliche und das Verwandeln von Materie in Form, der physisch-sinnliche Aspekt – der in Kunstkritik und Kunstgeschichte gern vernachlässigt wird –, das Faktische und das Illusionäre stehen in einem wechselseitigen Verhältnis zueinander. Und je verwirrender die täuschende Welt der Bilder dank der verführerischen Kraft der Massenmedien die Dinge selbst überlagerte, das Als-ob „the real thing" ersetzte, das Gesehene über das Erfahrbare triumphierte, die Rede über die Tat, desto stärker wurde ihm die Notwendigkeit, eine Begegnung mit dem Elementaren zu suchen, mit jenem Moment des Handelns, der Simultanität von Ergreifen und Begreifen verkörpert. Malerei ist so gesehen das vielleicht wichtigste Medium in der Kunst der Mediengesellschaft.

Vieles hat den Entschluss Joachim Hillers natürlich vorbereitet, unbewusst zum Teil, aber zunehmend auch abgestoßen von den Gaukelkünsten seines beruflichen Umfelds. Die entbehrungsreichen Nachkriegsjahre mit ihrem Hunger nach Kunst und Kultur und dem verbreiteten Bedürfnis nach Orientierung waren vorüber, die elementaren Lebensbedürfnisse gestillt, das Verlangen nach Ablenkung und Unterhaltung stieg in dem Maße, wie im Kielwasser des Koreakriegs die Margen des Sozialprodukts im sogenannten Wirtschaftswunderland emporschnellten und die Menschen, getrieben vom sich ausbreitenden Wohlstand, die Flucht aus der Realität übten. Unter den kritischen Geistern der Kriegs- und Nachkriegsgeneration häuften sich schon die Proteste gegen die geschliffenen Leitbilder einer Gesellschaft, die im Taumel des Konsums alles, was nicht in ihr Bild passte, verleugnete und verdrängte: politisch, sozial und kulturell – vor allem ihre horrende Leibfeindlichkeit. Deren Ursachen lagen zwar auf der Hand, wurden aber zugleich strikt ausgeblendet. Als eine aseptische, sexfreie Zeit bleiben die fünfziger Jahre den damals Heranwachsenden in Erinnerung.

Malerei hingegen ist eine körperliche Tätigkeit, ein handgreifliches Handeln in und mit Materie, ein Prozess des aktiven Verwandelns und Anverwandelns, des Schichtens und Abtragens, des Formens und Verformens, des Gelingens und Misslingens, des beständigen Risikos. Joachim Hiller vollzieht dieses Handeln mit seinem ganzen Körper und nicht nur mit den Händen, indem er die Malfläche nicht auf eine Staffelei platziert, sondern ebenerdig auf den Fußboden, und die Leinwand als Feld der Entscheidungen und des Handelns betrachtet. Als er seine Entscheidung für die Malerei traf, war das Votum nicht gleichbedeutend mit einer Entscheidung für die Kunst, im Gegenteil; jedenfalls nicht im Sinne des Systems Kunst und des Kunstbetriebs mit seinen Moden, Zwängen und Abhängigkeiten sowie dem unvermeidlichen Hang zum Markenzeichen. Vermutlich wäre er auch vom Regen in die Traufe geraten. „Sie können", sagte Kollege Georg Baselitz, „in Deutschland keine seriöse Karriere im System machen, sondern nur eine Außenseiterkarriere. Sie können sich darin nicht frei entfalten."

Nein, wie Fitzcarraldo schuf Hiller sich ein Fundament, abseits der etablierten Kunstszene und unbeeindruckt von ihren Diskursen und Kapriolen. Er eignete sich in pragmatischem Zugriff die Technik des Malens an, experimentierte, scheiterte und reüssierte, setzte von Neuem an, scheiterte und reüssierte abermals, während sich gleichzeitig in der westlichen Gesellschaft ein umfassender Wandel im Sozialtypus abzeichnete: Vom Menschen, der sein Verhalten einem inneren Kompass unterordnet, zum Menschen, der mit ausgefahrenen Antennen sein Verhalten an den Signalen der Außenwelt ausrichtet. Hiller brachte sein Schiff der Malerei über den Berg, um, zunächst einmal, für sich selber zum beglückenden Kunsterlebnis zu gelangen.

Die Kunst und ihre Geschichte lieferten ihm nicht weniger Anregungen als die Anschauung der Natur. Ich vermeide bewusst das Wort Einflüsse, weil es in puncto künstlerischer Arbeit statt Erfahrung Fremdbestimmung behauptet, statt souveräner Durchdringung hirnlose Kopie. Aus den ihm verfügbaren Inspirationsquellen in Natur und Kultur hat Hiller über Jahrzehnte im bewährten Verfahren von „trial and error" eine eigenständige und prägnante künstlerische Sprache entwickelt. Ihre komplexen Verbindungen und Verzweigungen beschreibt und analysiert Peter Lodermeyer kompetent, subtil und einleuchtend. Erst nachdem der Künstler seine Sprache in der Malerei gefunden hat, hat sich Joachim Hiller entschlossen, sie an andere zu adressieren; wie Werner Herzog es mit seinem *Fitzcarraldo* getan hat. Die wichtigste Botschaft seiner Kunst ist gleichwohl: Sehen ist kein passiver Vollzug. Optisches Wahrnehmen ist ein physiologischer Akt und wer das nicht zu begreifen vermag, der (oder die) wird auch nie den Wunsch verspüren, die Oberfläche eines gemalten Bildes mit den Händen berühren zu wollen. In einer vollendeten Malerei schießt das Sehen in die Fingerspitzen.

Klaus Honnef
Bonn, Dezember 2008

From the sources of inspiration at his disposal in nature and culture, Hiller developed an individual and pithy artistic language over years of trial and error.

Foreword

Not everybody

is as crazy a guy as Fitzcarraldo. He transports an entire steamship across a mountain in the Brazilian jungle, only because the proceeds from the lucrative rubber trade have enabled him to set up an opera house there. Unforgettable, that incredibly free laugh of his, when the aria of Enrico Caruso he so worships finally resounds, although his undertaking has ultimately failed. A more joyous face than actor Klaus Kinski's at that moment cannot be found elsewhere in the history of film. Fitzcarraldo is only a film figure. But his creator really did transport an entire steamship over a mountain in the Brazilian jungle, merely for the sake of making this grandiose film happen. A crazy guy, this is what American photographer Ryan McGinley, younger by a generation, has justifiably called film artist Werner Herzog, the man for whom it was always important to instill in us that art is a physiological thing and not only an event of the "as-if" (as though something were like it is being portrayed).

The painter Joachim Hiller must surely also be such a crazy guy. For just when from all sides in the Western hemisphere, those constantly renewed promises of a better life were showing up and finally seemed to be coming true in West German postwar society rather mundanly, Hiller pulled back from society. He quit a profession whose task it was to show in nice words, and no less nice pictures, how the longed-for paradise could be furnished: with the glittering objects of consumerdom and their inherent demand for more and more. It was a seemingly happy life that could be effortlessly reached if the elementary demands of existence would only disappear among all the purported fulfillments and satisfactions of the as-if.

A vacation lasting three months on a Dalmatian island brought the graphic designer Joachim Hiller his inner Damascus. Even today, says his wife Ingetraud, she could lead anyone to the very cliffs he began to draw at the time with an unbelievable meticulousness and intensity. The turning point in his life: from now on he dedicated himself exclusively to painting, a genre, which according to the terms of the Modern finds fulfillment in itself. Hiller, born in 1933 and in possession of an arts-and-crafts degree from Berlin, had also painted on the side during the time he was a successful art director.

But now it became clear to him that painting could no longer be incidental in his life, if he did not in turn wish to be ensnared in the webs of the as-if of art. A fortunate circumstance came in handy for him. A multitude of references and accordances exist between his artistic source of inspiration, nature in its diverse and constantly changing forms of appearance, and the chosen medium of his art, painting. The process of becoming and making, the changeable and the changing of matter into form, the physical and sensual aspect we tend to neglect in art criticism and art history, and the factual and the illusionary all stand in reciprocal and interdependent relationships. And the more confusing the illusionist world of the pictures masked the things themselves owing to the seductive power of the mass media, the more the as-if replaced "the real thing", and what was seen triumphed over what was experienced, and speech prevailed over action, then the stronger the necessity became for him to seek an encounter with the elementary, that moment of action embodying the simultaneousness of touching and grasping. From this perspective, painting is perhaps the most important medium in the art of the media society.

There was, of course, a lot in advance that led up to Joachim Hiller's decision, part of it unconscious, but he was also increasingly repulsed by the showiness of his occupation. The lean postwar years with their hunger for art and culture and the widespread need for orientation were over, the elementary vital needs satisfied. The desire for diversion and entertainment grew in the wake of the Korean War proportionately to the extent the growth margins of the social product in the land of the so-called economic miracle soared, and people, driven by the spreading wealth and economic success, practiced escaping reality. Among the critical voices of the war and postwar generation, there were increased protests against the smooth models of a society that—driven by the blind rush of consumption—denied and suppressed everything that did not fit to its notions and standards; politically, socially, and culturally—above all, as shown by its horrendous phobia of the body. The causes were clear enough, but at the same time they were categorically ignored. People growing up then keep remembering the 1950s as an aseptic time, free of sex.

Painting, by contrast, is a physical activity, actively and concretely getting involved in and with matter, a process of actively transforming and assimilating, of layering and scraping off, of forming and deforming, of achieving and failing, of taking constant risks. Joachim Hiller accomplishes this action with his entire body, not just with his hands, because he does not place his surface to be painted on an easel, but on the ground, on the floor, viewing his canvas as a field of decisions and action. When he opted in favor of painting, this was not equivalent to a decision in favor of art; on the contrary, in any event it was not a decision in favor of the art system and art business with its fashions, constraints, and dependencies as well as the inevitable preference for the label. Probably he would have jumped out of the frying pan and into the fire. "You cannot," says his colleague Georg Baselitz, "have a serious career within the system in Germany, but rather only a career as an outsider. You cannot develop freely within."

No, like Fitzcarraldo, Hiller created a basis for himself, away from the established art scene and undeterred by its discourses and whims. Pragmatically he acquired the technique of painting, experimented, failed and succeeded, began again, failed and succeeded again while at the same time a comprehensive change in the social type was taking place in western society: from a person whose behavior was guided by an inner compass to a person with directional antennas, who took his or her signals from the outside world. Hiller brought his ship of painting across the mountain first and foremost to please himself for having achieved such an artistic feat.

Art and its history do not provide him with less stimuli than looking at nature. I consciously avoid using the term influences, because in matters of artistic work, it suggests determination from the outside instead of one's own experience, a brainless copy instead of sovereign internalization. From the sources of inspiration at his disposal in nature and culture, Hiller developed an individual and pithy artistic language over years of trial and error. Its complex connections and ramifications are competently described and analyzed by Peter Lodermeyer in a subtle, but clear way. Only after the artist found a language in painting did Joachim Hiller also decide to address it to others; like Werner Herzog did with his Fitzcarraldo. *Nevertheless, the most important message of his art is: seeing does not come about passively. Optical perception is a physiological act and the person who fails to understand this will also never feel the desire to touch the surface of a painted picture with his or her hands. If a painting is successful, the seeing process runs through the fingertips.*

Klaus Honnef
Bonn, December 2008

Frühe Studie auf Papier, *Early sketch on paper*

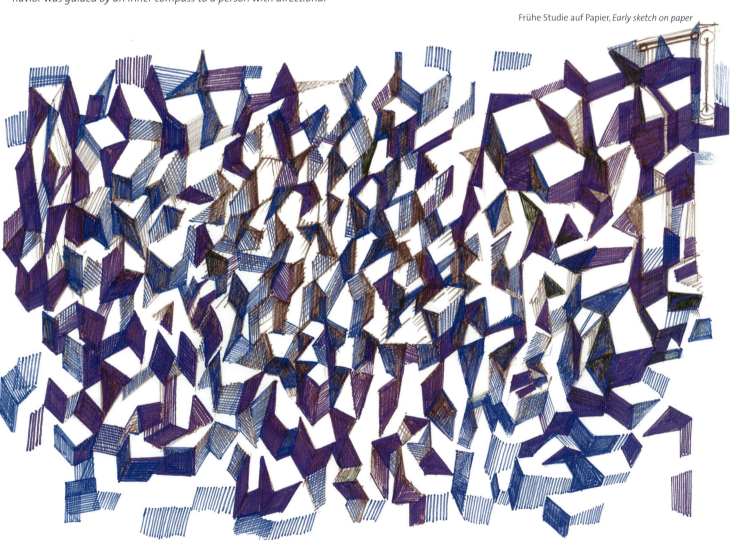

Acryl und Sand auf Leinwand/*Acrylics and sand on canvas*, 70 x 80 cm, 1967

Peter Lodermeyer
Hiller

Einleitung	8
Introduction	
Prägungen (1933–1949)	18
Formative Experiences (1933–1949)	
Ausbildung und Beruf (1949–1969)	27
Education and Profession (1949–1969)	
Die Begegnung mit Chargesheimer	30
The Encounter With Chargesheimer	
Die Anfänge eigenständiger Malerei (1966–1968)	34
The Beginnings of Independence in Painting (1966–1968)	
Die Suche nach der gültigen Form (1969–1970)	41
The Search for a Valid Form (1969–1970)	
Neue Wege der Malerei	47
New Paths of Painting	
Zerbrochenes Glas	52
Broken Glass	
„Malen wie die Natur"	60
"Painting Like Nature"	
Erosionen	68
Erosions	
Prozesse in Echtzeit – Die kinetischen Objekte	77
Processes in Real Time—The Kinetic Objects	
Malerei als Prozess	81
Painting as Process	
Exkurs: Hiller und das Informel – Einige kunsthistorische Überlegungen	92
Excursus: Hiller and Art Informel—A Few Art Historical Thoughts	
Ein Cézanne-Intermezzo	108
A Cézanne Intermezzo	
Exkus: Gedanken zum Quadrat	116
Excursus: Thoughts on The Square	
Gemalte Reliefs	128
Painted Reliefs	
Wasser und Wellen	144
Water and Waves	
Wolken	155
Clouds	
Wasser – Farbe	160
Water—Color	
Natur, Freiheit, Individualität	171
Nature, Freedom, Individuality	
Zum Schluss	185
At Last	

Einleitung

Gerade heute morgen ist mir beim Rasieren folgender Satz eingefallen, machen Sie damit, was Sie wollen: Die „objektive Wirklichkeit" sollte man wie ein Bettlaken sorgfältig zusammenfalten und in einem Wandschrank einschließen, ein für allemal ...
Pablo Picasso[1]

Kunst kann eine Haltung zur Welt aufzeigen, wenn sie mehr ist als marktorientiertes Produzieren oder eine höhere Form von Dekoration. Sie kann Möglichkeiten bereitstellen, die Wirklichkeit auf eine Weise wahrzunehmen, wie sie unser unbedachter Alltag nicht kennt. Das utopische Potenzial, das Kunst immer noch und immer wieder neu entfaltet, besteht darin, dass etwas, was keinen anderen Ort hat als „nur" ein Bild, so *real* und auf eine Art *wirklich* und *notwendig* erscheinen kann, dass es der sogenannten „objektiven" Wirklichkeit in nichts nachsteht. Dies gehört zu den faszinierendsten, vielleicht nie vollständig zu verstehenden Sinnpotenzialen der Kunst. Sie kann uns bewusst machen, dass wir ohnehin nie etwas anderes haben werden als *Bilder*, also Vorstellungen und Interpretationen von Wirklichkeit. Das künstlerische Werk von Joachim Hiller ist ein groß angelegter Versuch, sich ein Bild der Welt zu machen, d.h., sich dem Unverfügbaren unseres Weltbezugs zu nähern, für das wir, mangels adäquater Begriffe, kaum ein besseres Wort finden als: Natur. „Natur" steht für die Gesamtheit der Welt, das Seiende in all seiner Unbegreiflichkeit, für die ungeheure Komplexität an Formen und Vorgängen, die wir nicht selbst hervorgebracht haben.

[1] Brassaï, Gespräche mit Picasso, Reinbek bei Hamburg 1986, S. 109.

Introduction

Just this morning, while I was shaving,
this sentence came to me, and I'll give it to you:
"objective reality" must be carefully folded,
the way one folds a sheet and
locks it away in a closet once and for all.
Pablo Picasso[1]

Art, when it is more than mere market-oriented production or a higher form of decoration, can show us an attitude towards the world. It may present possibilities for perceiving realities otherwise unknown in our thoughtless everyday world. The utopian potential that art continues to unfold every day anew consists in the fact that something having no other place of existence than its "mere" picture can appear so real, *and in some way* true *and* necessary, *so that it is no way inferior compared to the so-called "objective" reality. This is one of art's most fascinating potentials for conveying meaning, one we will perhaps never fully understand. It can make us aware that, at any rate, we will never have anything but* pictures, *i.e. notions and interpretations of reality. The artistic work of Joachim Hiller is a large-scale attempt to obtain a picture of the world; that is, the artist approaches something unattainable in our idea of the world, for which, lacking an adequate concept or a better word, we must refer to as: nature. "Nature" stands for the sum total of the world, for what it is in all its incomprehensibility, for the unbelievable complexity of forms and processes we ourselves have not produced.*

[1] Brassaï, *Conversations with Picasso*, translated by Jane Marie Todd, Chicago, 2002, p. 197.

Öl auf Leinwand/*Oil on canvas*
95 x 75 cm, 1967 (Ausschnitt/*Detail*)

Öl auf Leinwand/*Oil on canvas*

75 x 95 cm, 1967

Wenn Hiller wiederholt äußerte, dass er nicht die Natur malen, sondern malen wolle „wie die Natur", so macht dies deutlich, dass er nicht die äußere, sichtbare Erscheinungswelt wiedergeben, sondern sich mit künstlerischen Mitteln formalen Strukturen nähern möchte, wie sie sich in der Natur finden. Genauer bedeutet dies, dass er Strukturen präsentiert, die sich naturhaft, d. h. selbsttätig ergeben aus den Materialien mit denen er umgeht und aus den Arbeitsprozessen, die er initiiert. Diese Art der Malerei hat, neben ihren unbestreitbaren sinnlichen Qualitäten, einen stark gedanklichen, um nicht zu sagen: philosophischen Gehalt. Sich diesem Gehalt anzunähern und die künstlerische wie inhaltliche Originalität des Werks von Joachim Hiller zumindest ansatzweise zu erschließen, ist die Aufgabe des vorliegenden Essays.

Zu dem Gesamtphänomen Hiller gehört ganz wesentlich auch seine ungewöhnliche Karriere. Hiller hat fast vier Jahrzehnte lang, von 1969 bis 2006, nur für sich selbst gearbeitet und seine Bilder und Reliefs in seinen Archivräumen vor den Augen der Mitwelt verborgen. Außer zwei Auftragsarbeiten und dem Kontakt zu einer kleinen Anzahl von Privatsammlern gab es keinerlei „Marktpräsenz" für ihn.

Es ist oft gesagt und beklagt worden, dass die Kunst in den letzten Jahrzehnten eine Phase der rigorosen Ökonomisierung durchgemacht habe. Da der Preis eines Kunstwerks sein einzig messbarer, also quantifizierbarer und objektiv vergleichbarer Parameter ist, hat sich als Maß für den Erfolg eines Künstlers immer mehr dessen Marktwert etabliert. Mit der „postmodernen" Relativierung aller Qualitätsmaßstäbe für die Kunst (die manchen Kuratoren und Theoretikern, aber auch vielen Künstlern, heute altmodisch und daher entbehrlich erscheinen), hat sich die Kunstkritik zunehmend in eine Kunstmarktberichterstattung verwandelt. Oft genug nach dem Vorbild der Sportnachrichten auf Zahlen und Rekorde bedacht, werden Hitlisten und Rangfolgen erstellt.

Dass Hiller nach mehr als 35 Jahren freiwilliger Selbstisolation mit einem riesigen, nach Inhalt und Umfang noch gar nicht umfassend gesichteten Werk an die Öffentlichkeit trat, ist ein Unikum zu einer Zeit, in der sich schon Akademiestudenten mit Karriereplanung und Marktanalyse beschäftigen, um sich frühzeitig eine Position im Kunstgeschehen zu sichern.

The fact that Hiller has repeatedly claimed he does not paint nature, but rather wants to paint "like nature" makes clear that he does not wish to reproduce the external, visible world of appearances, but rather by using artistic means, approach formal structures as they occur in nature. More precisely, this means that he presents structures which result from the materials he deals with, and from the work processes he initiates in a natural way, i.e. the structures come about on their own. In addition to its uncontested sensual qualities, this type of painting has a strongly intellectual, if not to say, philosophical content. To understand this content and the artistic as well as substantial originality of the work of Joachim Hiller, at least partially, is the purpose of this essay.

A deeply essential aspect of the overall phenomenon of Hiller is his unusual career. For nearly four decades, from 1969 to 2006, Hiller only worked for himself, hiding his pictures and reliefs away in his archives from the eyes of his fellow citizens. Except for two commissioned works and the contact to a small number of private collectors, he did not have any "market presence" at all. It has often been stated and lamented that in recent decades art has gone through a phase of rigorous economization. Since the price of a work of art is its only measurable, i.e. quantifiable and objectively comparable parameter, an artist's market value has increasingly established itself as the measure of his or her success. With the "postmodern" leveling of all measures of the quality of art (which seems old-fashioned and therefore, redundant today to some curators and theoreticians, but also to many artists), art criticism has increasingly metamorphosed into reporting about the art market. Often enough modeled after sports reporting and geared to numbers and records, hit-charts and rankings are established. That Hiller, after more than 35 years of self-willed isolation, has come public with a gigantic œuvre, to date yet unexamined in terms of contents and scope, is truly unique at a time when academy students are already thinking in terms of career planning and market analyzis in order to secure early a place for themselves on the art scene.

Man kann nur hoffen, dass die bittere Analyse des Kunstwissenschaftlers Beat Wyss eine Übertreibung zum Zweck der Verdeutlichung ist: „Die Studenten, die sich für Kunst entscheiden, tun dies in einer Gesellschaft, für die Autorennfahrer, Tennisspieler und der Skandaladel als Vorbilder durch die Klatschpresse geistern. […] Im Gegensatz zu allen bürgerlichen Erwerbsformen bietet das Künstlertum die Aussicht, sich aus dem Nichts in die Talkshows beamen zu können. Das Künstler-werden-Wollen ist der etwas anspruchsvollere Weg, dem sozialen Wunschtraum nachzugehen: Wie knacke ich den Jackpot? Die Kunstakademie gibt Nachhilfestunden für das Glück, vielleicht Millionär zu werden."[2]

Wie weltenfern stehen solche Sätze gegenüber der Realität des Kunststudenten Joachim Hiller zu Beginn der 50er-Jahre! Dass man mit Kunst Geld verdienen, geschweige denn wohlhabend werden könnte, lag damals jenseits des Vorstellbaren. Dass sich seine Kunst in irgendeiner Weise ökonomischen Erwartungen anpassen sollte, war und ist für Joachim Hiller eine völlig absurde Vorstellung. In dem gegenwärtigen Klima der vollständigen Vermengung von künstlerischen und ökonomischen Belangen stehen Werk und Karriere Joachim Hillers eher unzeitgemäß da. Was niemanden verdrießen muss – im Gegenteil: Spätestens seit Friedrich Nietzsche ist „Unzeitgemäßheit" kein Makel mehr: „unzeitgemäß – das heißt gegen die Zeit und dadurch auf die Zeit und hoffentlich zu Gunsten einer kommenden Zeit – zu wirken."[3]

Es ist ein Anliegen des Malers Joachim Hiller, mit seinen Bildern eine ganze Welt abzuschreiten, die Malerei als einen dynamischen Prozess der Welterfahrung zu betreiben, der von Neugier, Lebendigkeit, Sinnlichkeit, Experimentierlust, geistigem Abenteurertum und nicht zuletzt auch von Verspieltheit angetrieben ist. Eine solche Haltung kennt keine Halbheiten. Wo Kunst, mit einem Wort von Kandinsky gesagt, zu einer „inneren Notwendigkeit" wird[4], kann sie nicht mehr nur nebenbei, nicht als Zugabe zu einem Brotberuf ausgeübt werden. Also war es für Hiller unvermeidlich, 1969, im Alter von fast 36 Jahren, seinen Beruf als Grafiker und Artdirector aufzugeben und alles auf die Karte Malerei zu setzen. Ich kenne viele Künstlerinnen und Künstler, für die ein Leben ohne eine solche eigenartige Tätigkeit schlicht nicht vorstellbar ist, weshalb sie freiwillig auf alle Annehmlichkeiten eines bürgerlichen Berufs mit Monatslohn und Rentenversicherung verzichten. Aber Joachim Hiller ist insofern ein ganz rarer Fall, als er, nach einigen gescheiterten, da eher halbherzig betriebenen Versuchen, in den Kunstbetrieb hineinzukommen, sich ohne Wenn und Aber vollständig aus der Öffentlichkeit zurückgezogen und sich dazu entschlossen hat, ohne Galerievertretung, ohne jede Ausstellungsmöglichkeit, ja sogar ohne Austausch mit Kollegen zu arbeiten.

2 Beat Wyss, Zwischen Reliquienkult und Fondsmanagement, in: *Monopol. Magazin für Kunst und Leben*, Nr. 6/2008, Juni, S. 84–87, Zitat S. 84.
3 Friedrich Nietzsche, Unzeitgemäße Betrachtungen II. Vom Nutzen und Nachtheil der Historie für das Leben, in: *Nietzsche Werke. Kritische Gesamtausgabe*. Herausgegeben von Giorgio Colli und Mazzino Montinari, Bd. III, 1, Berlin/New York 1972, S. 239–330, Zitat S. 243.
4 Wassily Kandinsky, *Über das Geistige in der Kunst* [1917], Bern-Bümpliz, 4. Auflage, 1952, S. 68.

We can only hope that the bitter analyzis of art theorist Beat Wyss is an exaggeration meant to drive home the message: "The students, who decide to do art, do so in a society for which race car drivers, tennis players and members of the scandal-ridden high-society waft through the rainbow press as role models. […] Contrary to all we would consider a normal way to earn a living, being an artist bears a potential of beaming yourself from nothing straight into talk shows. Wanting to be an artist is a somewhat more demanding way of pursuing the social dream come true: how do I hit the jackpot? The art academy provides tutoring for how to maybe get lucky and become a millionaire."[2] These statements are a far cry from the reality of Joachim Hiller as an art student at the beginning of the 1950s! That you could earn money with art, let alone get rich, was at the time beyond anyone's comprehension. That his art should somehow adapt to economic expectations was and is for Joachim Hiller a completely absurd notion. In the present climate of the complete mixture of artistic and economic interests, the œuvre and the career of Joachim Hiller present themselves as rather out-of-season. And this is something which need not make anyone unhappy—quite the contrary: At the latest since Friedrich Nietzsche, "out-of-season" is no longer derogatory: ".... its inappropriateness for the times, that is, in opposition to the age, thus working on the age, and, we hope, for the benefit of a coming time."[3]

One of the intentions of Joachim Hiller as a painter is to move through an entire world with his pictures, propagating painting as a dynamic process of experiencing the world, driven by curiosity, liveliness, sensuality, a joy of experimentation, intellectual adventure, and last but not least, also by playfulness. Such an attitude is not halfhearted. Whenever art becomes, to put it in Kandinsky's words, an "inner necessity"[4] it can no longer be incidental, not be practiced in addition to gainful employment. Thus, it was inevitable for Hiller to give up his profession as a graphics designer and art director in 1969, at the age of nearly 36 years, and to put all of his eggs into one basket, painting. I know many artists who are simply unable to imagine a life without this peculiar activity, and it is the reason they willingly forego all the amenities of a normal job with the money coming in every month and pension insurance. But Joachim Hiller is an extremely rare case inasmuch as, failing several times in half-hearted attempts to enter the art business, he completely and unequivocally withdrew from the public, deciding to work as an artist, without being represented by a gallery, without any possibilities for exhibiting, and even without any exchange with colleagues.

2 Beat Wyss, Zwischen Reliquienkult und Fondsmanagement, in: *Monopol. Magazin für Kunst und Leben*, Nr. 6/2008, June, p. 84–87, quote p. 84, (translation, e.v.).
3 Friedrich Nietzsche, Unzeitgemäße Betrachtungen II. (Untimely Meditations) Vom Nutzen und Nachtheil der Historie für das Leben, in: *Nietzsche Werke. Kritische Gesamtausgabe*. Edited by Giorgio Colli and Mizzino Montinari, Vol. III, 1, Berlin/New York 1972, p. 239–330, quote p. 243.
4 Vassily Kandinsky, *Über das Geistige in der Kunst* [1917] Bern-Bümpliz, 4th edition, 1952, p. 68.

Öl auf Leinwand/*Oil on canvas*
95 x 75 cm, 1967 (Ausschnitt/*Detail*)

Öl auf Leinwand/*Oil on canvas*

70 x 90 cm, 1968

Ein solcher Rückzug für mehr als dreieinhalb Jahrzehnte war für den Maler unabdingbar. Ohne ihn hätte er nicht die nötige Konzentration auf sein Werk aufbringen können, ohne ihn hätte er nicht die Freiheit verspürt, die er für sein Werk unbedingt brauchte. „Freiheit" scheint ein merkwürdig anachronistischer Begriff in der heutigen Kunstwelt und ist doch unverzichtbar für das Verständnis des Werks von Joachim Hiller. Die Lebensdevise des Philosophen René Descartes „Bene vixit, bene qui latuit – Glücklich lebte, der sich gut verborgen hielt" könnte sehr gut auch das Motto des Malers Joachim Hiller sein. Sie war die Voraussetzung für das Entstehen dessen, was ich in einem früheren Text über ihn als die „Kunst des Eigensinns" bezeichnet habe.[5] Dass Hiller – wenn mir dieses Heidegger'sche Wortspiel erlaubt ist – endlich doch aus der Verborgenheit in die Unverborgenheit des Kunstbetriebs getreten ist, ist ein Glücksfall für das interessierte Publikum, dem sich nun das einzigartige Vergnügen bietet, sich in diesem labyrinthisch verzweigten künstlerischen Werk wie in einem plötzlich sich eröffnenden unbekannten Gelände zu bewegen. Ziel dieses Essays ist es, dem Betrachter einige Wege und Verbindungslinien zu erschließen, die sich über lange Zeiträume hinweg entwickelt haben. Es ist der Versuch, sich der technischen Vielfalt und Wandlungsfähigkeit einer Kunstauffassung zu nähern, die aus der genauen Aufmerksamkeit auf die Strukturbildung der Natur kommt.

Dieser Versuch hatte von Beginn seiner Niederschrift an den Untertitel „Werkbiografie", auch wenn dieser Begriff alles andere als eindeutig ist. Dass es eine Künstlerbiografie im klassischen Stil von „Leben und Werk" werden würde, verbot sich von selbst. Es wäre nicht im Sinne des Betreffenden bzw. in diesem Falle Betroffenen gewesen, es würde auch dem Werk Hillers nicht gerecht werden. Das Eigenartige ist, dass die biografischen Stationen, die es zu erwähnen gilt, alle zur *Vorgeschichte* seiner künstlerischen Tätigkeit gehören. Kindheit und Jugend während der Nazizeit, die Erfahrungen der Nachkriegsjahre, die frühe Aufnahme eines Kunststudiums, Ausbildung und Beruf, der sich allmählich vorbereitende Entschluss zum Künstlertum ... Das alles geht ganz sicher in das Werk mit ein. Doch sobald Hiller den Weg einer eigenständigen Künstlertätigkeit eingeschlagen hatte, traten alle erzählbaren und mitteilenswerten biografischen Fakten zurück. Sein Werk *ist* die Biografie des Künstlers Joachim Hiller.

This withdrawal for more than three and a half decades was vitally necessary for the painter. Without it he would not have been able to summon the concentration needed for his works, would not have felt the freedom he so absolutely needed for his work. "Freedom" seems to be a strangely anachronistic term in today's world of art, and yet it is important for the understanding of Joachim Hiller's work. The life motto of the philosopher René Descartes: "Bene vixit, bene qui latuit—he lived well, who kept himself well hidden" could also serve very well as the motto of the painter Joachim Hiller. It was the precondition for the birth of what I refer to in an earlier article about him as the "art of idiosyncrasy".[5] The fact that Hiller—allowing for one of Heidegger's plays on words—has, after all, finally emerged from his "hiddenness" to come into the "unhiddenness" of the art world, means good fortune for an interested audience now having the unique pleasure of moving through this labyrinth of art works as if through an unknown terrain which has suddenly opened up before us. This essay aims at identifying for the viewer a few paths and connecting lines, which have developed over the course of a long period of time. It is an attempt to approach the technical diversity and changeability of an art concept that derives from a precise observation of how nature forms its structures.

From the moment of its inception, this attempt bore the title "The Work as Biography", even though this concept is anything but clear. That it might evolve into an artist's biography in the classic sense of the "Life and Work" was out of the question from the onset. It would not have been in keeping with the will of the person concerned and neither would it have done justice to Hiller's works. The odd thing is that the biographical stations are all part of the prehistory of his work as an artist. His childhood and youth during the Nazi regime, the post-war experiences, taking up his studies of art in early years, his education and profession, gradually preparing for the decision to become an artist ... all of these have certainly entered his work. But as soon as Hiller embarked upon his path as an independent artist, any narrative facts seem to become secondary. His work is *the biography of the artist Joachim Hiller.*

---

5 Peter Lodermeyer, Die Kunst des Eigensinns, in: *Joachim Hiller. Die Kunst des Eigensinns.* Ausstellungskatalog 25 Jahre Walter Bischoff Galerie: Retrospektive Joachim Hiller, Soest 2008.

5 Peter Lodermeyer, The Art of Idiosyncrasy, in *Joachim Hiller. Die Kunst des Eigensinns.* Exhibition catalogue for the 25th anniversary of the Walter Bischoff Galerie: Joachim Hiller Retrospective, Soest 2008.

Wäre eine Werkbiografie also die „Biografie" des Werks? Ja und nein. Ja, weil es in diesem Essay hauptsächlich um das Werk und seine wichtigsten Intentionen geht. Nein, weil es sich nicht in der Form einer linearen Biografie beschreiben lässt. Hillers Werk kann unterteilt werden in die frühen Anfänge, in das zentrale Naturerlebnis an der dalmatinischen Küste 1969, in die folgenden etwa zehn Jahre der Suche nach den künstlerischen Techniken, die diesem Erlebnis angemessen waren, sowie in die Zeit der Entfaltung seines künstlerischen Ansatzes. Doch diese Einteilung ergibt nur scheinbar eine lineare Abfolge. Die synchrone Arbeit an verschiedenen Werkserien, das gleichzeitige Entwickeln unterschiedlichster Techniken, die aufeinander einwirken, einander durchdringen und beeinflussen, machen Hillers Werk eher zu einem Rhizom, einem vielfach verzweigten und verschlungenen Wurzelgeflecht. Dass dessen Darstellung hier grob vereinfacht wurde, um in griffige Kapitel eingeteilt zu werden, ist nur der Darstellung geschuldet und schien mir aus Gründen der besseren Lesbarkeit gerechtfertigt.

Schwerwiegender als diese Frage der Vereinfachung scheint mir das Problem der Datierung zu sein. Hiller hat, zum Schrecken des Kunsthistorikers, seine Werke mit ganz wenigen Ausnahmen undatiert gelassen. Dies ist offenbar ein Teil des Eigensinns dieses Künstlers. Ohne die Hilfe seiner Ehefrau Ingetraud Lehnen-Hiller wäre eine halbwegs zuverlässige Datierung der Arbeiten unmöglich oder bestenfalls ein Ratespiel gewesen. Anhand zahlreicher eindeutig datierbarer „Leitfossilien" hat sie die Entstehungsdaten der hier gezeigten Werke nach bestem Wissen und Gewissen zusammengestellt. Das wissenschaftlich korrekte Verfahren, die zweifelsfreien Daten zu markieren und die abgeleiteten Jahres-

So would a work biography thus mean the "biography" of the work? Yes and no. Yes, because this essay is mainly about the work and its most important intentions. No, because it is not possible to describe it in the form of a linear biography. Hiller's work may be divided into the early beginnings, the key experience of nature on the Dalmatian coast in 1969, the approximately ten years that followed while he was searching for artistic techniques suited to this experience, as well as the time when his artistic approach came into its own. But this division only provides a linear succession at first glance. The synchronous work on various series, the simultaneous development of the most highly varying techniques, which affect one another mutually, permeating and influencing one another at the same time, make Hiller's work rather a rhizome, the diversely branching and entwined wickerwork of roots. The fact that its portrayal has been greatly simplified here to divide the work into handy chapters is solely for reasons of facilitating the characterization and seemed legitimate to me since it makes the text more readable.

Of greater concern than this issue of simplification was the problem of dating the works. With only a few exceptions Hiller, to the horror of the art historian, has left his work undated. It is apparently a part of the idiosyncrasy of this artist. Without the help of his wife Ingetraud Lehnen-Hiller, it would have been impossible, or at best an educated guess, to create a halfway reliable dating of the works. Using numerous "fossils" that could clearly be dated, she has compiled the dates of the works shown here to the best of her knowledge and conviction. The scientifically correct procedure, namely to mark the dates that were certain and to cite the derived dates including the extent of their uncertainty did not appear to me justifiable within the framework of this text, which is a "mere" first

Öl auf Leinwand/*Oil on canvas*, 70 x 90 cm, 1967

zahlen samt dem Grad ihrer Unsicherheit zu benennen, schien mir im Rahmen des vorliegenden Textes, der „nur" ein erster umfassender Darstellungs- und Interpretationsanlauf sein möchte, nicht angezeigt. Diese Aufgabe muss der noch ausstehenden Arbeit der Erstellung eines Werkverzeichnisses überlassen bleiben.

Dass der hier vorliegende Versuch als eine erste Annäherung nur höchst vorläufig sein kann, ist dem Verfasser durchaus bewusst. Das kann angesichts der Faktenlage, einschließlich der Tatsache, dass noch längst nicht alle Arbeiten gesichtet sind, nicht anders sein. Doch dieser Mangel hat auch sehr erfreuliche Aspekte. Ich kann mich an keinen meiner zahlreichen Besuche im Atelier Joachim Hillers in Nierstein erinnern, bei dem er mir nicht seine neuesten Arbeiten gezeigt hätte. Oft waren sie noch in unfertigem Zustand auf der Staffelei und oft genug waren sie frappierend anders als die Werke, die ich bereits kannte. Ich habe keine Zweifel, dass in der Zeit der Niederschrift dieser Zeilen wieder neue, überraschende Arbeiten entstehen, die in dieser Dokumentation ohnehin nicht berücksichtigt werden können. Das Unfertige dieses Buches über Joachim Hiller ist also zugleich ein Versprechen für die Zukunft seines Werks.

Bonn, November 2008

comprehensive attempt at a portrayal as well as an interpretation. This task remains to be tackled in connection with the compilation of a work inventory, something still waiting to be carried out.

The author is wholly aware that this book is a first approach and as such, it is yet highly provisional. It cannot be regarded otherwise considering the state of the factual knowledge, including the fact that by far not all of the works have even been examined yet. But this lack also poses very pleasant aspects. I am unable to recall a single of my numerous visits to Joachim Hiller's studio in Nierstein, where he did not show me his latest works. Often they were there on the easel, unfinished, and often enough, they were astonishingly different than works I was already familiar with. I do not doubt for a moment that as I write these lines, new and surprising works are coming about, which anyway may not be accounted for in this documentation. What remains unfinished in this book about Joachim Hiller is thus at the same time a promise for the future of his art work.

Bonn, November 2008

Formative Experiences
(1933–1949)

It would be worth our while to systematically examine the extent that formative experiences of childhood have influenced artists in terms of obsessions with form. "You only ever portray what you experienced in childhood," admits German artist Anselm Kiefer, winner of the Peace Prize of the German Book Trade, in an interview in 2008: "There is nothing else. All of the material that you use, and this applies to writers as well, comes from childhood, when the brain was formed. Even if I took a trip to the moon, I would find analogies to my childhood there."[6] We know of similar statements made, for example, by British sculptor Henry Moore and American minimalist Carl Andre, who referred to his childhood experiences as "quarry of [his] art": "Henry Moore said that the work of art is to recover the vividness of our earliest experiences. Those earliest experiences are the quarry of my art."[7] Is it a coincidence that artists such as Moore and Andre who work in three dimensions and a painter such as Kiefer who greatly concerns himself with material consider the connection between childhood experience and artistic form so significant? Does the plastic process in "forming the brain" have an immediate effect upon the sculptural treatment of materials?

Such questions go beyond the expertise of an art historian, but they keep our imagination busy with respect to works such as those Joachim Hiller produces, who has been oscillating for decades between the poles of painting and relief, driven by a lasting fascination for the possibilities of form inherent to the materials themselves. The deep interest in the forms of nature and the structures they themselves form doubtlessly comes from far back in terms of his biography. Joachim Hiller remembers very vividly how, as a small boy, he was fascinated one day when he caught sight of cracks forming in mud as it dried, the network patterns forming on their own as the dampness and then heat made their impact on the dirt. Or, an even older memory that Hiller can put an exact date to, namely the end of August 1939: how astonished he was when he let sand trickle from his hand, shapes "like fir trees" formed, over and over again and all by themselves. Sand's tendencies to form shapes was to become a repeated theme decades later in the most varying contexts of his work as an artist. Equally vivid in his memory is how, when working

---

6 Anselm Kiefer, Ich arbeite am Mythos, Interview with G. Czöppan und S. Sattler, in: *Focus* No. 33, 11 August 2008, p. 56–59, quote p. 57.

7 Carl Andre, *Cuts: Texts 1959–2004*. With an introduction by James Meyer, Cambridge, MA 2005, p. 83.

Acryl und Sand auf Styropor/*Acrylics and sand on Styrofoam*

150 x 150 cm, 2008

Acryl auf Leinwand/*Acrylics on canvas*

100 x 100 cm, 1997

… der Blick über die Wasserfläche, die Reflexionen des Sonnenlichts, die schaukelnden Bootsfahrten –
diese Erinnerungen bildeten viel später ein starkes Motiv dafür, mehrere Serien über das Thema Wasser zu malen.

… with the view across the surface of the water, the reflections of the sunlight and the rocking boat trips—
these memories were later to provide a strong motif for doing several series on the theme of water.

selbst, Formen „wie Tannenbäume" ergaben. Die Form bildenden Eigenschaften von Sand wurden Jahrzehnte später in unterschiedlichsten Kontexten immer wieder Thema seiner künstlerischen Arbeit. Ebenso lebhaft ist Hiller in Erinnerung, wie er in der Malklasse während seines Studiums an der Berliner „Meisterschule für das Kunsthandwerk" beim freien figürlichen Malen nicht wie seine Kommilitonen Landschaften und Aktdarstellungen wählte, sondern die Herausforderung suchte, möglichst naturgetreu ein Stück Baumrinde wiederzugeben. Oder die Tage am Wannsee, der Blick über die Wasserfläche, die Reflexionen des Sonnenlichts, die schaukelnden Bootsfahrten – diese Erinnerungen bildeten viel später ein starkes Motiv dafür, mehrere Serien über das Thema Wasser zu malen.

Es wäre eine Frage an die Hirnforscher und Vertreter des neuen Fachs „Neuroästhetik", die sich in den letzten Jahrzehnten immer weiter auch in die klassischen Gebiete der Geisteswissenschaften vorgewagt haben – nicht selten mit dem deutlich erkennbaren Anspruch, eine neue Leitdisziplin zu etablieren –, warum die Formen der Natur überhaupt eine solch ästhetische Faszination auf uns ausüben. Ob Meereswellen, Schneekristalle, das Blattwerk von Bäumen, Holzmaserungen, geologische Verwerfungen oder was auch immer: Die Strukturenvielfalt der Natur fasziniert uns, oft genug finden wir diese Formen ästhetisch anziehend. Warum eigentlich? Die Standarderklärung von Evolutionsbiologen angesichts kultureller Phänomene, dass wir schätzen, was uns Überlebensvorteile verschafft, greift hier wohl kaum. Wäre es denkbar, dass wir sie schön finden, weil unser Denken und Empfinden auf ganz ähnlichen Strukturen beruht? Wer etwa die Mikroaufnahmen von Neuronen betrachtet, findet Strukturmerkmale, wie man sie auch in der Natur immer wieder sehen kann: komplexe, netzartig zusammenhängende Gebilde, Gespinste von Nervenverbindungen. Finden wir die Strukturen der Natur ästhetisch ansprechend, weil unser Gehirn, unsere Erkenntnisorgane selbst aus solchen Strukturen aufgebaut sind? Eine spekulative Frage, gewiss, aber eine Frage, die überaus anregend ist, wenn wir uns – immer im Blick auf das Werk von Joachim Hiller – die Frage stellen, wo und wie die Zusammenhänge, die Schnitt- und Verbindungsstellen zwischen Natur und Kunst zustande kommen. Ebenso spekulativ wie die generelle Frage nach den Gründen der ästhetischen Wirkung von Naturformen ist die spezielle, warum und wie Kindheitserfahrungen sich so dominant durchsetzen, dass sie sich zu einer lebenslangen Beschäftigung entwickeln können.

on free and figurative exercises during his painting class at the Berlin "Meisterschule für das Kunsthandwerk", he did not choose landscapes and nudes for his portrayals as his fellow students did, but opted for the challenge of depicting a piece of tree bark as true to nature as possible instead. Or there were the days at Lake Wannsee with the view across the surface of the water, the reflections of the sunlight and the rocking boat trips—these memories were later to provide a strong motif for doing several series on the theme of water.

It would be a question for brain researchers and experts in the new field of "neuroaesthetics", who have been increasingly advancing into the classical realms of the liberal arts—often enough with the clearly stated claim of establishing a new leading discipline— concerning why the forms of nature hold such an aesthetic fascination for us at all. No matter if they be waves on the sea, snowflakes, the foliage of trees, grain of wood, geological formations, or anything else: nature's structural diversity fascinates us and we often find these forms to be aesthetically attractive. Why is this so? The standard explanation evolutionary biologists use concerning cultural phenomena, namely that we value what enhances our chances of survival may hardly apply here. Would it be conceivable that we find them beautiful because our thoughts and sensitivities are based on very similar structures? The person who, for example, examines microphotographs of neurons, finds structural features of the kind we also keep witnessing in nature: complex, web-like formations, webs spun of nerve synapses. Do we find the structures of nature aesthetically attractive because our brains, our sensory organs are made up of such structures themselves? Granted, this is a speculative, but very stimulating question if—always with a view to the works of Joachim Hiller—we ask where and how the connections, interfaces, and connecting points come about between nature and art. No less speculative than the general question concerning the reasons for the aesthetic effect of natural forms is the special question concerning why and how childhood experiences manage to prevail so dominantly that they may develop into a lifelong preoccupation.

Zement und Acryl auf Holz / *Cement and acrylics on wood*
50 x 50 cm, 1985

Gar nicht spekulativ, sondern gut nachvollziehbar ist hingegen die Prägung, die durch die Lebensumstände und die geschichtlich-politischen Verhältnisse in Kindheit und Jugend auf den Künstler eingewirkt und sich unvermeidlich in seiner Auffassung von Kunst niedergeschlagen hat. Joachim Hiller wurde am 13. Oktober 1933 in Berlin-Lichterfelde geboren – zu einer Zeit und an einem Ort also, an dem die Katastrophe des Dritten Reiches mit der Machtergreifung Adolf Hitlers wenige Monate zuvor seinen Lauf genommen hatte. Seine ersten Lebensjahre verbrachte Joachim Hiller mit seinen Eltern, einem Apotheker und dessen im sozialen Dienst tätigen Ehefrau, seinem anderthalb Jahre älteren Bruder und zwei jüngeren Schwestern in Berlin-Schöneberg. 1940 wurde er in Berlin eingeschult, doch schon bald danach kriegsbedingt auf Schulen in Schlesien, Ostpreußen und Thüringen geschickt. Dass er, das Stadtkind, die Zeit zwischen dem siebten und dem zwölften Lebensjahr auf dem Land verbracht hat, bezeichnet er als eine entscheidende Prägung (Hiller benutzt überhaupt gern diesen von dem Verhaltensforscher Konrad Lorenz geprägten Begriff).

On the other hand, what is not speculative at all, but easy to comprehend are the formative experiences resulting from the living conditions and the historical and political circumstances of the artist's childhood and youth, which inevitably influenced his conception of art. Joachim Hiller was born in Berlin-Lichterfelde on October 13th, 1933—in a time and place where the catastrophe of the Third Reich had begun with Adolf Hitler's coming to power just months before. Joachim Hiller's first years of life were spent in Berlin-Schöneberg with his parents, an apothecary and his wife who worked for the social services, his one-and-a-half-year elder brother, and two younger sisters. In 1940 he began primary school in Berlin, but soon thereafter, due to the war, he was sent to schools in Silesia, Eastern Prussia, and Thuringia. The fact that he, a child of the city, spent the period between the ages of seven and twelve in the countryside is something he labels a decisive formative experience (Hiller is fond of using the term "Prägung" in German, which had been coined by the behavioral scientist Konrad Lorenz).

Acryl und Polyester auf Leinwand/*Acrylics and polyester on canvas*

100 x 100 cm, 1979 (Ausschnitt/*Detail*)

Zement und Acryl auf Holz/*Cement and acrylics on wood*

50 x 50 cm, 1985

Den Untergang des nationalsozialistischen Deutschlands, die Zeit der endlosen Bombardierungen und des erbitterten Kampfes um Berlin im Frühjahr 1945 erlebte Hiller in Schlesien. Der Zusammenbruch der Ostfront und die allgemeine Flucht der Landbevölkerung nach Westen machten eine Rückkehr nach Berlin notwendig. Die Zeit bis 1949 verbrachte er mit seinen Geschwistern in dem Jugendheim in Berlin, in dem seine Mutter eine Kindergruppe betreute. Joachim Hiller nennt die Jahre nach dem Zweiten Weltkrieg den Lebensabschnitt, der ihn, neben seiner Kindheit, am stärksten geprägt habe. Wer wie der Verfasser mit zwei Jahrzehnten Abstand geboren wurde, kann sich nur höchst unzureichend vorstellen, was es für einen Zwölfjährigen bedeutet, in einer weitgehend zerstörten Stadt groß zu werden. Was sind die Auswirkungen, wenn man zu einer Zeit, in der man, als Person noch unfertig, gerade erst beginnt sich selbst zu entdecken, mit Verwüstungen ungeheuren Ausmaßes, mit dem ganzen komplexen Gemisch der Gefühlswelt der ersten Nachkriegszeit, mit ihren Entbehrungen, dem Hunger, den Aufräumarbeiten, den Kriegsheimkehrern, dem aus authentischen Erinnerungen, Schweigen und Verdrängen gemischten seelischen Aufarbeiten der Nazidiktatur konfrontiert wird? Welche Ängste, welche bewusst und unbewusst wahrgenommenen Realitäten, welche Abenteuer auch und welche Phantasmen, ausgelöst durch die Trümmerberge, die ausgebrannten Häuser mit ihren verkohlten Balkengerippen? Womöglich ist eine kleine, zementgraue, ein wenig an Anselm Kiefers apokalyptische Malerei erinnernde quadratische kleine Bildtafel mit einem bedrohlich ins Bildfeld ragenden Stück verbrannten Holzes als eine späte, aus den Tiefen der Erinnerung aufgetauchte Reminiszenz an jene Zeit zu verstehen. Aufschlussreich ist hier eine Äußerung des Künstlers von 2004 über die Themen seiner Bilder: „Zunächst hieß bei mir die Trias: Erde, Wasser, Luft. Später kam Feuer hinzu; das Feuer hatten sie mir, dem Berliner Kriegskind, erst mal ausgetrieben."[8]

At the time of the downfall of Nazi Germany, the time of endless bombings and bitter fighting for Berlin in the spring of 1945, Hiller was in Silesia. The collapse of the Eastern Front and the general flight of the population to the west then made it necessary for him to return to Berlin. The time until 1949 was spent together with his siblings in a home for youths in Berlin, where his mother was in charge of a group of children. Joachim Hiller refers to the years after World War II as the years that, next to his childhood, constituted the most formative experiences. A person like the author who was born two decades after all this happened cannot begin to fathom what it means for a 12 year old to grow up in a city that had largely been destroyed. What are the effects at a time when you yourself are yet not fully formed as a person and are just beginning to discover yourself, if you are confronted with devastation of horrendous scope, the whole complex mixture of feelings that prevailed in the time right after the war, all the deprivation, the hunger, clearing away the rubble, men returning home from the war, your soul coming to grips with the Nazi dictatorship through a mix of authentic memories, silence, and suppression? What fears, what consciously and unconsciously-perceived realities, but also what adventures and what phantasmagorias, triggered by the mountains of rubble, the burnt out buildings with their skeletons of charred beams? It is quite possible that a small cement-gray, square panel picture, faintly reminiscent of Anselm Kiefer's apocalyptic painting, and with a piece of burnt wood menacingly protruding into the picture area, may be understood as a late reminiscence from that time, culled from the depths of memory. In this respect a statement the artist made in 2004 sheds light on the themes of his pictures: "Initially, for me there was a triad of earth, water, and air. Only later was fire added to this; for me, the war child from Berlin, they had first driven the fire out."[8]

8 Roland Held, *Joachim Hiller*, Katalog Galerie Nero, Wiesbaden 2006, S. 12.

8 Roland Held, *Joachim Hiller*, Catalogue of the Galerie Nero, Wiesbaden 2006, p. 12.

Es ist diese generationsspezifische Erfahrung einer geschichtlichen Ausnahmesituation, die Hiller in den literarischen Werken von Walter Kempowski so treffend beschrieben findet. Was Hillers frühe Biografie von der des vier Jahre älteren Autors grundlegend unterscheidet: Hiller war gegen Ende des Krieges noch jung genug, um nicht als Flakhelfer oder gar als zwangsweise rekrutierter Frontsoldat direkt mit der Realität des Kriegs und dem Irrsinn eines längst aussichtslosen Endkampfs konfrontiert zu werden.

Die mit dem Zusammenbruch des Dritten Reiches einhergehende Zerstörung war paradoxerweise eine einmalige Chance für die Persönlichkeitsentwicklung. Wo die Welt in Trümmern lag wie die zerbombte ehemalige Reichshauptstadt, entstand für die jüngere Generation zugleich ein bis dato unbekanntes Maß an Freiheit. Die Vergangenheit schien mit einem Untergangsszenario abgeschlossen zu sein, vor den Jugendlichen lag eine noch völlig unbestimmte Zukunft – und damit ein nicht festgelegtes, erst noch zu erkundendes Terrain. Dies ist die ambivalente Ausgangslage für eine ganze Generation, zu der Joachim Hiller gehört: Die geschichtliche Katastrophe war zugleich eine historische Chance auf eine Freiheitserfahrung, wie sie andere Generationen so nicht gekannt hatten. (Dies gilt zumindest für den Westteil der Stadt, in der sowjetisch besetzten Zone bereitete sich schon die nächste Form von Zwangsherrschaft auf deutschem Boden vor.) Dieses – selbstverständlich stets gefährdete, verletzliche – Freiheitsgefühl, durch den Verlust traditioneller Bindungen ermöglicht, war in der Kunst zugleich auch die geistige Grundlage für den wichtigsten Malstil der Nachkriegsjahre, das Informel, das für Hiller Ausgangspunkt für seine Malerei werden sollte.

In der chaotischen Endphase des Zweiten Weltkriegs war ein geregelter Schulalltag nicht möglich. Es ist den besonderen Umständen jener Jahre zu verdanken, dass Joachim Hiller ohne Abitur oder vergleichbaren Schulabschluss im Alter von erst 15 Jahren an den Abendsemestern der „Meisterschule für das Kunsthandwerk" in Berlin-Charlottenburg teilnehmen konnte. Mit 16 absolvierte er seine Aufnahmeprüfung. Den Lehrern erschienen die eingereichten Arbeiten jedoch so erwachsen, dass sie Zweifel daran hatten, ob der Junge wirklich der Autor dieser Blätter gewesen sein konnte. Also musste er unter Aufsicht weitere Proben seines zeichnerischen Könnens abgeben. Als jüngster der Klasse hatte Hiller bei seinen Kommilitonen bald den Spitznamen „Benjamin".

It is this generation-specific experience of a historically-exceptional situation, which Hiller finds so aptly described in the literary works of Walter Kempowski. But there is something that makes Hiller's early biography fundamentally different from that of the writer who is four years older: Hiller was still young enough around the end of the war not to be inducted as an antiaircraft helper or forcibly recruited as a front line soldier to directly face the reality of the war and be confronted with the madness of the final fighting in a war long since lost.

Paradoxically, the destruction that accompanied the collapse of the Third Reich also meant a once-in-a-lifetime chance for personal development. Where the world lay in rubble, as the former capital of the Reich did, a hitherto unknown measure of freedom came about for the younger generation at the same time. The past seemed to have ended in a downfall scenario, but the future for the young people was yet completely undetermined—and as such it was a free terrain that had yet to be explored. This is the ambivalent departure point for the entire generation to which Joachim Hiller belongs: the historical catastrophe was at the same time a historical chance for experiencing freedom, the likes of which had been unknown to other generations. (At least this applies to the western sector of the city. In the Soviet occupied zone, the next form of dictatorship was being prepared on German soil.) Of course, this always endangered and vulnerable feeling of freedom, made possible by the loss of traditional ties, was also at the same time in art the determining factor that allowed the most important painting style of the post-war years to come about, Informel. This in turn was to become the departure point for Hiller with his painting.

In the chaotic end phase of World War II a normal school routine was no longer possible. Because of the special circumstances of those years, Joachim Hiller was able to attend the evening classes at the "Master School for Arts and Crafts" in Berlin-Charlottenburg without an Abitur-graduation diploma, and this already at the young age of 15. At the age of 16 he took his entrance exams there. The works he submitted seemed so mature to the teachers that they doubted that the young man could actually have been their author. For this reason he had to supply further samples of his draftsmanship under the careful scrutiny of watchful eyes. As the youngest of his class, Hiller was soon dubbed "Benjamin" by his fellow students.

Werbeagentur/*Advertising agency*, Hamburg, 1965

Ausbildung und Beruf (1949–1969)

Die Ausbildung an der „Meisterschule für das Kunsthandwerk" in Charlottenburg (das stark kriegszerstörte und danach nur vereinfacht wieder aufgebaute Gebäude beherbergt heute eine Dependance der Universität der Künste (UdK), der ehemaligen Hochschule der Künste) war damals nicht so spezialisiert wie heute, wo in der Studienrichtung Visuelle Kommunikation das Fach Grafik-Design mit seinen vielen neuen, vor allem elektronischen Entwurfsmethoden angesiedelt ist. Grundlage der Ausbildung war ein ganz elementarer Unterricht in Malerei, die selbstverständlich noch gegenständlich ausgerichtet war und klassische Fächer wie Aktzeichnen, Anatomie, Geometrisches Zeichnen und Farbenlehre umfasste. Auf dieser Basis wurden die angewandten Künste gelehrt, druckgrafische Techniken unterrichtet usw. Die Vorstellung, die Joachim Hiller, dessen Lieblingsfach die Gebrauchsgrafik war, von seinem künftigen Berufsfeld entwickelte, war sehr stark durch sein Interesse für das Kino geprägt. Kinowerbung, überhaupt die Plakate, hatten es ihm angetan. Geprägt von der Umgebung der zerstörten Stadt und ihren tristen, vom Krieg gezeichneten Mauern, entwickelte er die Vorstellung, den Alltag mit farbigen, gut gestalteten Plakaten freundlicher zu machen. Plakate waren ein wichtiges Medium in der jungen Bundesrepublik. In Kassel etwa wurde 1948 unter Hans Leistikow die „Schule für Plakatkunst,

Education and Profession (1949–1969)

The building in which the "Master School for Arts and Crafts" was located in Berlin-Charlottenburg was heavily destroyed in WW II and then only rebuilt in reduced form, Today it houses a branch of the "Universität der Künste" (UdK), the Academy of Arts, formerly known as "Hochschule der Künste". When Hiller studied at this school, the education was not yet as specialized as it is today, where the course of study "Visual Communication" includes the subject of graphics design, an area affording many new, above all computer aided, design methods. The basis of his education was extremely rudimentary instruction in painting, still figurative of course, and consisting of classic subjects such as life drawing, anatomy, technical drawing and color theory. The applied arts as well as printing techniques were taught on this basis. The ideas that Joachim Hiller, whose favorite subject was commercial art, entertained with respect to his future professional field were greatly influenced by his interest in the cinema. Cinema advertising and poster art in general impressed him very much. Being equally greatly influenced by the city in ruins with its sad, war-pocked facades, he had the idea of making daily life friendlier with colorful, well-designed posters. Posters were an important medium in the young Federal Republic of Germany. In Kassel, for example, Hans Leistikow founded the "School for Poster Art, Book, and Magazine Graphics" in 1948. In those initial years of

Buch- und Zeitschriftengrafik" gegründet. Politische Plakate zum Beispiel wurden in den Anfangsjahren der parlamentarischen Demokratie noch nicht auf fotografischer Basis erstellt, sondern waren grafische Produkte, wurden gemalt oder gezeichnet. In den Jahren des sich langsam anbahnenden Wirtschaftswunders und damit des mehr und mehr zunehmenden Konsums waren Werbeplakate für Produkte aller Art, für Reisen und Freizeitveranstaltungen wie etwa das Kino en vogue. Plakatkunst und Werbegrafik waren in Deutschland stark gefragt.

Nach vier Jahren Studium schloss Hiller 1953 seine Ausbildung an der Meisterschule mit einem Diplom ab. Mit der Idee, auf künstlerisch anspruchsvollem Niveau Plakatgestaltung und Werbegrafik zu betreiben, startete der erst 20-Jährige einen Versuch, sich mit einem Grafikstudio selbstständig zu machen. Das Unterfangen scheiterte unter anderem an unzureichendem Startkapital. Also verließ Joachim Hiller Berlin, ging für knapp ein Jahr in die Lüneburger Heide nach Walsrode, wo er in einer Firma für Verpackungsmaterial eine Stelle als Gebrauchsgrafiker fand und sich ein Büro mit mehreren Kollegen teilen musste.

parliamentary democracy, political posters were not yet using photography, but rather conveyed their messages via graphics, either painted or drawn. In the ensuing years of what would slowly become the economic miracle, with its increasing consumer behavior, poster advertising was very much sought after for all kinds of products, and for travel and leisure activities such as cinema. Thus consequently, there was a growing demand for poster art and advertising graphics design in Germany at the time.

After four years of studies Hiller received 1953 his diploma from the Master School. Having in mind the production of high-quality posters and advertising graphics, the young man, only 20 years old, went into business for himself with a graphics studio. This undertaking failed, among other things due to a lack of start-up capital. And so Joachim Hiller left Berlin and went to Walsrode on the Lüneburg Heath for almost a year, where he found a position as commercial artist in a company that produced packaging materials, sharing an office with several colleagues.

Öl auf Leinwand/*Oil on canvas*
40 x 40 cm, 1969

Mag sein, dass aus dieser Zeit Hillers Vorliebe für die frühen Romane Arno Schmidts stammt, dessen autobiografisch gefärbte Kriegsheimkehrergeschichten meist in der Lüneburger Heide spielen. Der zurückgezogenen Lebensweise von Arno Schmidt zugunsten einer gesteigerten Konzentration auf seine künstlerische Arbeit wird sich Hiller später auf gewisse Weise annähern. 1957 ging er nach Frankfurt am Main und die Jobwechsel folgten im Jahrestakt. Eine lukrative Anstellung als Layouter bei J. W. Thompson, einer der seinerzeit bedeutendsten amerikanischen Werbeagenturen in Franfurt, eine noch heute weltweit agierende Firma, machte den Anfang. 1958 erfolgte der Wechsel zu Masius & Ferguson und 1959 zu Heumann. Anfang der 60er-Jahre dann zog es ihn nach Hamburg, wo er u. a. im Februar 1962 die legendäre Sturmflut miterlebte, die mehr als 300 Todesopfer forderte. Im selben Jahr kehrt Hiller an den Main zurück, wird Artdirector wiederum bei der nun als Heumann/Ogilvy firmierenden erweiterten alten Agentur. Hier war er hauptsächlich für die Werbekampagnen für die Lufthansa zuständig.

In den 60er-Jahren war die Lufthansa noch eine junge Firma, in gewissem Sinne Symbol für den wirtschaftlichen Aufschwung der Bundesrepublik Deutschland und die schrittweise Rückkehr in die Weltgemeinschaft. 1951, nach der Liquidation des Restvermögens der alten, 1926 gegründeten Lufthansa AG, wurde das Luftfahrtunternehmen in den folgenden Jahren neu aufgebaut, bevor mit der Erlaubnis der Alliierten am 1. März 1955 der erste Probeflug und ein Monat später der reguläre Linienluftverkehr stattfand. Der 1. April 1955 ist die fliegerische, wenn auch nicht die juristische Geburtsstunde des deutschen Luftfahrtunternehmens.[9] Die Aufgabe von Joachim Hiller bestand darin, Werbekampagnen für das junge Unternehmen zu gestalten. In diesem Zusammenhang konnte er zum Beispiel auch an einem der frühen Flüge nach Japan teilnehmen, die 1961 aufgenommen wurden. Für eine Woche hielt er sich in Tokio auf. Doch seine Vorstellung, in diesem Unternehmen auf künstlerisch anspruchsvollem Niveau Werbung gestalten zu können, stellte sich als Illusion heraus. Die Enttäuschung darüber, dass seine besten Ideen im zermürbenden Kampf um Zustimmung aus den Chefetagen zerredet und bis zur Unkenntlichkeit banalisiert wurden, entwickelte sich im Laufe der Jahre zu immer größer werdender Unzufriedenheit mit seiner Profession.

It may be that Hiller's predilection for the early novels of Arno Schmidt whose autobiographically influenced stories of soldiers returning from the war mostly took place on Lüneburg Heath, stem from this time. Arno Schmidt's reclusive lifestyle so that he could concentrate fully on his work as an artist is something Hiller later himself emulates to a certain extent. In 1957 he went to Frankfurt on Main, where from now on he changed jobs each year. He set out lucratively employed as a layout designer at J. Walter Thompson, one of the day's most important American advertising agencies in Frankfurt, a company that still exists worldwide today. In 1958 he changed to Masius & Ferguson and again in 1959 to Heumann. At the beginning of the 1960s then he was lured to Hamburg, where he lived through the legendary storm floods that cost more than 300 lives. In the same year, Hiller returned to the Main, becoming Art Director at his old agency which had now expanded to become Heumann/Ogilvy. Here he was chiefly responsible for the advertising campaigns for Lufthansa.

In the 1960s, Lufthansa was still a young company, in some ways a symbol of the economic upswing of the Federal Republic of Germany and the gradual return to the community of states. After the liquidation in 1951 of the remaining assets of the old Lufthansa AG which had been founded in 1926, the airline was re-established with a new structure in the ensuing years before receiving permission from the Allies to make a first test flight on March 1, 1955. A month later the regular airline service commenced, meaning that April 1, 1955 is the aviational though not legal birthday of the German aviation company.[9] It was Joachim Hiller's responsibility to create advertising campaigns for the young company. In this connection, for example, he was able to take one of the early flights to Japan, which began in 1961. He stayed in Tokyo for a week. But the dream that he would ever be able to create artistically demanding advertising under the auspices of this company became a dwindling illusion for him. He was subjected to the bitter experience of having his best ideas torn apart and made banal beyond recognition by upper management in an exhausting fight for approval, this leading over the years to an ever-increasing discontent with his profession.

---

9 Zu den Aufbaujahren der Lufthansa vgl. Klaus-Jochen Rieger, *50 Jahre Lufthansa. Eine Erfolgsgeschichte in Fakten, Bildern und Daten*, Königswinter 2005, S. 8–25.

9 Concerning the formative years of the Lufthansa, see Klaus-Jochen Rieger, *50 Jahre Lufthansa. Eine Erfolgsgeschichte in Fakten, Bildern und Daten*, Königswinter 2005, p. 8–25.

Foto/*Photo*: Chargesheimer
Frankfurt am Main/*Frankfurt on Main*, 1966

Die Begegnung mit Chargesheimer

Zu den uneingeschränkt positiven Erlebnissen jener Zeit gehört die Begegnung mit dem berühmten Fotografen Chargesheimer, dem „Bohemien aus Köln", mit dem er im Rahmen einiger Lufthansa-Werbekampagnen für mehrere Monate zusammenarbeitete. Von seinen Freunden wurde der Fotograf folgendermaßen charakterisiert: „Chargesheimer war ein Unersättlicher, dem nichts genügte, der sich verzehrte, ein Unglücklicher mit einem ganz verrückten Leben, der so gern glücklich war und für Augenblicke auch herrlich rheinisch närrisch sein konnte […]. Er war ein Kneipengänger, Kettenraucher, Autofahrer, Fanatiker der Arbeit, trug einen dicken Schnauzbart und einen Hut mit breitester Krempe. Er machte es sich und seinen Mitmenschen so schwer wie möglich."[10] Oder: „Alles Spießige, Bürgerliche, Stinknormale und Dummheit waren ihm ein Greul. Sie verachtete er, darüber konnte er seinen Spott ausschütten. Und ironisch, bissig, sarkastisch, das konnte er sein."[11]

10 Gregor Ramseger, zitiert nach: Bodo von Dewitz, *Chargesheimer. Bohemien aus Köln*, in: Chargesheimer. Bohemien aus Köln 1924–1971, herausgegeben von Bodo von Dewitz, Köln 2007, S. 9–17, Zitat S. 17.
11 Wolfgang Kristen, zitiert nach: ebd..

The Encounter With Chargesheimer

Among Hiller's thoroughly positive experiences from this time, however, is his encounter with the famous photographer Chargesheimer, the "Bohemian from Cologne", whom he worked with for several months on a Lufthansa advertising campaign. The photographer's friends described him like this: "Chargesheimer was insatiable, never satisfied, wasting away, an unhappy person with a completely crazy life, but who so loved being happy and who, for an instant, could be wonderfully, Rhenishly foolish […] He loved going to bars, chain-smoking and driving cars, and he was fanatical about his work, sported a thick moustache and a hat with the widest of brims. He made life as difficult as possible for himself and those around him."[10] Also: "Everything bourgeois, middle class, and too normal or stupid he abhorred. He hated all of this, and made fun of it all. And ironic, mean, and sarcastic, he could be all of that."[11]

10 Gregor Ramseger, quoted in: Bodo von Dewitz, *Chargesheimer, Bohemien aus Köln*, in: Chargesheimer. Bohemien aus Köln 1924–1971. Edited by Bodo von Dewitz, Cologne 2007, p. 9–17, quote p. 17.
11 Wolfgang Kristen, quoted in: Ibid.

Chargesheimer war für Hiller ein Beispiel für die Freiheit eines Künstlerlebens …
For Hiller, Chargesheimer was a paragon of the freedom of an artist's life …

Es ist nicht verwunderlich, dass Hiller diesen Querkopf mochte. Chargesheimers unkonventionelle Art, seine ironische Haltung gegenüber Hierarchien, sein anarchischer Witz und nicht zuletzt seine Trinkfestigkeit machten ihn für Hiller zu einer erfreulichen Ausnahmeerscheinung im Werbealltag. An Eigensinn standen sich die beiden in nichts nach. Ihre kritische Haltung gegenüber der Nachkriegsgesellschaft teilten sie, ebenso das Leiden an der Verödung der Städte durch die geistlose Nachkriegsarchitektur (Chargesheimer hatte sie in eindrücklichen Fotoreportagen geschildert). Hiller erinnert sich an die turbulenten Auftritte von Chargesheimer bei der Lufthansa, an das Befremden, das er regelmäßig beim Personal auslöste, wenn er sich plötzlich aus Gründen der besseren Perspektive auf den Boden warf, um zu fotografieren. Auch die Schnäpse zum Aufwärmen während der Arbeitszeit sind Hiller unvergesslich. Hiller hat eine Fotografie aufbewahrt, die Chargesheimer während der gemeinsamen Arbeit von ihm aufgenommen hat. Selbst ein solcher Schnappschuss zeigt Chargesheimers formales Können, den Sinn für stimmige Kompositionen und den richtigen Augenblick. Das stark untersichtig aufgenommen Foto zeigt Hiller im Profil mit konzentriertem Blick auf ein außerhalb des Bildfeldes befindliches Gegenüber. Der rechte Arm ist horizontal-vertikal stabilisiert, während die diagonal aufsteigende Linke und der Blick in die Ferne weisen: Die „Dirigentenpose" verbindet Statik und Dynamik auf perfekte Weise.

Hillers Nähe zu Chargesheimer wird umso verständlicher, als der Fotograf, der heute für seine Porträtfotos und Städtereportagen berühmt ist, stets auch mit rein künstlerischen Arbeiten beschäftigt war. Von den späten 40er-Jahren an experimentierte er mit abstrakten, informellen „Lichtgrafiken", mit „Formen aus der lichtempfindlichen Gelatineschicht von unbelichteten Glasnegativen oder Filmen."[12] Diesen „photochemischen Malereien" oder „Chemogrammen" stehen manche der späteren Strukturexperimente Hillers erstaunlich nahe. Christine De Naeyer hat diese Arbeiten als „den Versuch" charakterisiert, „die Zufälligkeiten des Chaos zu kontrollieren, um eine universelle und archetypische Form (von Chargesheimer als ‚kollektiv' beschrieben) zu schaffen, ähnlich den von der Natur hervorgebrachten Formen […]."[13] Doch

It is not too surprising that Hiller liked this contrary person. Chargesheimer's unconventional ways, his ironic attitude towards hierarchies, his anarchic humor, and last but not least, his ability to hold his drink made him a fortunate exception in everyday advertising life. Neither artist lacked in idiosyncrasy. They shared a critical attitude towards post-war society and both suffered greatly under the desolation of the cities due to the mindless post-war architecture. (Chargesheimer captured this in impressive photo reportages.) Hiller remembers the turbulent shows Chargesheimer put on at Lufthansa, the general astonishment he regularly triggered with the personnel, when he would suddenly throw himself to the ground to get a better perspective for his photographs. Also the times they drank schnapps during work hours to warm-up is indelibly written in Hiller's memory. Hiller has kept a photograph that Chargesheimer once took of him while they were working together. Even a snapshot like this one shows Chargesheimer's formal prowess, his sense for harmonious composition and the right moment. The photograph, shot from an extreme view from below, shows Hiller in profile with his gaze focused on something outside the field of the picture. The right arm has been stabilized in the horizontal-vertical position while his gaze and his left arm extend upwards at a diagonal pointing to the distance: This "conductor's pose" perfectly connects the static and the dynamic.

Hiller's closeness to Chargesheimer is understandable to us, because the photographer, known today for his portrait photographs and city reportages, was always equally concerned with creating works of pure art. Beginning in the late 1940s he was experimenting with abstract, informal "graphics of light", their "forms stemming from the light-sensitive gelatin layer of unexposed glass negatives or films".[12] These "photochemical paintings" or "chemograms" show an uncanny likeness to some of Hiller's later experiments with structure. Christine De Naeyer noted "an attempt" in these works "to control the randomness of chaos in order to create a universal and archetypal form (described as "collective" by Chargesheimer), similar to the forms nature produced […]."[13] But not only this will have interested Hiller; from the 1960s until his early death, Chargesheimer also created kinetic objects, the so-called "meditation wheels", which play

---

12 Christine De Naeyer, Theater des Unsichtbaren: Ausbrüche einer Innenwelt im Aufstand. Fotografische Erprobungen, in: von Dewitz [Anm. 10], S. 97–101. Zitat S. 98.
13 Ebd.

12 Christine De Naeyer, Theater des Unsichtbaren: Ausbrüche einer Innenwelt im Aufstand. Fotografische Erprobungen, in: von Dewitz (footnote 10), quote p. 98.
13 Ibid.

Federzeichnung auf Karton/*Ink drawing on cardboard*, 40 x 30 cm, 1969

nicht nur das musste Hiller interessieren, Chargesheimer hat während der 60er-Jahre bis zu seinem frühen Tod auch kinetische Objekte hergestellt, sogenannte „Meditationsmühlen", die mit den optischen Effekten von Licht und Glas spielen.[14] Womöglich waren sie eine Anregung für Hillers eigene Experimente mit kinetischen Objekten in den späten 70er-Jahren. Chargesheimer starb unter bis heute nicht völlig geklärten Umständen. „Mit an Sicherheit grenzender Wahrscheinlichkeit hat er sich in der Silvesternacht vom 31. Dezember 1971 in Köln das Leben genommen."[15] Zu diesem Zeitpunkt hatte Hiller gerade die ersten Jahre seiner freien künstlerischen Arbeit hinter sich. Im Gespräch betont der Maler, wie oft er die Gesellschaft des Kölner Fotografen schon vermisst habe.

Chargesheimer war für Hiller ein Beispiel für die Freiheit eines Künstlerlebens, das hat sicherlich seine eigenen Entscheidungen in dieser Richtung bestärkt. Die Unzufriedenheit mit seinem Brotberuf wuchs sich für Hiller über die Jahre immer mehr zu einer krisenhaften Situation aus. Es wurde ihm immer deutlicher, dass seine Vorstellungen von künstlerischer Freiheit in diesem Rahmen nicht umsetzbar waren. Daher malte er, sooft die Arbeit es zuließ, in seiner Freizeit, an den Feierabenden, den Wochenenden und im Urlaub. Die Bilder aus den mittleren 60er-Jahren lassen deutlich sein Ringen um einen malerischen Ansatz erkennen, den Versuch, sich eine Formidee zu erarbeiten, von der aus sich ein gangbarer Weg erschließen könnte. Der Schritt von der Angestelltensituation in die Selbstständigkeit als freier Grafiker war der Versuch, noch einmal einen beruflichen Neuanfang zu wagen und sich in neue Aufgaben zu stürzen. Das Gegenteil geschah. Die Unzufriedenheit mit einer Situation, die ein freies kreatives Arbeiten unmöglich machte, war von einem gewissen Zeitpunkt an nicht länger zu ertragen. 1969 quittierte Joachim Hiller seinen Beruf und ging, ohne klare Vorstellungen über seine Zukunft, zunächst einmal ins Ausland, in das damalige Jugoslawien, das zu der Zeit, noch unter dem Regime Titos, alles andere als touristisch erschlossen war.

14 Vgl. Barbara Engelbach, Chargesheimers Kristallwelt, in: von Dewitz [Anm. 10], S. 293–297.
15 Von Dewitz [Anm. 10], S. 9.

with the optic effects of light and glass.[14] Possibly they served as an impetus for Hiller's own experiments with kinetic objects in the late 1970s. Chargesheimer died under circumstances still not entirely explained. "It is highly likely, if not entirely certain, that he committed suicide in Cologne on New Year's Eve, December 31, 1971."[15] At the time it happened, Hiller was just completing his first years out on his own as an artist. In passing conversation, the painter remarks how often he has missed the company of the Cologne photographer.

For Hiller, Chargesheimer was a paragon of the freedom of an artist's life and certainly lent weight to his own decisions in this direction. His professional discontent had continued to deteriorate increasingly into a crisis situation for Hiller over the years. It became clearer and clearer that he would not be able to realize his ideas of artistic freedom under these conditions. For this reason he painted as often as his work would allow in his free time, after work, on weekends, and on vacation. The pictures dating from the mid-1960s clearly reveal his grappling with a painterly approach, attempt to work out a form idea of his own, from which a path would emerge that he could take. Stepping out of an employment situation into the independence of a freelance, self-employed graphics artist marked the attempt to have a fresh start in his professional career and throw himself into a new task. It failed and quite the opposite happened; his discontent with a situation that made any freely creative work impossible became unbearable for him after a certain point. In 1969 Joachim Hiller relinquished his profession and just left with no clear ideas about his future, first going off to what was known as Yugoslavia at the time, a country then still under the Tito regime, and anything but tourist friendly.

14 See Barbara Engelbach, Chargesheimers Kristallwelt, in: von Dewitz [footnote 10], p. 293–297.
15 Von Dewitz [footnote 10], p. 9.

Farbe ist hier nicht nur Kolorit, sondern Material,
das mit seiner aufgerauten Oberfläche an den Tastsinn des Betrachters appelliert.
Paint here is not only color; it is also the material
whose roughened surface appeals to the viewer's sense of touch.

Die Anfänge eigenständiger Malerei (1966–1968)

Dass der Aufenthalt in Jugoslawien von enormer Bedeutung sein würde – künstlerisch wie privat – war freilich nicht abzusehen. Bevor ich auf die Zeit Hillers auf der Insel Sveti Clement näher zu sprechen komme, soll erst einmal ein Blick auf seine künstlerische Produktion aus der Zeit der zweiten Hälfte der 60er-Jahre geworfen werden. In ihr zeigen sich keimhaft bereits gewisse Themen und formale Vorstellungen, die erst später klarer konturiert wurden. Aus ihnen erwuchs die sich über Jahrzehnte entfaltende Idee, mit naturhaften Strukturen zu arbeiten. Die Bilder, die sich ungefähr in die Jahre 1966 und 1967 datieren lassen, sind noch mit Öl auf Leinwand gemalt. Später wird Joachim Hiller die flexiblere, sehr viel schneller trocknende Acrylfarbe bevorzugen und nur gelegentlich wieder zur Ölmalerei zurückkehren.

The Beginnings of Independence in Painting (1966–1968)

No one could have foreseen that the stay in Yugoslavia would be of such fateful significance—both from an artistic as well as a private point of view. But before we launch into the time Hiller spent on the island of Sveti Clement, we should cast a glance first of all at his production dating from the second half of the 1960s. Here we may already find the seeds of certain themes and formal notions which will only clearly germinate later. From them an idea was to grow that developed over the course of decades, namely, to work with nature-like structures. The pictures, roughly datable in 1966 and 1967, are still painted in oil on canvas at this point. Later Joachim Hiller came to prefer the acrylics, which were easier to work with and had the additional advantage of drying much quicker, from now on only rarely returning to oil painting.

Öl auf Leinwand/*Oil on canvas*

75 x 90 cm, 1967

Acryl auf Leinwand/*Acrylics on canvas*

83 x 83 cm, 1967

Ende der 60er-Jahre ist Hiller damit befasst, zu einer gültigen, in sich stimmigen Form zu finden. Nichtgegenständliche Malerei muss, wenn sie nicht beliebig sein und das heißt letztlich: ins Gefällige oder Dekorative abgleiten will, eine nachvollziehbare Motivation aufweisen. Die Nachkriegsabstraktion bot dafür zwei klassische Lösungen an: Einerseits eine auf geometrische Flächenteilungen basierende konstruktive Malerei (man denke vor allem an Max Bill und seine Vorstellungen von konkreter Kunst) und andererseits eine auf spontane, intuitive, gestische Impulse vertrauende Malerei, die in ihren höchst unterschiedlichen Spielarten meist als Tachismus, Informel, lyrische Abstraktion oder abstrakter Expressionismus bezeichnet wird. Hillers frühe Arbeiten stehen durchaus in dieser Tradition. Ich denke, sie lassen sich als Auseinandersetzungen mit dem Werk Serge Poliakoffs (1900–1969) begreifen, das erst wenige Jahre zuvor (1964) auf der *documenta III* in Kassel gezeigt wurde. Hiller bewunderte an Poliakoffs Malerei immer die souveräne Art der Formfindung. Typisch für die Malerei des Russen, der 1962 die französische Staatsbürgerschaft annahm, war eine Fügung von ineinander „verhakten" individuellen, d. h. sich nicht wiederholenden Farbformen, die dem Bild einen inneren Zusammenhang verliehen, der weder von errechneter Geometrie noch von gestischen Intuitionen herrührte.

At the end of the 1960s, Hiller's concern was with finding a valid, harmonious form. If it is not to be random, which ultimately means if it is not degenerate into the category of the saccharine-sweet or the decorative, non-objective painting must necessarily reveal a motivation we are able to comprehend. Post-war abstraction proffered two classical solutions to this: on the one hand a constructive painting based upon the geometric portioning of the picture surfaces (Max Bill and his notions of concrete art come to mind above all here) and on the other hand, a great variety of spontaneous, intuitive painting relying on gesture impulses, known, for the most part, as tachisme, art informel, lyrical abstraction, or abstract expressionism. Hiller's early works certainly stand in this tradition. In my opinion they may be regarded as dialogues with the work of Serge Poliakoff (1900–1969), who had been shown only a few years earlier at the documenta III in Kassel (1964). Hiller always admired in Poliakoff's painting the masterly invention of forms. Typical for the painting of the Russian, who assumed French citizenship in 1962, was an assembly of individual, i.e. non-repetitive, forms that "hooked" on one another and which lent an inner coherence to the picture stemming neither from calculated geometry nor from intuitive gesture impulses.

Öl auf Leinwand/*Oil on canvas*

40 x 40 cm, 1969

Roland Held hat die Machart der frühen Hiller-Bilder an einem Beispiel beschrieben: „Man sieht dem Bild nicht mehr an, dass sein erster Zustand lediglich aus […] Farbpfützen [bestand], die neben- und übereinandergegossen wurden. Hillers Eingriffe mit Feder und Tusche haben strukturgebend abgeholfen, haben daraus eine Komposition gemacht, etwa in der Form eines durchgerüttelten Kreuzes."[16] Das „durchgerüttelte Kreuz" verweist auf eine im Wesentlichen horizontal-vertikale Grundstruktur (mit eindeutiger Betonung der Vertikalen), in die immer wieder leicht diagonal versetzte, widerspenstige Formpartikel „eingehakt" sind. An dieser Formidee ist die Beschäftigung mit Poliakoff am deutlichsten zu erkennen. Möglicherweise ist auch die dunkle, ins Monochrome tendierende Farbgebung der Bilder auf ihn zurückzuführen. Poliakoff hatte in seinen letzten Lebensjahren seine Palette immer mehr gedämpft und bevorzugte in jener Zeit dunkle Farbtöne.

Was auch immer Hillers frühe Abstraktionen dem Russen zu verdanken haben, sie lassen bereits gewisse Merkmale erkennen, die für seine späteren Arbeiten typisch sind. Zunächst gilt dies für die Materialität der Farbe. Die Ritzungen mit der Feder verleihen der Ölfarbe einen schrundigen Charakter. Farbe ist hier nicht nur Kolorit, sondern Material, das mit seiner aufgerauten Oberfläche an den Tastsinn des Betrachters appelliert. Das Changieren zwischen Malerei und Relief, das in diesen frühen Bildern noch ganz verhalten aufscheint, wird einen großen Teil der späteren Werke ganz entscheidend bestimmen. Des Weiteren weisen die an Naturformen, an Baumrinde oder – eher noch – an Gesteinsschichten, Schieferplatten oder Ähnliches erinnernden Strukturen auf kommende, über viele Jahre sich erstreckende thematische Konstanten hin. Die weitgehend auf erdige Grau- und Brauntöne reduzierte Palette dieser Bilder wird sich in ungezählten Arbeiten bis weit in die 8oer-Jahre hinein immer wieder finden. Die Beschäftigung mit Gesteinsstrukturen, mit geologischen und mineralogischen Formvarianten, wird sich schon sehr bald zu einem Lebensthema verdichten, das Hiller wie kein anderes ausgeschöpft hat.

16 Held [Anm. 8], S. 22.

Roland Held has described the way the early Hiller paintings were executed using the following example: "You can no longer tell that the picture's initial state merely consisted of […] puddles of color poured next to and over one another. Hiller's interventions with pen and ink have helped to provide the structure, have made a composition out of it, for example in the form of a cross thoroughly shaken-up."[16] By "shaken up cross" Held refers to what is essentially a basic horizontal and vertical structure (with the vertical being clearly emphasized), in which unruly particles of form set at a slight diagonal are repeatedly "hooked". This form idea reveals Hiller's studies of Poliakoff very clearly. Possibly the dark colors of the pictures tending towards monochromy may also go back to his influence. In the last years of his life, Poliakoff reduced his colors more and more, preferring dark colors by this time.

Whatever Hiller's early abstract works owe to the Russian, they also allow us to recognize already certain features that are typical of his later works. First there is the material quality of his paint. The scratchings made with a pen lend the oil paint a fissured character. Paint here is not only color; it is also the material whose roughened surface appeals to the viewer's sense of touch. The alternation between painting and relief, restrained yet in the early pictures, becomes very decisive in a major portion of the later works. Moreover, the structures that are reminiscent of natural forms, tree bark or—rather—strata of rock, slabs of slate, or the like, indicate persisting themes that will accompany him over many years. The color palettes of these pictures, largely reduced to earthy gray and brown tones, are to be found repeatedly in countless works until far into the 1980s. His studies of rock structures, with geological and mineralogical variations of form, will soon develop into a lifelong theme, one which Hiller has put through all the declensions in a way no other artist has.

16 Held [footnote 8], p. 22.

Öl auf Leinwand/*Oil on canvas*
75 x 95 cm, 1968

Die Beschäftigung mit Gesteinsstrukturen, mit geologischen und mineralogischen Formvarianten,
wird sich schon sehr bald zu einem Lebensthema verdichten, das Hiller wie kein anderes ausgeschöpft hat.
His studies of rock structures, with geological and mineralogical variations of form,
will soon develop into a lifelong theme, one which Hiller has put through all the declensions in a way no other artist has.

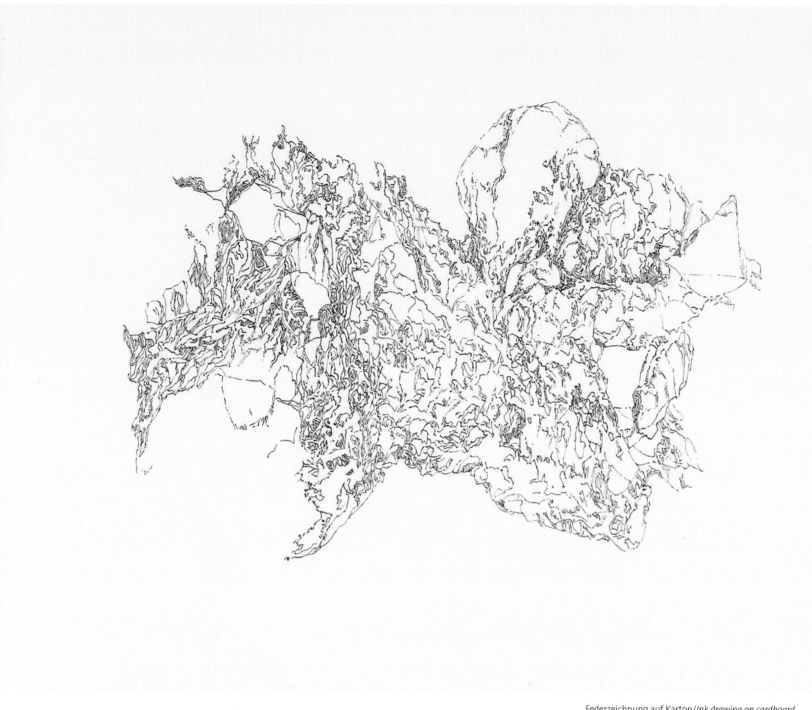

Federzeichnung auf Karton/*Ink drawing on cardboard*

30 x 40 cm, 1969

Die Suche nach der gültigen Form (1969–1970)

Die Geburt des Künstlers aus dem Geiste der beruflichen Krise: Es ist selten, aber nicht ohne Vorbild, dass der Durchbruch zum freien Künstlertum erst nach erfolgreichem Absolvieren eines bürgerlichen Berufs geschafft wird. Man denke nur, als ein Beispiel von unbestrittenem internationalem Rang, an den französischen Maler Jean Dubuffet. Der Altmeister der Art Brut hatte bis zu seinem 41. Lebensjahr als Weinhändler gearbeitet, bevor er die seit seiner Jugendzeit vernachlässigte Malerei wieder aufnahm. Zwei Jahre später hatte er seine erste Ausstellung. Bei Joachim Hiller liegt der Fall insofern anders, als er immerzu gemalt hatte, der Malerei aber nicht den ihr zustehenden Platz in seinem Leben einräumen konnte. Sein Durchbruch zur freien Künstlerexistenz bedurfte eines fundamentalen Neuanfangs als Voraussetzung der Notwendigkeit, sein Leben radikal zu ändern.

Diesen Neuanfang setzte Hiller mit dem Abschied vom Berufsleben und den zwei Dutzend Federzeichnungen von verwitterten Steinen und Felsen, die er 1969 an der dalmatinischen Küste und auf der kroatischen Insel Sveti Clement anfertigte. Mit ihnen wurden die ersten Schritte in Richtung auf ein an strukturellen Formen der Natur und einer prozesshaft mit den Materialgegebenheiten arbeitenden Malerei getan. Diese Zeichnungen kann man, obwohl sie vor der Landschaft entstanden, kaum als gegenständlich bezeichnen. Denn was Hiller an seinen Motiven interessierte, waren nicht die klassischen Themen der Landschaftsmalerei, etwa das Verhältnis von Hauptmotiv und Umgebung, die Entfaltung des Landschaftsraums oder gar der atmosphärische Stimmungsgehalt eines Landschaftsprospekts.

The Search for a Valid Form (1969–1970)

An artist born out of the spirit of a professional crisis: it is rare, but not unheard of, that the breakthrough to becoming an independent, practicing artist is only attained after successfully practicing a bourgeois profession. To cite just one example of uncontested, international rank, we need only think of the French painter Jean Dubuffet. The grand old man of Art Brut had worked as a wine dealer until he was 41, before taking up the painting again he had neglected since his youth. Two years later he had his first exhibition. The case is different with Joachim Hiller in as much as he had always painted, though he was unable to give it the place it deserved in his life. His breakthrough to establishing a free existence as an artist called for a fundamentally new start, the necessary prerequisite for changing his life radically.

This new beginning was marked by his farewell to professional life and the two dozen pen and ink drawings of weathered stones and rocks that he made in 1969 along the Dalmatian coast and on the Croatian island of Sveti Clement. With these drawings he took his first steps in the direction of the structural forms of nature and a kind of painting that worked with processes inherent to the materials used. Although they were done directly before the landscape, these drawings may hardly be referred to as objective, representative art. What interested Hiller with respect to his motifs were not the classic themes of landscape painting, for example the relationship of the main motif to the environment, or laying out the landscape space, or even the atmosphere of a landscape view.

Was Hiller stattdessen von den Felsformationen mit ihren Licht- und Schattenpartien aufnahm, waren allein die Strukturen, die sich im Stein zeigten, die Brüche, die Sedimentspuren, die Körnung, die Linienverläufe usw. In diesen Zeichnungen herrscht ein hoher Abstraktionsgrad, daher kann man ihren gegenständlichen Bezug meist auch gar nicht mehr zweifelsfrei erkennen. Räumlichkeit ist, bis auf Andeutungen von Licht- und Schattenpartien und einige Formüberschneidungen, praktisch eliminiert; die teils verdichteten, teils in summarische Linien auslaufenden Formen wirken ganz in die Fläche vermittelt. Dadurch bleibt oft auch völlig unklar, in welchem Maßstab diese Zeichnungen angelegt sind. Ob es sich um Binnenstrukturen einzelner Steine handelt oder um großräumige Felspanoramen, bleibt bei den meisten dieser Arbeiten ungewiss. Dieser Effekt des Changierens zwischen mikro- und makrostruktureller Bildanlage ist eine Eigenschaft, die bei den Hiller'schen Arbeiten über Jahrzehnte und über viele Werkreihen hin immer wieder zu beobachten ist. Ihre ästhetische Besonderheit besteht darin, dass sie die interpretierende Mitarbeit, die produktive Vorstellungskraft des Betrachters aktiviert.

Hiller hat sich seine Wertschätzung für diese rund 25 Federzeichnungen bis heute bewahrt. Das kommt sehr deutlich darin zum Ausdruck, dass er in jeder Einzelausstellung, die seit 2006 stattfand, möglichst gleich am Eingang jeweils eine Auswahl dieser Arbeiten platzierte. Worin besteht nun die Wichtigkeit dieser Zeichnungen? Es ist wohl die Tatsache, dass der Künstler hier nicht aktiv nach einer Form suchte, sondern – im Gegenteil – bestrebt war, eine bereits vorhandene, in sich stimmige Form aufzunehmen. Ganz rezeptiv nur Empfänger einer Form zu sein, die sich mit Notwendigkeit entwickelt und doch gänzlich unvorhersehbar, war eine Übung, die ihm bewusst werden ließ, dass sich in der Natur Formen bilden, die man mit bloßem Willen und Vorstellungskraft allein niemals hätte hervorbringen können. Die Formen, die er mit der Zeichenfeder festhielt, waren also kein Produkt künstlerischer Kreativität, sondern vielmehr Entscheidungshilfen, um das Prinzip der Formfindung ganz neu zu überdenken. Die Erkenntnis, dass dafür erst noch die notwenigen technischen Mittel gefunden werden mussten, sollte sich erst später langsam entwickeln.

Instead, what Hiller gleaned from these rock formations with their light and shadow areas were the structures themselves revealed in the stone, the chips, the traces of sediment, the grain, the way the lines progressed, etc. In these drawings a high level of abstraction prevails and thus, for the most part, it is scarcely possible to even recognize their objective context. Space has practically been eliminated, except for hints of light and shadow areas and several overlaps of form; the forms, sometimes condensed, and other times summarily sketched, are seemingly conveyed entirely on the surface. This is why the actual scale of these drawings often remains completely unclear. Ambiguity prevails in most of these works as to whether we are dealing with the interior structures of individual stones or with large-scale rock panoramas. The effect of this alternation between micro- and macrostructures in the pictures is a phenomenon we have been witnessing in Hiller's works over decades and in many series. Their particular aesthetic attraction consists in the fact that they activate the interpretative cooperation, the productive imagination of the viewer.

Hiller still maintains his esteem for these approximately 25 pen and ink drawings today. This is clearly demonstrated in his placing a selection of these works as close to the entrance as possible in every exhibition that has taken place since 2006. Why are these drawings so important? Most likely it is because here the artist had not been actively searching for a form, but rather—to the contrary—he was striving to take up a harmonious form already in existence. Being wholly receptive, the mere receiver of a form developing out of necessity and yet entirely unpredictable, was an exercise which made him aware that forms come about in nature, which a person could never have produced with mere will and imagination. The forms he captured with his drawing pen, were thus, not the product of artistic creativity, but rather tools to completely review the principle of finding forms. The recognition that in order to be able to accomplish this, the necessary technical means would first have to be found was something that only slowly developed later.

Acryl auf Leinwand/*Acrylics on canvas*, 125 x 90 cm, 1972

Doch so sehr Hiller als Zeichner „Empfänger" und „Übersetzer" einer Naturform war, verhielt er sich doch nicht bloß passiv. Die Blätter entfalten ihren ästhetischen Reiz nur aufgrund einiger eminent wichtiger *künstlerischer* Entscheidungen. Zunächst ist es die Wahl eines bestimmten Mediums, nämlich der Federzeichnung mit all ihren historischen Reminiszenzen (Hiller erwähnt gern die minutiösen Naturstudien Caspar David Friedrichs), hinzukommen die kompositorischen Entscheidungen, wo das Aufnehmen der Formen jeweils endet, welchen Anteil die Leerstellen des Zeichenblattes einnehmen usw. Die Beschränkung auf die rein linearen Strukturen und die willkürlichen Formgrenzen lassen die entstehenden Strukturen losgelöst von der materiellen Beschaffenheit des Motivs erscheinen. So entstehen Gebilde, die sich in amorpher Ausbreitung wie organische Substanzen, manchmal S-förmig, manchmal annähernd sternförmig über die Blätter „bewegen" und so nachdrücklich auf die Vorstellungskraft des Betrachters einwirken.

Eine ähnliche Doppeldeutigkeit weisen die Umsetzungen dieser Erfahrungen in die Ölmalerei auf, die Hiller noch im selben Jahr 1969 mit einer Reihe von kleinen, nur 40 mal 40 Zentimeter messenden Leinwänden in Angriff nahm. Auch auf diesen Ölstudien sind die Formen meist isoliert und nicht bis an die Bildgrenzen durchgezogen. Durch diese Heraushebung aus dem landschaftlichen Kontext gewinnen sie die Qualität von Materialproben. Die Dominanz heller Ocker- und Rottöne (die bei der Sonnenstrahlung sicherlich völlig realistisch wiedergegeben sind) bewirkt, dass der Steincharakter weitgehend verloren geht und die Formen eine irritierend organische Qualität erhalten. Mit ihren Höhlungen und Einschlüssen und ihren spitzen Binnenformen lassen sie unvermeidlich an Gewebeproben oder zerrissene Fleischstücke denken. Schon an diesen frühen Arbeiten kann man in aller Deutlichkeit erkennen, dass Hillers Beschäftigung mit Naturformen niemals etwas „Naturalistisches" hatte, nie nur die Wiedergabe einer visuellen Erscheinungswirklichkeit war, sondern vielmehr eine Offenheit und Deutungsambivalenz beinhaltet, die sich als Konstanten bis in die jüngsten Arbeiten hinein verfolgen lassen.

But as much as Hiller as a draftsman was the "receiver" and "translator" of a natural form, he did not merely remain passive. The pages unfold their aesthetic attraction only because the artist has made several eminently important artistic *decisions. First there is the choice of a certain medium, namely the pen and ink drawing with all of its historical reverberations (Hiller is fond of referring to the minute natural studies of Caspar David Friedrich). Then there are the compositional decisions where the inclusion of the forms ends each time, as to what portion the empty spaces of the pages should have, etc. The limitation to the purely linear structures and the random limitations of the forms allow the resulting structures to seem detached from the material quality of the motif. Thus structures come about that "move" across the pages like organic substances in amorphic expansion, sometimes s-shaped, sometimes nearly star-shaped, thus making a lasting impression upon the imagination of the viewer.*

A similar ambiguity is shown when these experiences are transposed into oil painting, which Hiller set to work in the same year 1969 with a series of small canvases measuring only 40 by 40 cm. The forms are likewise largely isolated in these oil studies as well and do not extend to the edges of the pictures. Since they have been excerpted from a landscape context, they take on the quality of material samples. The dominance of light ochre and red tones (which are certainly completely realistic given the intense sunlight) has the effect that the character of the stone is for the most part lost, the forms retaining a confusingly organic quality. With their hollows and intercalations and their sharp interior shapes they unmistakably evoke tissue samples or torn pieces of meat. Already these early works allow us to recognize in all clarity that Hiller's occupation with natural forms was never something "naturalistic", never merely the reproduction of a visual appearance of reality, but rather had an openness and ambivalence of interpretation, which has continued to accompany even the most recent works.

Öl auf Leinwand/*Oil on canvas*
60 x 90 cm, 1968

Ich habe weiter oben erwähnt, dass der Aufenthalt 1969 an der dalmatinischen Küste künstlerisch wie privat von enormer Bedeutung war. Der private Teil bestand darin, dass Joachim Hiller hier Ingetraud Lehnen kennenlernte. Mit ihr lebte er anschließend unter Beibehaltung einer gewissen räumlichen Distanz in Frankfurt zusammen. 1984 heirateten die beiden.

Wie wichtig der fast dreimonatige Aufenthalt in Jugoslawien für den Künstler war, zeigt sich daran, dass er in den folgenden Jahren immer wieder für mindestens einen Monat dorthin zurückkehrte, um zu zeichnen und zu malen. In einem Interview betonte er, dass diese Aufenthalte für ihn eine Art „Kontrolle" waren. Sich vor Ort immer wieder mit den einzigartigen Strukturen der Steine und Felsformationen zu beschäftigen, bewahrte ihn, so betont er, vor Manierismen, Wiederholungen und bloßer Routine.[17]

I mentioned above that the stay at the Dalmatian coast was of enormous significance both artistically and privately. The private matter was that it was here where Joachim Hiller and Ingetraud Lehnen met. Afterwards he lived with her in Frankfurt, though they maintained a certain distance. In 1984 the couple married.

Just how important for the artist that nearly three-month stay in Yugoslavia was is attested to by his repeated visits there in the years that followed, each time at least for a month, so that he could draw and paint. In an interview he emphasized that these stays were for him a type of "check". Being able to study the unique structures of the stones and rock formations on location guarded him against mannerism, repetitions, and mere routine, he said.[17]

17 Joachim Hiller in einem Interview anlässlich der Retrospektive in der Walter Bischoff Galerie, Berlin, 15.8.2008.

17 Joachim Hiller in an interview on the occasion of his retrospective at the Walter Bischoff Galerie, Berlin, 15 August 2008.

Acryl auf Leinwand/*Acrylics on canvas*, 120 x 100 cm, 1971

Neue Wege der Malerei

Was man, mit einer Paraphrase von Peter Handkes Hommage an Paul Cézanne, als die „Lehre von Sveti Clement"[18] bezeichnen könnte, war Joachim Hiller zwar klar geworden: Die notwendigen motivierten, in sich stimmigen Formen, nach denen er suchte, waren weder in geometrischen noch in gestischen Verfahren zu finden. Sie waren überhaupt nicht in einem Willensakt und in einem subjektiven Schaffensprozess herzustellen. Die Natur bringt in einem hochkomplexen Spiel von Strukturen bildenden und Strukturen auflösenden Prozessen unablässig solche „notwendigen" Formen hervor. Dies geschieht zwar nach konstanten Gesetzen, aber wegen der jeweils besonderen Bedingungen in immer neuen Formen. Die Natur wiederholt sich nicht. Aber wie sollte diese Lehre in die malerische Praxis umgesetzt werden? Das akribische zeichnerische oder malerische Abbilden vorgefundener Strukturmomente war eine notwendige Übung, aber noch kein befriedigendes künstlerisches Konzept. Was jetzt fehlte, war das Ausarbeiten von Techniken, die eine Anwendung der „Lehre von Sveti Clement" ermöglichen.

Hillers frühe Arbeiten, die Zeichnungen und Ölstudien aus Sveti Clement eingeschlossen, sind trotz ihrer Tendenz zur Abstraktion und zur strukturellen Fokussierung noch traditionell in dem Sinne, dass hier Figur-Grund-Verhältnisse eine Rolle spielen, vor allem aber, weil Hiller hier noch immer mit der von Hand ausgeführten Umsetzung visueller Eindrücke beschäftigt war. Seit den frühen 70er-Jahren zeigte Hiller immer stärker die Tendenz, die Palette seiner Arbeitsmaterialien zu erweitern und sie zu Mitspielern im ästhetischen Erscheinungsbild seiner Werke zu machen. Dies führte zugleich zu einer verstärkten Objektivierung der künstlerischen Verfahrensweisen.

18 Peter Handke, *Die Lehre der Sainte-Victoire*, Frankfurt a. M. 1980.

New Paths of Painting

What we might refer to as the "Lesson of Sveti Clement", to paraphrase Peter Handke's homage to Paul Cézanne,[18] had become clear to Joachim Hiller: the necessary, motivated forms of intrinsic harmony he had been looking for could not be found either in geometric or in gestural processes. They were not to be found in an act of will at all, nor could they be produced in a subjective process of creation. It is nature which continuously produces such "necessary" forms in a highly complex play of processes that build and dissolve structures. Granted, this takes place according to never-changing laws, but it always finds new forms due to the respective particular conditions. Nature does not repeat itself. But how was such a lesson to be transformed into painterly practice? The minutely-drawn or painted portrayals of instances of structures he had found were a necessary exercise, but did not yet yield a satisfying artistic concept. Missing now was to work out the techniques, which would make it possible to apply the "Lesson of Sveti Clement".

Despite their tendency towards abstraction and structural focus, Hiller's early works, including the drawings and oil studies from Sveti Clement, are still traditional in the sense that here the relationships between figure and ground play a role. But above all, this is because Hiller was still using them to study the transformation of visual impressions into something he could do by hand. Since the early 1970s, Hiller has revealed a growing tendency for expanding the range of the materials he worked with, making them figure in the aesthetic appearance of his works. At the same time this led to an increased objectification of the artistic processes.

18 Peter Handke, Die Lehre der Sainte-Victoire, (The Lesson of Mount Sainte-Victoire), Frankfurt a. M. 1980.

Sehr deutlich kommt dies in einer Serie von Arbeiten aus der ersten Hälfte der 70er-Jahre zum Ausdruck, die in einer Technik ausgeführt ist, die Hillers Absicht zeigt, den Gestaltungsprozess zu versachlichen, von der persönlichen Handschrift zu befreien und die Eigengesetzlichkeit der angewandten Materialien und Arbeitsmethoden zu thematisieren. Das Arbeiten mit der Spritzpistole war ein wichtiger Schritt in diese Richtung. „Airbrush", wie die Technik des Zerstäubens von dünnflüssiger Farbe meist genannt wird, hatte zu dieser Zeit noch kaum den Ruf eines künstlerischen Verfahrens. Sie war und ist bis heute ein typisches Arbeitswerkzeug von Grafikdesignern und Illustratoren. In den 60er-Jahren fing sie, vermittelt vor allem durch die amerikanische Pop-Art und den Fotorealismus, langsam an, sich auch in der Malerei zu etablieren. Was Hiller an der Technik des Airbrush interessierte, war nicht die Möglichkeit, auf einfache Weise homogene Farbflächen oder effektvolle Farbverläufe zu kreieren, sondern die Tatsache, dass der Farbstrahl aus der Pistole *gerichtet* ist. Dies bedeutet, dass die Farbpartikel wie der Lichtkegel einer Taschenlampe von einem Punkt aus trichterförmig abstrahlen. Wenn nun ein Hindernis zwischen Spritzpistole und Leinwand bzw. Papier liegt, entstehen hellere und dunklere Zonen. Anders jedoch als beim Lichtstrahl erscheinen die „Schatten"-Zonen auf der Seite, die der Farbquelle zugewandt ist. Mit Gegenständen, die Hiller auf der Malfläche platzierte, entstanden quasi gegenständliche Formenerscheinungen von geisterhafter Plastizität, vergleichbar der Präsenz von Gegenständen auf Fotonegativen.

Hiller experimentierte insbesondere bei den Arbeiten auf Papier mit verschiedenen Formen, mit in einfachen geometrischen Konfigurationen angeordneten Steinen, mit Alltagsgegenständen, die auf dem Papier verteilt sind und mit gebogenen Kartonstreifen. Wo der Künstler Ensembles geschwungener Formen von verschiedenen Seiten her hell und dunkel „angestrahlt" hat, bekommen die Bilder oft etwas irritierend Organisches, durch die entsprechend warme Tonigkeit auch Erotisches, an rätselhaft verschlungene Frauenkörper erinnernd. Die Tendenz zur Gegenständlichkeit ist bei diesen Bildern eher eine Nebenerscheinung, ein Effekt, der sich aus den „Laborbedingungen" der Bildherstellung ergibt.

This is very clearly expressed in a series of works from the first half of the 1970s, carried out in a technique revealing Hiller's intention of making the process of creation more factual, of freeing it of any personal signature, and of making a theme of the intrinsic laws of the materials and working methods used. Working with a spray gun was an important step in this direction. "Airbrushing", as this technique for spraying on highly liquid paint is mostly called, hardly had a reputation as an artistic method at the time. It was and still is today a typical tool graphics designers and illustrators use. In the 1960s, above all due to American pop art and photo realism, it began to establish itself slowly in painting. What interested Hiller about the airbrush was not the possibility of creating homogenous surfaces or effective color progressions, but the fact that the squirt of paint sprayed from the gun is focused. *This means that the particles of paint radiate from a certain point like an inverted funnel, similar to the cone of light from a flashlight. If you place an obstruction between the spray gun and the canvas or paper, lighter and darker zones come about. But unlike with a ray of light, the "shadow" zones appear on the side turned toward the source of paint. Through objects that Hiller placed on the paint surface, semi-objectlike appearances of ghostlike plasticity came about, comparable to the presence of objects on photograph negatives.*

Especially with the works on paper, Hiller experimented with various forms, with stones laid out in simple geometric configurations, with everyday objects distributed over the paper, and with pieces of bent cardboard. Wherever the artist "illuminated" from various sides ensembles of curving forms in light and dark shades, these pictures often take on something confusingly organic and due to the corresponding warm tones, they may even seem erotic, reminding us of the mysteriously entwined bodies of women. The tendency towards the objective is more of an incidental occurrence in these pictures, an effect arising from the "laboratory conditions" of the picture creation.

Acryl auf Papier/Acrylics on paper
50 x 50 cm, 1970

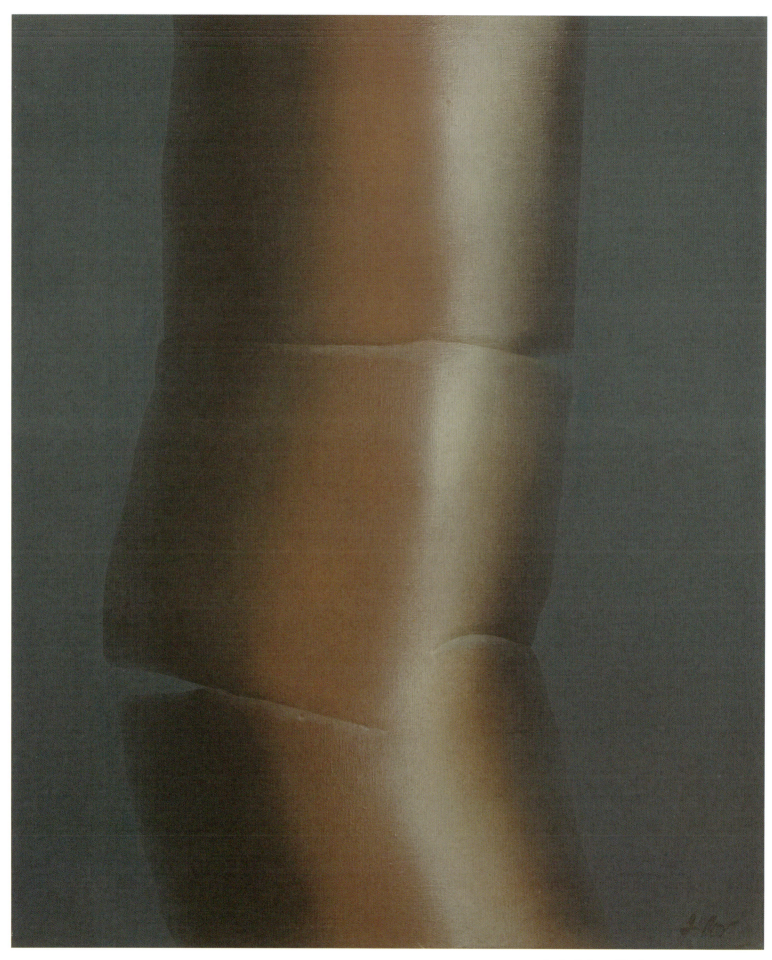

Acryl auf Leinwand/*Acrylics on canvas*, 120 x 100 cm, 1971

Dennoch steht diese Phase in Hillers Werk eher isoliert da. Die Lehre aus seiner Beschäftigung mit den Steinen an der dalmatinischen Küste war zwar insofern befolgt, als er die Formen aus den Bedingungen der Versuchsanordnung erwachsen ließ (nicht anderes macht ja das „Labor" der Natur), aber die Resultate waren inhaltlich noch nicht auf der Höhe seines Anspruchs, vergleichbar der Natur vorzugehen. Denn in gewisser Hinsicht waren diese Arbeiten „surrealistisch". Die merkwürdige Ambivalenz zwischen steinerner und organischer Anmutung in den Ölstudien von Sveti Clement war nicht gesucht. Sie ergab sich aus dem genauen Abbilden dessen, was er vor Augen hatte, sowie aus der Isolation des Motivs. Es war ein unbeabsichtigter und daher umso wirkungsvollerer Nebeneffekt. Doch was Hiller mit den „anthropomorphen" Spritzpistolenbildern tat, war ein aktiver Vorgang, ein Hineinsehen von organischen und insbesondere erotischen Vorstellungen. Es ist, bei aller Objektivierung der Mittel, in diesen Arbeiten noch sehr viel Subjektivität und Projektion im Spiel, wie man es von den Surrealisten kennt, die ebenfalls in zufällige Formfunde psychische – und insbesondere sexuell geladene – Energien leiteten.

Was diese Arbeiten der frühen 70er-Jahre für Hiller jedoch zukunftweisend macht, ist die Erweiterung der malerischen Mittel. An die Stelle der traditionellen Ölmalerei mit Pinsel und Palette treten neue, unerprobte Materialien und malerische Verfahrensweisen. Die Verwendung von Acrylfarbe und Spritzpistole war Hiller aus seiner Arbeit als Grafiker vertraut. Wenn der Malerei ein neues Feld an Motiven und Strukturen erschlossen werden sollte, waren die entsprechenden Mittel und Techniken zu finden. Hiller zeigte nie Berührungsängste mit ungewöhnlichen, als kunstfremd erachteten Arbeitsmaterialien. Sowenig für ihn eine unüberbrückbare Kluft zwischen Malerei und Grafik herrscht, sowenig gibt es einen kategorischen Unterschied zwischen Malerei und Relief. Gerade aus dem Spannungsfeld zwischen der flächigen Malerei und dem in die dritte Dimension ausgreifenden Relief entstanden immer wieder neue formale Lösungen und technische Innovationen, die sein Werk prägen sollten.

And yet this phase stands isolated in Hiller's work. Granted, the lesson learned from his studies of rocks on the Dalmatian coast was followed to the extent that he allowed the forms to grow out of the conditions of the experimental arrangement (nature's "laboratory" does the same), but in substance the results did not yet meet his expectations of working in a manner comparable to nature. The reason why is because in a certain respect these works were "surrealistic". He had not been looking for the strange ambivalence between stony and organic appearance as in the oil studies of Sveti Clement. It resulted from the exact portrayal of what was before his eyes, as well as from the isolation of the motif. It had been an unintentional and therefore all the more effective side effect. But what Hiller was doing with the "anthropomorphic" spray gun pictures was an active process, looking into organic and especially erotic notions. For all the objectivity of the means, there is still a lot of subjectivity and projection at play in these works, such as we know from the surrealists, who also directed psychic—and in particular sexual—energies into random form findings.

The thing that was forward-looking in these works of the early 1970s is the expansion of the painterly means. Instead of the traditional oil painting with brush and palette, we now find new and unexplored materials and painting processes being used. Hiller had been familiar with acrylics and the spray gun from his works as a graphics designer. If a new field of motifs and structures was to be opened to painting, he had to find the respective means and techniques. Hiller never shied from trying out unusual materials to work with that were considered as foreign to art. Just as there is for him no insurmountable gap between painting and graphics, there is also no categorical difference between painting and relief. Precisely from this field of tension between the flat painting and the relief extending into the third dimension, he repeatedly came up with new formal solutions and technical innovations that would become characteristic of his work.

Zerbrochenes Glas

Enorme Wichtigkeit für die Ausarbeitung einer der Formung von Naturstrukturen analogen Malerei kommen den Reliefs mit Glasplatten zu, die Hiller von etwa 1974 an bis zum Beginn der 8oer-Jahre fertigte. Manchmal hilft der Zufall der Kunst auf die Sprünge. Genau dies geschah, als Joachim Hiller einmal versehentlich eine Glasscheibe zerbrach. Die Linienverläufe der Brüche ergaben eine Flächenteilung, eine „Komposition", die in sich absolut stimmig wirkte. Eine Glasplatte zerbricht nach Maßgabe der Naturgesetze, in Abhängigkeit von Art, Stärke und Richtung des einwirkenden Drucks und der mineralischen Beschaffenheit des Glases. Innerhalb von Sekundenbruchteilen „entscheidet" das Glas über die Verlaufsform der Brüche und kreiert ein Liniennetz. So entsteht eine lineare Struktur als Flächenteilung, die man sich so nie hätte ausdenken können. Aus dieser Beobachtung erwuchs Hillers Idee, Glasplatten auf einem flexiblen Untergrund, zum Beispiel auf Hartschaumplatten, zu platzieren, zu zerbrechen und die Bruchstücke mit einem geeigneten Klebstoff zu fixieren. So entstanden Flachreliefs, die, je nach der Art ihrer „Behandlung", sanfte tektonische Brüche aufweisen oder aber in dramatischer Weise aufklaffen, tiefe Verletzungsspuren zeigen – bleibende Dokumente einer schockhaften, plötzlichen Krafteinwirkung.

Eine merkwürdige Ambivalenz besteht zwischen der Herstellungsweise, da die Glasplatten selbstverständlich in horizontaler Lage zerbrochen wurden, und ihrer Präsentation in vertikaler Lage als Bilder an der Wand. Durch diese Anordnung verlieren sie etwas von ihrer faktischen Objekthaftigkeit und werden als *Bilder* wahrgenommen, das heißt als Zeichen für etwas anderes. Indem Hiller die meisten dieser Arbeiten sehr hell gefärbt hat, weiß, eisblau oder in sanften Erdfarben, wirken sie sehr stark auf die Einbildungskraft der Betrachter. Unvermeidlich versucht man beim Betrachten dieser reliefartigen Bilder, die als Effekte einer physischen Krafteinwirkung dastehen, auf deren Ursache zurückzuschließen. Wie bei den Zeichnungen an der dalmatinischen Küste verschieben sich die Grenzen der Maßstäblichkeit, ein typischer „Hiller-Effekt" stellt sich ein: Das Verschwimmen der Grenzen zwischen Mikro- und Makrowelt. Man kann an Spuren im Eis bzw. in Sandwüsten denken oder aber – im großen Maßstab – an riesige, durch gewaltige Kräfte aufgetürmte Eisschollen (vergleichbar denen auf Caspar David Friedrichs berühmtem Bild „Das Eismeer"). Man kann an Einschusslöcher denken oder aber an gewaltige, durch einen Meteoritenhagel verursachte Einschlagkrater oder an tektonische Einbrüche in Wüstenlandschaften, die aus großer Höhe fotografiert wurden … Immer wieder finden sich im Werk von Joachim Hiller diese Sprünge zwischen der Faktizität der Bilder und der in der Vorstellung des Betrachters erfolgenden Ausweitung in erdgeschichtliche Großdimensionen.

Broken Glass

Of utmost importance for working out a new painting analogous to the forming of natural structures are the reliefs using sheets of glass, which Hiller was making from around 1974 until the beginning of the 1980s. Sometimes it is pure chance that helps art along. This is precisely what happened when Joachim Hiller accidentally broke a sheet of glass. The lines formed in the breakage divided the surface into a "composition" seeming to possess an absolute inner harmony. A sheet of glass breaks according to the laws of nature, depending on its type, thickness, and direction the prevailing pressure came from, as well as the mineral content of the glass. In the split of a second, the glass "decides" how the breaks will progress, and thus, creates a network of lines. A linear structure spreads across the surface that we could never have thought up on our own. It was from this observation that Hiller had the idea of placing and breaking sheets of glass upon a flexible ground, for example rigid foam boards, and then affixing the pieces with the right adhesive glue. The result was flat reliefs, which, depending on their "treatment", display gentle tectonic fissures, or else, gape dramatically with deep traces of injury, the remnants documenting the shock of a sudden impact of force.

A strange ambivalence exists between the manners of production, since the sheets of glass were, of course, broken in a horizontal position and their vertical presentation as pictures on the wall. Because of this arrangement they lose some of their factual objectivity and are then perceived as pictures, *that is, as signs for something else. Since Hiller has colored most of these works in very light shades, white, ice-blue, or in soft earth tones, these pieces have a very strong effect on the viewer's imagination. In gazing at these relief-like pictures resulting from the impact of physical force, we inevitably attempt to deduce its cause. Like with the drawings on the Dalmatian coast the scale shifts, and a typical "Hiller-effect" occurs, a blurring between the micro and macro world. You can think of traces in the ice, or in sand deserts—or on a large scale—of giant blocks of ice piled up by massive forces (like those on Caspar David Friedrich's famous painting "Das Eismeer"—The Wreck of Hope). You can think of the pockmarks of bullets or of mighty craters caused by a meteor shower or of tectonic breaks in desert landscapes, photographed from a high altitude … Over and over again in the works of Joachim Hiller we find these mental jumps between the factual appearance of the picture and its expansion to large-scale dimensions of the natural history of the earth occurring in the mind of the viewer.*

Relief, Glas und Sand/*Relief, glass and sand*

120 x 120 cm, 1976

Glas und Sand auf Hartschaum/*Glass and sand on Styrofoam*

120 x 120 cm, 1976

… so kann man Hillers Arbeit mit dem Zerbrechen der Glasplatten als ein Aufbegehren,
als ein Aufbrechen (im wörtlichen Sinne) der traditionellen Vorstellung von Malerei und Bildbegriff verstehen.
*… we can also regard Hiller's work with his breaking the sheets of glass as a protest,
as breaking out (literally) of the traditional notion of painting and picture conception.*

Joachim Hiller hat einmal erwähnt, die Idee zu seinen Glasplattenreliefs sei auch durch die Erinnerung an die Studentenrevolte von 1968 ausgelöst worden. Frankfurt, wo Hiller lebte und sein Atelier in Bahnhofsnähe mitten im Rotlichtbezirk hatte, war damals das Zentrum der Unruhen. Hiller erinnert sich noch sehr gut an die eingeschlagenen Schaufensterscheiben von Banken und Juwelierläden. Betrachtet man das Relief von 1974 mit seinen spitzen, auf das schwarze Bildzentrum gerichteten Glassplittern, kann man diese Erinnerung sehr gut nachvollziehen. Es wäre sicher völlig verfehlt, zwischen Hillers künstlerischen Experimenten und den Studentenunruhen der 68er-Jahre irgendeine inhaltliche Beziehung herzustellen. Dennoch gibt es eine strukturelle Gemeinsamkeit: So wie die Studenten gegen die – wirklichen oder vermeintlichen – Verkrustungen der bürgerlichen Gesellschaft revoltierten, so kann man Hillers Arbeit mit dem Zerbrechen der Glasplatten als ein Aufbegehren, als ein Aufbrechen (im wörtlichen Sinne) der traditionellen Vorstellung von Malerei und Bildbegriff verstehen. Die Reinheit und Perfektion einer unversehrten quadratischen Glasplatte mit Hammerschlägen zu traktieren, durch einen Sprung mit beiden Füßen zu zertreten, ist ein Akt von durchaus symbolischer Kraft. Das Bild als offenes Fenster („finestra aperta") zur Welt ist eine seit der Frührenaissance verwendete Leitmetapher für die Auffassung der neuzeitlichen Malerei. Die Transparenz und Klarheit des Glases kann zudem als Metapher für reine Geistigkeit begriffen werden. Als solche, als Träger konzeptueller Begrifflichkeit, wurde sie auch von Künstlern wie Joseph Kosuth verwendet. Wenn Hiller nun Glasplatten in einem elementar physischen Akt zertrümmert, als *Action painting* in einem bis dato nicht praktizierten Sinn, dann zeigt dies auch eine Aggressivität gegen den herkömmlichen Kunstbegriff, eine Ungeduld mit traditionellen Weisen der Bildgestaltung.

Joachim Hiller once mentioned that the idea for his plate glass reliefs was also evoked by his reminiscence of the student revolt of 1968. In Frankfurt where Hiller lived and had his studio near the central station in the middle of the red-light district, was the center of all the unrest. Hiller still remembers very well the smashed windows of banks and jewelry stores. If we look at the relief of 1974 with its sharp glass splinters pointing to the black center of the picture, we can follow this memory very well. It would certainly be wrong to establish any relationship of content between Hiller's artistic experiments and the student unrest of 1968. And yet they are comparable in one facet. Like the students revolting against the—actual or presumed—crust that had formed over bourgeois society, we can also regard Hiller's work with his breaking the sheets of glass as a protest, as breaking out (literally) of the traditional notion of painting and picture conception. Maltreating the purity and perfection of an intact square sheet of glass by pounding it with a hammer or jumping on it with both feet is certainly an act of symbolic force. The picture as a window opening to the world ("finestra aperta") has been a leading metaphor for the understanding of modern painting since early renaissance times. In addition, the transparency and clarity of the glass may also be considered a metaphor for what is purely spiritual. It has also been used like this, as vehicle for conceptual thinking, by artists such as Joseph Kosuth. If Hiller now shatters sheets of glass in an elementary physical act, as an action painting in a sense unheard of until that time, then this also reveals an aggression towards the customary concept of art, and impatience with traditional ways of picture creation.

Selbstverständlich sind vergleichbare Haltungen aus der modernen Kunst bekannt. Man erinnere sich an Picassos Satz, dass bei ihm die Malerei aus einer „Summe von Destruktionen" bestehe. (Nicht zufällig bezieht sich daher der Scherz, den sich Hiller einmal erlaubte, indem er die Anordnung der Glassplitter nicht den physikalischen Kräften überließ, sondern sie zu einem Gesicht formte, als Hommage an die facettierten, aus Linienstücken zusammengesetzten Porträts aus Picassos Phase des analytischen Kubismus.)[19] Oder man denke an Lucio Fontanas Schnitte in die Leinwand, an Alberto Burris aus verbranntem Sackleinen gefertigte Bilder oder an Yves Kleins oder Heinz Macks Verfahren, mit Flammenwerfern Löcher und Flecken in die Bilder zu brennen. Der Kunsttheoretiker Boris Groys hat diese Tendenz der Moderne als die eines „grausamen Martyriums des Bildes" beschrieben: „Zumindest seit dem Anfang dieses [des 20.] Jahrhunderts wird das Kunstwerk den Torturen ausgeliefert, die sich nur mit denen vergleichen lassen, deren Spuren die Körper der christlichen Märtyrer aufweisen. Das Bild wird (symbolisch oder real) verbrannt, zerschnitten, verunstaltet, beschmutzt und auf andere unterschiedlichste Weisen körperlich misshandelt." Bis dahin lassen sich Groys' Worte auch auf Hiller anwenden, doch wenn der Theoretiker schließt: „Alle diese Torturen hinterlassen auf der Oberfläche des Kunstwerks Wunden, Narben und Spuren der Gewaltanwendung, die die Materialität des Kunstwerks als lebendiges Fleisch einer in ihm verborgenen Subjektivität aufweisen" und diese Materie als „Träger eines geistigen Unbewussten" deutet, dann mag er damit einen gewissen Zug in der Entwicklung der modernen Kunst beschreiben. Doch Hillers Exerzitien haben eine andere Stoßrichtung als die „Vergeistigung der eigenen Materie des Kunstwerks".[20] Es geht ihm ja gerade um die Materie selbst, um die Formpotenziale, die noch unentdeckt im Material schlummern. Vergeistigung, das „Geistige in der Kunst", das seit Kandinskys gleichnamigem Essay[21] eine der Richtkräfte der Moderne ausmacht, ist für Hiller keine Lösung. Es führt kein Weg an der Materialität, d. h. am Naturcharakter des Bildmaterials vorbei. Die Dichotomie von Geist und Körper, ein philosophisch stets kontrovers diskutiertes Verhältnis, begrifflich ungeklärt und voller verborgener ideologischer Antagonismen, spielt für Hiller als solche keine Rolle.

19 Abb. in: *Joachim Hiller. Die Kunst des Eigensinns* [Anm. 5], S. 12.
20 Boris Groys, Der Tod steht ihr gut, in: *Kunst ohne Geschichte? Ansichten zu Kunst und Kunstgeschichte heute*. Herausgegeben von Anne-Marie Bonnet und Gabriele Kopp-Schmidt, München 1995, S. 13–22, alle Zitate S. 17.
21 [Anm. 4].

Of course, we are familiar with similar attitudes in modern art and need only think of Picasso's statement that for him painting consists of a "sum of destructions". (It is no coincidence that the joke Hiller once played by not leaving the arrangement of the splinters of glass up to physical forces, but by making them into a face referred as an homage to the multifaceted portraits composed of linear pieces from Picasso's phase of analytical cubism).[19] Or we think of Lucio Fontana's slashes in the canvas, of Alberto Burri's pictures made of charred sackcloth, or Yves Klein's or Heinz Mack's techniques of burning holes and spots into the pictures with flame throwers. Art theorist Boris Groys has described this tendency of the modern as one of the "horrible martyrdoms of the picture": "At least since the beginning of this [the 20th] century, the work of art has been subjected to tortures, only comparable to those displayed by the bodies of Christian martyrs. The picture (either symbolically or in reality) is burnt, slashed, disfigured, dirtied, and bodily mistreated in other, extremely varying ways." Up to this point Groys's words also apply to Hiller, but when the theorist closes with "All of these tortures leave behind on the surface of the art work wounds, scars, and traces of the use of force which feature the materiality of the art work as the living flesh of a subjectivity hidden within", interpreting this matter as the "carrier of a spiritual unconscious," then it may be that he is characterizing a certain feature in the development of modern art. But Hiller's spiritual exercises have a different thrust than the "spiritualization of the intrinsic matter of the work of art".[20] His concern is precisely for the matter itself, for the form potential yet slumbering undiscovered in the material. Spiritualization, the "spiritual in art" known to us since Kandinsky's essay with the same title[21] as one of the directional forces of the modern, is not a solution for Hiller. There is no way around materiality, i.e. the natural character of the picture material. The dichotomy of spirit and body, always discussed as a philosophically controversial relationship, conceptually undefined and full of hidden ideological antagonisms, does not play such a role for Hiller.

19 Depicted in: *Joachim Hiller. Die Kunst des Eigensinns* [footnote 5], p. 12.
20 Boris Groys, Der Tod steht ihr gut, in: *Kunst ohne Geschichte? Ansichten zu Kunst und Kunstgeschichte heute*. Edited by Anne-Marie Bonnet and Gabriele Kopp-Schmidt, Munich 1995, p. 13–22, all quotes p. 17.
21 [footnote 4].

Glas und Kunststoff/*Glass and plastics*
100 x 100 cm, 1975 (Ausschnitt/*Detail*)

Glas und Sand auf Hartschaum/*Glass and sand on Styrofoam*

120 x 120 cm, 1976

Dass die Natur der Materialien aufgrund der ihnen innewohnenden physikalischen Kräfte Formen bilden, die uns wiederum emotional berühren, und zwar auf die vielfältigste Weise, ist das Faszinosum, das seine Kunst in Gang hält. Das, was die Naturwissenschaft mit dem Begriff der Selbstorganisation beschreibt, die Fähigkeit der Natur, mit nur vier Grundkräften (starke Wechselwirkung, elektromagnetische Wechselwirkung, schwache Wechselwirkung und Gravitation) eine ungeheuer komplexe Formenwelt hervorzubringen, ist mit dem Geist-Körper-Dualismus nicht angemessen zu beschreiben. Wenn Joachim Hiller also mit dem Zertrümmern von Glasplatten eine höchst dynamische, um nicht zu sagen aggressive Art der „Malerei" erfindet, dann wendet er sich gewiss gegen eine erstarrte und fragwürdig gewordene Auffassung von Kunst und einen Malereibegriff, der ohnehin in den 60er- und 70er-Jahren von allen Seiten kritisiert wurde (ich werde darauf weiter unten zurückkommen). Doch dies geschieht nicht im Namen einer Denunziation des Materiellen, sondern im Gegenteil aus einem lebhaften Interesse an den der Materie innewohnenden Gestaltungskräften. Hillers Naturbegriff ist unsentimental, denkbar weit entfernt etwa vom Naturbegriff der Impressionisten mit ihrer Idylle für Sonntagsausflügler, ihren Parks und Blumenwiesen im Sonnenschein. Die Natur bildet Formen, transformiert und zerstört sie wieder, sie ist konstruktiv-destruktiv, im Großen wie im Kleinen ebenso vertraut wie unheimlich, so faszinierend wie unbegreiflich.

The fact that the nature of materials due to their intrinsic physical forces builds forms that in turn move us emotionally and in the most diverse ways, is the fascinating thing which keeps his art going. What the natural sciences describe as self-organization, nature's ability to produce a tremendously complex world of forms using only four basic forces (a strong reciprocal action, electromagnetic correlation, weak correlation, and gravitation), may not be suitably described using the dualism of spirit and body. Thus, when Joachim Hiller invents a highly dynamic if not aggressive way of "painting" in shattering his sheets of glass, then he is certainly turning against a petrified and increasingly questionable notion of art and a concept of painting which was anyway criticized from all sides in the 1960s and 70s (I will return to this subject later on). But this does not take place in the name of denouncing the material things; on the contrary, it is driven by a lively interest in the matter's intrinsic forces of creation. Hiller's concept of nature is unsentimental, obviously a far cry from the Impressionist concept of nature, for example, with their pastoral scenes for Sunday excursionists, their parks, and flower meadows in the sunshine. Nature constructs forms, transforms, and destroys them again. It is constructive and destructive, in big and small things familiar and unfamiliar alike, fascinating as well as incomprehensible.

…bleibende Dokumente einer schockhaften, plötzlichen Krafteinwirkung.

…the remnants documenting the shock of a sudden impact of force.

„Malen wie die Natur"

Natur und Kunst, sie scheinen sich zu fliehen
Und haben sich, eh man es denkt, gefunden …[22]
Johann Wolfgang v. Goethe

Das Aufbrechen des Bildes war für Hiller eine Notwendigkeit auf dem Weg, die technischen Mittel zu finden, die eine angemessene Umsetzung der „Lehre von Sveti Clement" ermöglichten. Knapp ein Jahrzehnt des Experimentierens und Suchens dauerte es, bis der Künstler die richtigen Folgerungen aus seinen Beobachtungen ziehen konnte. In den 80er-Jahren vollzogen sich diese dann explosionsartig. Nicht das Abbilden und Nachahmen der Natur war die Lösung, sondern das Arbeiten mit den Materialien und den ihnen immanenten Formkräften. Materie ist in der Lage, selbsttätig Strukturen zu bilden, man muss sie nur in diese Richtung lenken und Ausgangsbedingungen schaffen, unter denen sich ihr Formpotenzial verwirklichen kann. In den 80er-Jahren entwickelte Hiller eine ganze Reihe von technischen Innovationen und erarbeitete völlig ungewöhnliche Methoden, Farbe auf die Leinwand bzw. aufs Papier zu bringen, Formen zu erzeugen und neue, ungekannte Wege der Malerei zu beschreiten. Diese technischen Verfahren haben sich im Laufe der Jahre verfeinert und verändert, haben untereinander neue Mischformen hervorgebracht und Transformationen durchlebt, wodurch eine historische Sichtung und Datierung nicht eben erleichtert wird.

"Painting Like Nature"

Nature and art seem each other to flee
Yet, each finds the other before one can tell …[22]
Johann Wolfgang v. Goethe

Hiller regarded it as necessary to break up the picture with the goal of finding the technical means that would enable a suitable transformation corresponding to the "Lesson of Sveti Clement". It took just short of a decade of experimenting and searching before the artist was able to draw the right consequences from his observations. In the 1980s this all happened like an explosion. Not the depicting or copying of nature was the solution, but rather working with the materials and their immanent forces of form. Matter is in a position to form structures on its own. You only need to point it in this direction and create the conditions for it to commence, upon which it may realize its potential for form. In the 1980s Hiller developed an entire series of technical innovations and came up with completely unusual methods for applying paint to the canvas, or respectively the paper, for creating forms, and for striking out in new unknown directions of painting. These technical procedures have been refined and changed over the years, have produced new mixed forms, and undergone transformations, all meaning that the task of regarding them historically and putting a date to them is not made any easier.

22 *Goethes Gedichte in zeitlicher Folge*, 2. Auflage Frankfurt a. M. 1982, S. 510.

22 *Goethes Gedichte in zeitlicher Folge*, 2nd edition, Frankfurt a. M. 1982, p. 510.
English translation: Robert Richards, *The Romantic Conception of Life. Science and Philosophy in the Age of Goethe*, Chicago 2002.

Acryl auf Leinwand/*Acrylics on canvas*

100 x 100 cm, 1987

Acryl auf Leinwand/*Acrylics on canvas*

100 x 100 cm, 2007

Es soll im Folgenden nur soweit von Hillers künstlerischen Techniken die Rede sein, wie dies zur angemessenen Betrachtung der Kunstwerke unbedingt erforderlich ist. Die Frage, wie und mit welchen Mitteln ein Kunstwerk gemacht ist, ist vollkommen legitim und im Falle Hillers, der die Betrachter seiner Werke oft genug vor Rätsel stellt, ganz und gar verständlich. Die Mystifikation, das Verbergen und Verheimlichen der Methoden, mit denen ein Kunstwerk gefertigt wurde, gehört einem antiquierten Begriff von Genieästhetik an. Doch daraus darf man nicht den Umkehrschluss ziehen, dass ein Kunstwerk mit dem Offenlegen und Erklären seiner technischen Verfahrensweisen auch „verstanden" sei. Man muss hier überhaupt deutlich zwischen „Erklärung" und „Interpretation" unterscheiden; es ist dies ein wichtiger Unterschied, der in vielen kunsthistorischen und kunstkritischen Texten nicht genügend beachtet wird.[23] Wenn man biografische, psychologische, historische oder eben auch technische Einflussfaktoren für die Entstehung eines Kunstwerks benennt, so ist man mit *Erklärungen* beschäftigt. Aus dieser Perspektive betrachtet man Kunstwerke als Wirkungen, als produzierte Effekte. Doch wenn man nach *Interpretationen* von Kunstwerken fragt, betrachtet man diese umgekehrt als Ursachen, will heißen als Verursacher von sinnlichen und gedanklichen Prozessen, die bei der Betrachtung stattfinden.

In what follows, we will enter into a discussion of Hiller's artistic techniques only as far as it is absolutely necessary for understanding the works of art. The issue concerning how an art work is made and what medium has been used is entirely legitimate and understandable in Hiller's case, who often enough confronts the viewer of his works with mysteries. The mystification, hiding the methods used in making a work of art and keeping them secret, is part of an antiquated concept of the aesthetics of genius. But from this we may not assume that the opposite would apply, that an art work is "understood" merely when the technical processes have been exposed and explained. Anyway we must clearly distinguish between "explanation" and "interpretation", an important distinction which does not receive sufficient attention in many texts on art history and art criticism.[23] If we use biographical, psychological, historical, or even technical factors that influence the creation of a work of art, then we are explaining *it. Seen from this perspective we view works of art as effects, produced effects. But if we ask about* interpretations *of works of art, we view them conversely as causes, i.e. as the things that trigger the sensory and thought processes in the viewer.*

---

23 Instruktive Bemerkungen zum Unterschied zwischen kunstwissenschaftlicher Erklärung und Interpretation finden sich in: Oskar Bätschmann, *Einführung in die kunstgeschichtliche Hermeneutik*, Darmstadt 1986, S. 68–72. sowie ders., Einleitung in: Michael Baxandall, *Ursachen der Bilder. Über das historische Erklären von Kunst*. Mit einer Einführung von Oskar Bätschmann. Aus dem Englischen von Reinhard Kaiser, Berlin 1990, S. 7–17.

23 Instructive remarks concerning the difference between art historical explanation and interpretation may be found in: Oskar Bätschmann, *Einführung in die kunstgeschichtliche Hermeneutik*, Darmstadt 1986, p. 68–72, as well as in: the same: Introduction, in: Michael Baxandall *Ursachen der Bilder. Über das historische Erklären von Kunst*. With an introduction by Oskar Bätschmann. Translated into German by Reinhard Kaiser, Berlin 1990.

Im Folgenden sollen Erklärungen technischer Verfahrensweisen nur dann gegeben werden, wenn dies verhindern kann, dass die Interpretationen der Werke Hillers aufgrund unzutreffender Vermutungen in die falsche Richtung laufen. Der bekannte, meist Goethe zugeschriebene Satz „Man sieht nur, was man weiß" bzw. seine Variante „Man sieht nur, was man zu wissen *glaubt*" trifft vollkommen zu (und ist mittlerweile auch neurophysiologisch bestens belegt).[24] Wer mit falschen Vermutungen an Werke von Joachim Hiller herangeht, wird andere Bilder sehen als derjenige, der über ein Minimum an technischem Verständnis für ihre Entstehungsweise verfügt. Ein Beispiel: Die für die 90er-Jahre typischen „gemalten Reliefs" erinnern die meisten Betrachter an Luftaufnahmen. Daher glauben zahlreiche Ausstellungsbesucher, wie ich aus vielen Gesprächen weiß, dass diese Bilder durch fotografische Aufnahmen, durch Projektion auf die Leinwand oder Ähnliches entstanden seien. Wer diese Hypothese zur Grundlage der Betrachtung macht, wird Hillers Bilder anders wahrnehmen als die Betrachter, die – eine ebenso häufige Annahme – vermuten, die Arbeiten wären mit einer Bildsoftware am Computer entworfen worden.

Abgesehen davon, dass Joachim Hiller keinen Computer freiwillig anrührt, aber durchaus bekennt, dass er, wäre er wieder jung, heute seine Arbeiten sicher mit elektronischen Hilfsmitteln entwerfen würde – die Bilder haben weder etwas mit Fotografie noch mit Computertechnologie zu tun, sondern sind durch das Falten und Zerknittern der Leinwände entstanden. Das solchermaßen erzeugte Relief ist malerisch fixiert und danach die Leinwand wieder glattgezogen worden. Nur in Kenntnis solcher elementaren technischen Voraussetzungen kann eine „medienästhetische" Fehlinterpretation dieser Bilder vermieden werden.

Dass technische Erklärungen hier auf ein Minimum beschränkt werden soll, hat aber auch – das soll nicht verschwiegen werden – Kompetenzgründe. Kunsthistoriker und -kritiker verfügen im Allgemeinen nicht über ausgeprägte Kenntnisse künstlerischer Arbeitsweisen. Das ist auch nicht ihr Metier. Im Falle Joachim Hillers reichen maltechnische Grundkenntnisse ohnehin nicht aus. Schließlich hat er Dutzende von maltechnischen Verfahren ganz neu erfunden. Bei meinen zahlreichen Besuchen in seinem Atelier hat Hiller manche davon sehr detailliert geschildert, zum Teil auch praktisch vorgeführt. Andere hat er bloß beschrieben, wieder andere bestenfalls mit wenigen Worten angedeutet – und wer weiß wie viele überhaupt verschwiegen. Dass die Frage „Wie ist das technisch gemacht?" immer auch in intime Bereiche des Künstlers eindringt und zudem am Eigentlichen der Kunst vorbeizielt, ist mir bei diesen Gesprächen immer wieder deutlich geworden.

---

24 Zum Beispiel: Wolf Singer, Neurobiologische Anmerkungen zum Konstruktivismus-Diskurs, in: ders., *Der Beobachter im Gehirn. Essays zur Hirnforschung*, Frankfurt a. M. 2002, S. 87–111.

In what follows, the aim will be to provide explanations of technical processes only in as much as this prevents misinterpretations of Hiller's works due to inapplicable assumptions. The famous statement, mostly attributed to Goethe, "You only see what you know", and its variation "You only see what you think *you know" is entirely accurate (and has been neurophysiologically proven in the meantime: perception is the checking of hypotheses").[24] If we approach Joachim Hiller's works with false assumptions, we will see different pictures than those who have a bit of technical understanding concerning the way these works have been made. To give an example: the "painted reliefs", typical for the 1990s, evoke aerial photographs in most of the viewers. For this reason, as I learned from many conversations, numerous visitors to the exhibition simply assumed that these pictures came about using photographs projected onto the canvas, or by using similar processes. If you make this hypothesis the basis of your viewing, you will perceive Hiller's works differently than the viewer who—just as frequently—assumes that the works came about using picture software at the computer.*

Apart from the fact that Joachim Hiller does not willingly touch a computer, though he admits that if he were young again, he would certainly be designing his works with the aid of electronics today—the pictures have nothing to do with either photography or with computer technology, but owe their existence rather to the folding and creasing of the canvas. The relief produced in this way has been fixed with painterly means, the canvas then being stretched taut and smooth again. Only by knowing such elementary technical prerequisites can we avoid a "media-aesthetic" false interpretation of these pictures.

The fact that technical explanations are limited to a minimum here is also for reasons of competence and should not be concealed. Art historians and critics do not generally possess detailed knowledge of artistic working procedures. It is not their field. And anyway, in Joachim Hiller's case, basic painterly knowledge would not be enough. After all, he invented dozens of innovative painterly techniques and procedures. During my countless visits to his studio, Hiller explained some of them in great detail, even demonstrating them sometimes in practice. Others he merely described and others yet again he at most hinted at in a few words—and heaven knows how many things he chose to keep silent about. That the question of "How did you do this technically?", always intrudes into the artist's private sphere and in addition misses the point as to what art essentially is, is something which has become clear to me time and again in the course of these discussions.

---

24 For example: Wolf Singer, Neurobiologische Anmerkungen zum Konstruktivismus-Diskurs, in Ibid., *Der Beobachter im Gehirn. Essays zur Hirnforschung*, Frankfurt am Main 2002, p. 87–111, quote p. 104.

Acryl auf Leinwand/*Acrylics on canvas*

100 x 100 cm, 1987

Spachtelmasse, Sand, Acryl auf Leinwand/*Putty, sand, acrylics on canvas*

100 x 100 cm, 1984

Acryl auf Leinwand/*Acrylics on canvas*

100 x 100 cm, 2007 (Ausschnitt/*Detail*)

Erosionen

Nach der eher drastischen Zertrümmerungsästhetik der Glasplattenreliefs beruhigte sich Hillers zwischen Malerei und Relief angesiedelte Formensprache wieder, wurde subtiler und feiner in der Struktur. Anfang der 80er-Jahre entstand eine Vielzahl von Arbeiten mit Zement, den er manchmal grau in grau, manchmal farbig gefasst auf Holzplatten oder Leinwände auftrug. In unterschiedlicher Reliefstärke erscheint das flexible, sehr gut formbare Material zuweilen rau und schrundig oder aber glatt und mehrschichtig aufgetragen. Was diese Arbeiten dem Betrachter vermitteln, ist ein Gefühl für Zeit, für die erodierende Arbeit der Naturmaterialien. Es sind dies Prozesse, die jeder kennt, der aufmerksam darauf achtet, wie sich Betondecken, asphaltierte Gehwege, Wandverputze, Gebäudeanstriche usw. unter dem permanenten Einfluss der Witterungsverhältnisse, der Temperaturschwankungen und mechanischer Einwirkungen verändern, wie obere Schichten des Materials abplatzen und darunterliegende Strukturen freigeben, wie sich feine Haarrisse oder gröbere Brüche über die Fläche ziehen, ganz eigene Muster und Liniennetze bilden. Das Besondere an diesen Arbeiten besteht darin, dass sie unseren Blick für diese Dinge erweitern und eine eigentümliche ästhetische Schönheit des Materials entdecken lassen, wo sie uns im Alltag nur lästig ist. Das Zerbröckeln von Putz, das Zerspringen von Betondecken kann, außerhalb des Kontexts praktischen Nutzens betrachtet, faszinierende und ästhetisch höchst interessante Formen bilden.

Diesen Ansatz der Auseinandersetzung mit der formauflösenden-formbildenden Dialektik der Naturkräfte verfolgte Hiller bald auch mit anderen Mitteln weiter. Anstatt Zement benutze er feinere und leichtere Spachtelmasse, die er dünn auf die Leinwand auftrug. Mit Acrylfarbe eingefärbt und mit schwarzem Sand als „Kontrastmittel" versehen, zeigen diese Arbeiten ein starkes optisches Relief. Dieser Effekt entsteht dadurch, dass sich der Sand beim Bewegen der flach ausgebreiteten Leinwand bzw. durch Pusten an den Graten und in den Ecken des aufgespachtelten Materials sammelt. Dadurch wird das flache Relief optisch erheblich verstärkt und es entsteht ein Eindruck, wie man ihn z. B. von ruß- oder staubgeschwärzten, mit Rauputz versehenen Mauern kennt.

Erosions

Subsequent to the drastic aesthetics of demolition in connection with the reliefs made of sheets of glass, Hiller's language of forms, located somewhere between painting and relief, settled down again, becoming more subtle and refined in structure. At the beginning of the 1980s he made a multitude of works using cement, sometimes executed in gray-in-gray and other times colorfully, on wooden boards or canvas. In varying degrees of relief the flexible, highly formable material is sometimes rough and cracked, sometimes smooth and multi-layered. What these works convey to the viewer is a feeling for time, for the erosion of natural materials. These are processes everyone is familiar with who has ever noticed how concrete floors, asphalt footpaths, wall plastering, the paint on buildings, etc. are subject to change due to the permanent influence of weathering, temperature changes and mechanical effects, how the upper layers of material peel to reveal the structures beneath, how fine hairline cracks or rougher crevices spread across a surface, forming their own patterns and networks of lines. What is special about these works is that they broaden our view on things, allowing us to discover a strange aesthetic beauty of the material, where we would only be bothered by them otherwise in our everyday lives. The crumbling of plaster and the cracks in concrete floors can form fascinating and highly interesting aesthetic shapes if we take them out of the context of practical use.

This approach for dealing with the form-dissolving and form-shaping dialectics of natural forces was something Hiller soon pursued using other means as well. Instead of cement he used a finer and lighter caulking, which he applied thinly to the canvas. With acrylics used for color and black sand applied as a "contrast medium", these works display a strong optical relief. This effect comes about by the sand's collecting at the ridges and corners of the applied caulking compound when moving the spread out canvas or by blowing the sand across it. In doing so, the flat relief is considerably strengthened visually and the impression arises as we know it for example of walls with roughcast plastering, covered with soot or black dust.

Acryl auf Leinwand/*Acrylics on canvas*

150 x 150 cm, 2007

Was diese Arbeiten dem Betrachter vermitteln, ist ein Gefühl für Zeit,
für die erodierende Arbeit der Naturmaterialien.
What these works convey to the viewer is a feeling for time,
for the erosion of natural materials.

Acryl auf Leinwand/*Acrylics on canvas*

100 x 100 cm, 2007

Überhaupt ist das Mauer-Motiv für Joachim Hiller von nicht zu überschätzender Bedeutung. In den unterschiedlichsten Techniken formt er immer wieder Strukturen, die an verputzte oder roh aufgesetzte Steinmauern erinnern. In manchen Bildern oder Reliefs sind klar erkennbar Fugen zu sehen, die diesen Eindruck verdeutlichen. Selbstverständlich steht Hiller mit der Faszination für das Motiv „Mauer" nicht allein. Man findet ein vergleichbares Interesse allenthalben in der europäischen Kunst der ersten Nachkriegsjahrzehnte, etwa die textur- und materialbetonten Bilder der 40er- und 50er-Jahre von Jean Dubuffet oder Jean Fautrier in Paris. Oder die informellen Materialbilder eines Alberto Burri in Italien oder Antoni Tàpies in Spanien. Auch die schwere Materialität des pastosen Farbauftrags bei Emil Schumacher in Deutschland und die graffitiartige Zeichensprache seiner frühen Bilder müssen hier genannt werden. Doch im Unterschied zu Hiller war das Interesse der genannten Künstler höchstens beiläufig auf die Naturprozesse selbst gerichtet. Ihnen war vielmehr daran gelegen, ausgetretene ästhetische Pfade zu verlassen und der Malerei neue Ausdrucksmöglichkeiten zu erschließen. Die Mauer kann als Paradigma der objekthaften Malerei nach dem Zweiten Weltkrieg bezeichnet werden. Im Gegensatz zu der bereits erwähnten neuzeitlichen Auffassung des Bildes als „finestra aperta", d. h. als offenes Fenster, das eine illusionistische Öffnung zur Welt darstellt, verschlossen viele Künstler die Bildfläche, indem sie diese als materielle Fläche, als Wand, als Mauerstück auffassten. Beispielhaft tat dies der spanische Maler Antoni Tàpies, indem er Mitte der 50er-Jahre dazu überging, seinen Malmitteln Sand, Marmorstaub, Leim und Ähnliches unterzumischen.

The motif of the wall is infinitely important for Joachim Hiller. In the most varying techniques he forms structures over and over again that remind us of plastered walls or random rubble masonry. In some of the pictures or reliefs we clearly recognize the joints, which make this impression even stronger. Of course, Hiller does not stand alone in his fascination for the motif of the wall. We find comparable interest all over European art in the first few decades after the war, for example the pictures of the 1940s and 1950s emphasizing texture and material by Jean Dubuffet or Jean Fautrier in Paris or of the Informel material pictures of the likes of Alberto Burri in Italy or of Antoni Tàpies in Spain. Also, the heavy materiality of Emil Schumacher's pastose application of paint in Germany and the graffiti like language of drawing in his earlier pictures must be mentioned in this connection. But unlike Hiller the interest of the artists cited above was incidental at most in terms of focusing on the processes of nature itself. Their intention was rather to depart from the beaten aesthetic paths and find new expressions for painting. The wall may be designated as a paradigm of objective painting after World War II. Contrary to the renaissance notion of the picture as a "finestra aperta", i.e. as an open window, representing an illusionist opening to the world, many artists closed up the picture surface by understanding it as a material surface, a wall, or a piece of a wall. In the mid-1950s the Spanish painter Antoni Tàpies accomplished this exemplarily by resorting to mixing sand, marble dust, glue, and similar materials into his painting medium.

Mauer, Kroatien/ *Wall, Croatia*

Für Joachim Hiller hat das Motiv Mauer jedoch eine weit über die formalen Möglichkeiten hinausreichende Bedeutung. Die Mauer steht an der Schnittstelle zwischen Natur und Kultur. Mauern umgeben und schützen unsere Häuser und Städte, unsere privaten und öffentlichen Arbeits- und Lebensräume gegen die Gewalt der Natur. In der Regel selbst aus Naturmaterialien wie Sand und Stein gebaut, sind sie den Naturkräften Wind, Sonne und Regen ausgesetzt. Solche noch nah am Naturmaterial bleibenden Mauerstrukturen sah Hiller zum Beispiel während seiner vielen Reisen ins frühere Jugoslawien. Nur in wenigen Ausnahmefällen zeigen die Mauern „Spuren, die von vergangenen Generationen, hier in fahrlässiger Kritzelei, dort in planvoller Geometrie, auf uralten Hauswänden hinterlassen worden sind."[25] Die sichtbare Natur mit ihren Formkräften ist für Hiller das Thema. Nicht die Zeichen des menschlichen Geistes, sondern die Schrift der Natur, die Flecken, Risse und Krakeleen, die durch mechanische Kräfte entstehen. In seinen Bildern werden wir uns der Naturkräfte bewusst, die alle unsere Hervorbringungen früher oder später wieder in Natur zurückverwandeln. Entsprechend wirken Hillers „Mauer"-Bilder stets gesättigt mit Zeit.

For Joachim Hiller the motif of the wall has a significance that extends far beyond the formal possibilities. The wall stands at the interface between nature and culture. Walls surround and protect our homes and cities, our private and public working and living spaces against the force of nature. Themselves as a rule made of natural materials such as sand and stone, they are exposed to natural forces such as wind, sun, and rain. Hiller saw such wall structures that remained close to the natural materials used in building them for example during his many trips to what was then Yugoslavia. Only with a few exceptions do the walls reveal "traces left behind by earlier generations on the ancient walls of houses, here careless scribbles, there carefully planned geometric figures."[25] Visible nature with its forces of form is Hiller's theme. Not the signs of the human mind, but the handwriting of nature, the spots, cracks, and craquelés caused by mechanical forces. In his pictures we become conscious of natural forces that sooner or later transform all we have ever produced back into nature. Accordingly, Hiller's "wall" pictures always seem saturated with time.

25 Held [Anm. 8], S. 46.

25 Held [footnote 8], p. 46.

Acryl und Spachtelmasse auf Holz/*Acrylics and putty on wood*

60 x 60 cm, 2008

Zeit ist das Element der Natur, denn die Natur ist in unaufhörlicher Bewegung und sie bewirkt unentwegt Veränderung. Es ist eine eigentümliche Menschenferne, ein gewissermaßen „anthropofugaler" Zug in Hillers Mauerbildern, ja überhaupt in seinem Werk. Es gibt nicht den geringsten Hinweis darauf, dass es sich um Mauern von noch bewohnten Häusern handelt. Sie wirken eher wie archäologische Relikte aus einer weit zurückliegenden Vergangenheit. Schaut man die Mauerbilder der 80er-Jahre nacheinander an, gewinnt man den Eindruck, einem Auflösungsprozess zuzusehen, bei dem die Errungenschaften menschlicher Kultur schrittweise von der Natur aufgesogen und in naturhafte Formbildung zurückgenommen werden. Hillers Mauerbilder scheinen von der unsentimentalen Einsicht getragen, dass alle menschliche Kultur ihre Zeit hat und eines Tages vergeht und von der Natur zurückgenommen wird.

Sehr deutlich wird dieser Zustand der fortschreitenden Formauflösung in den beiden umfangreichen Serien von Bildern, bei denen Hiller mit zahlreichen übereinanderliegenden Farbschichten arbeitete. In der einen Serie werden die Farbschichten teilweise wieder abgeschliffen, sodass tiefer liegende Zustände zum Vorschein kommen. In der anderen verwendete Hiller flüssiges Wachs, mit dem er die Leinwand stellenweise bedeckte, dann neue Farbschichten auftrug, das Wachs mit einer Heißluftpistole wieder entfernte usw. Auf diese Art entstanden vielteilige fleckige Strukturen in unterschiedlichen Dichtegraden. Auch wenn man auf den meisten dieser Arbeiten noch ein horizontal-vertikales Grundraster zu erkennen vermag, ist dieses dennoch kaum noch als Spur eines planvollen menschlichen Handelns zu deuten. Es könnte sich ebenso gut um naturwüchsige Strukturen handeln. In diesen Arbeiten geht schrittweise auch der gegenständlich lesbare Bezug zur Mauer verloren. Von manchen Bildern fühlt man sich eher an Nahaufnahmen von Leder oder Baumrinde erinnert, wären da nicht die starken Farben, das zum Teil „impressionistische" Flirren und Flackern der in kleinste Flecken aufgelösten Farbpartikel. Oder handelt es sich um eine Mikrowelt, um riesenhaft vergrößerte mikroskopische Schnitte durch Mineralien, die im Gegenlicht funkeln? Hillers Bilder Mitte der 80er-Jahre stehen am äußersten Rand gegenständlicher Assoziationsfähigkeit. Form löst sich hier allmählich auf in reine Malerei.

Time is the element of nature, since nature is in perpetual motion and causes constant change. Strangely distant to man, there is a certain "anthropofugal" feature in Hiller's wall pictures and even in his work in general. There is not the slightest hint that these are walls of houses still lived in. Rather they seem like the archaeological relics of long ago. If we look at the wall pictures of the 1980s one after another, we gain the impression we are witnessing a process of dissolution where the achievements of human culture are being sucked up by nature step by step and reclaimed for the natural creation of forms. Hiller's wall paintings appear to be borne by the unsentimental insight that all human culture has its time and one day it will pass and be reclaimed by nature.

This progressive condition of form dissolution becomes very clear in the two comprehensive series of pictures in which Hiller was working with numerous layers of paint on top of each other. In the one series the layers of paint are partially sanded off again so that the layers underneath are exposed. In the other series Hiller used liquid wax to cover the canvas in parts, now applying new layers of paint and next removing the wax again with a hot-air gun, etc. In this way multi-part, spotted structures come about in various degrees of density. Even though we may still recognize a basic horizontal and vertical pattern in most of these works, nevertheless this may hardly be interpreted as the trace of planned human actions. It may just as well be naturally-grown structures. In these works the recognizable objective context of the wall increasingly gets lost, step by step. Some of the pictures would rather remind us of close-ups of leather or tree bark, if it were not for the strong colors, the partially "impressionistic" shimmering and flickering of the particles of paint that have dissolved into the most minute spots. Or is this a micro world, of gigantically enlarged microscopic cross-sections of minerals, which glitter against the light? Hiller's pictures from the mid-1980s define the outer limit for our capacity to associate them with objects. Here form gradually dissolves into painting.

Acryl, Sand, Hartschaum auf Holz/*Acrylics, sand, Styrofoam on wood*

150 x 150 cm, 2007

Es ist eine eigentümliche Menschenferne, ein gewissermaßen „anthropofugaler" Zug in Hillers Mauerbildern, ja überhaupt in seinem Werk.
Strangely distant to man, there is a certain "anthropofugal" feature in Hiller's wall pictures and even in his work in general.

In den späten 70er-Jahren baute Joachim Hiller eine Reihe kinetischer Objekte,
um dynamische Strukturprozesse dauerhaft anschaulich zu machen.
In the late 1970s Joachim Hiller built a series of kinetic objects to create a possibility
for making dynamic processes of structure enduringly visible.

  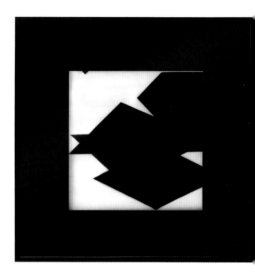

Glas, Elektromotoren und Aluminium/*Glass, electric motors and aluminium*

65 x 65 x 15 cm, 1979

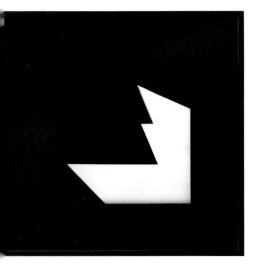
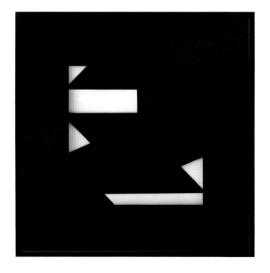
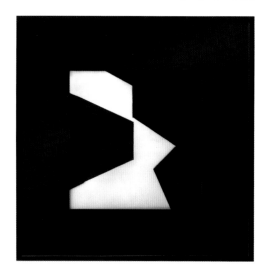

Prozesse in Echtzeit – Die kinetischen Objekte

Ich habe weiter oben behauptet, dass Joachim Hillers Mauerbilder gesättigt seien mit Zeit. Überhaupt muss Zeit notwendigerweise ein Thema sein, wenn man naturhafte Strukturen thematisiert. Denn Strukturen entstehen in der Zeit und verändern sich mit der Zeit. Naturstrukturen entstehen in Zeiträumen, die der menschlichen Beobachtung meist unzugänglich sind, ja sich der menschlichen Vorstellungskraft überhaupt entziehen. Viele Formbildungsprozesse, zum Beispiel die Auffaltung von Gebirgen, geologische Sedimentierungen usw. vollziehen sich über Jahrmillionen in einer Langsamkeit, die für menschliche Augen nicht nachvollziehbar ist. Andere Prozesse ereignen sich überaus schnell, z. B. das Zerbrechen von Glas. Der Verlauf der Bruchkanten geschieht in Millisekunden, zu schnell, um von uns betrachtet zu werden. Die Idee von Joachim Hiller war es, mit seinen erfindungsreichen malerischen Techniken Strukturen anschaulich zu machen, deren Bildung sich in der Natur gewöhnlich nicht beobachten lässt. Dennoch war es im Medium der Malerei bzw. des Reliefs unvermeidlich, dass nur die Ergebnisse von Prozessen zu zeigen waren, nicht aber die Prozesse selbst. So kann man die zerbrochenen und fixierten Glasscheiben sehen, nicht aber das Brechen; die gefalteten und zerknitterten Leinwände, nicht aber die Faltung selbst. Aus diesem Mangel entstand der Wunsch, einen permanenten Formbildungsprozess anschaulich zu machen. Paradoxerweise war dies nur mithilfe dessen möglich, was wir gewöhnlich als das Gegenteil von Natur ansehen, nämlich mit Maschinen, technischen Apparaten.

Processes in Real Time— The Kinetic Objects

I maintained above that Joachim Hiller's wall pictures were saturated with time. In general, time must necessarily be a theme if you are working with nature-like structures. Structures come about in time and change over time. Natural structures come about in periods of time that, for the most part, do not avail themselves to human observation, or even escape human imagination entirely. Many of the processes for creating forms, for example the anticline folds of mountains, geological sedimentation, etc. take place over millions of years at a rate invisible to human eyes. Other processes happen very quickly: breaking glass, for example. The progression of the breakage lines takes place in milliseconds, too quickly for us to see. It was Joachim Hiller's idea to make structures visible whose natural formation we may normally never witness, with the help of his inventive painterly techniques. And yet in the medium of painting, or respectively the relief, it was inevitable that only the results of the processes would be visible, not the processes themselves. Thus, we can see the broken and fixed sheets of glass, but not the breaking. Likewise, we can see the folded and crumpled canvases, but not the actual folding itself. Out of these shortcomings the desire grew to make visible a continuing creation process of forms. Paradoxically, this was only possible with the aid of what we would normally consider the opposite of nature, namely with machines and technical equipment.

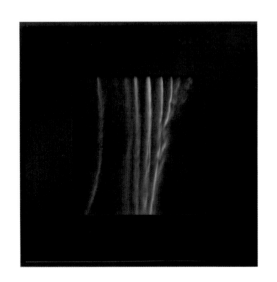
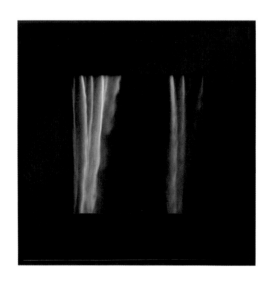
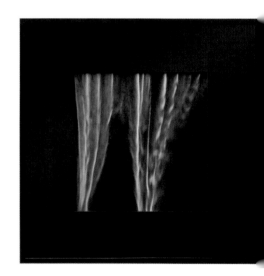

In den späten 70er-Jahren baute Joachim Hiller eine Reihe kinetischer Objekte, um dynamische Strukturprozesse dauerhaft anschaulich zu machen. Einer der Apparate transportiert zum Beispiel feinen weißen Sand nach oben, wo er hinter einer Plexiglasscheibe sichtbar herunterrieselt, neu aufgenommen, wieder nach oben befördert wird usw. Dem Betrachter bietet sich der Anblick eines sich ständig verändernden „Vorhangs" aus fallendem Sand. Ein anderer Apparat verschiebt in unterschiedlichen Geschwindigkeiten eine Reihe von einfachen Formen permanent gegeneinander, sodass sich dauernd ein anderer Anblick bietet, eine wechselnde Anordnung und Gewichtung von Schwarz und Weiß. Dass Hiller die aufwendige Arbeit an den kinetischen Objekten bald wieder aufgab, hatte in erster Linie praktische Gründe: Die Elektromotoren, die sich für seine Zwecke eigneten, waren sehr anfällig und bedurften ständiger Wartung und Reparatur. Auch wenn die Arbeit an den kinetischen Objekten sein Verständnis für den Prozesscharakter seiner Kunst vertieft hatte, waren sie doch auch ästhetisch letztlich nicht befriedigend und, verglichen mit seinen Gemälden und Reliefs, zu offensichtlich in der Wirkung und zu zeitraubend in der Konstruktion. So blieb die kinetische Kunst in Hillers Gesamtwerk eine interessante, aber doch sehr kurze Episode.

In the late 1970s Joachim Hiller built a series of kinetic objects to create a possibility for making dynamic processes of structure enduringly visible. One of the apparatuses, for example, transports fine white sand upwards, where we watch it trickle down behind a sheet of plexiglass, collect again, and be transported upwards once more, etc. The viewer gazes upon a constantly changing "curtain" of falling sand. Another apparatus pushes in various tempos a couple of simple forms constantly against one another, so that we are always looking at a different situation, a changing arrangement and ratio between black and white. That Hiller soon abandoned the extensive amount of work he was putting into the kinetic objects was mainly due to practical reasons: the electric motors that suited his purposes were extremely sensitive and called for constant care and repair. Even though the work on the kinetic objects deepened his understanding for the processual character of his art, nevertheless they were not ultimately satisfying from an aesthetic standpoint and, compared with his paintings and reliefs, they were too apparent in their effect and too time-consuming in the construction. Thus, the kinetic art remains an interesting but short-lived episode in Hiller's overall work.

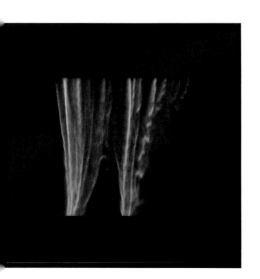 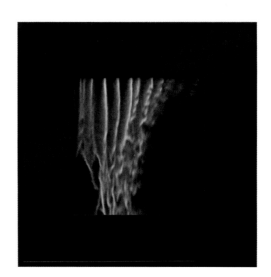 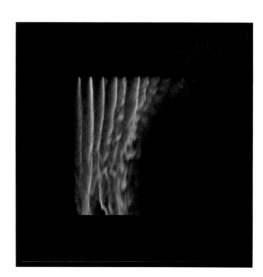

Glas, Sand, Elektromotoren und Aluminium / *Glass, sand, electric motors and aluminium*

65 x 65 x 15 cm, 1979

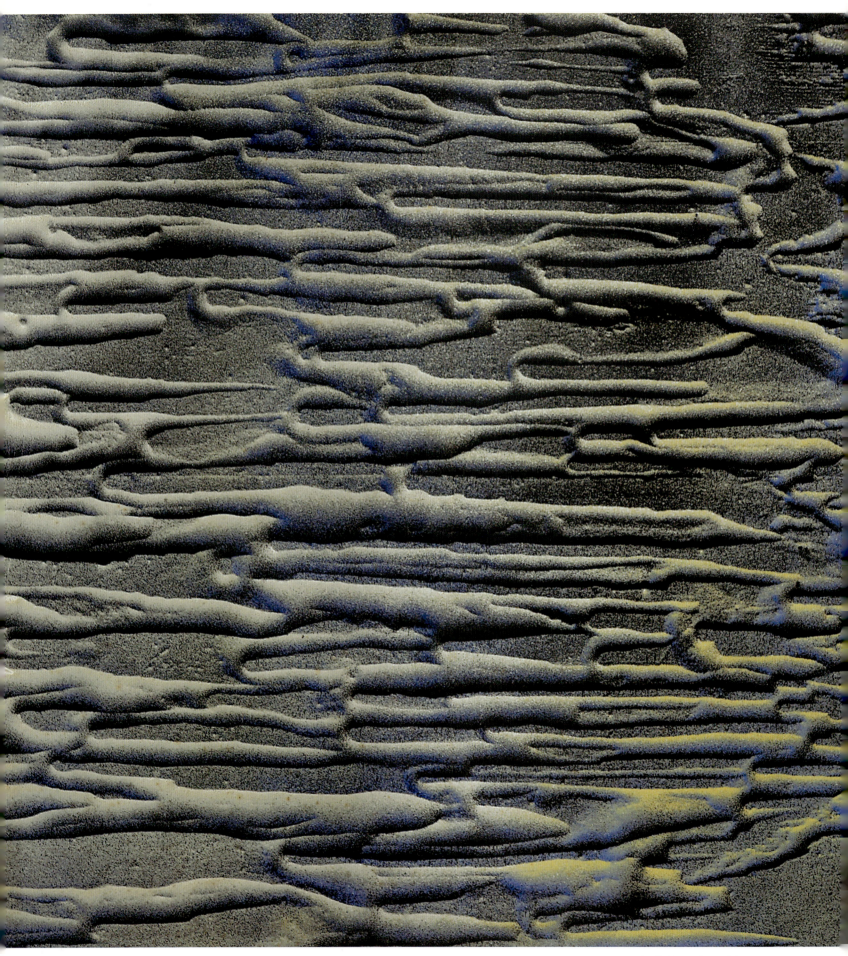

Acryl auf Folie/*Acrylics on foil*, 110 x 110 cm, 1972

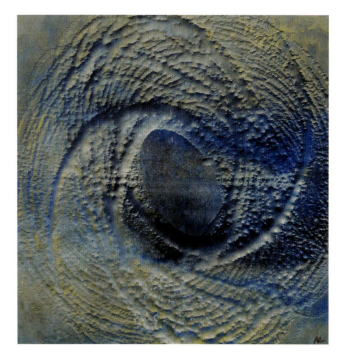

Acryl auf Folie/*Acrylics on foil*, 110 x 110 cm, 1972

Malerei als Prozess

Die Empfindung verwirklicht sich nicht im Material,
ohne dass das Material nicht vollständig in die Empfindung,
in das Perzept oder den Affekt übergeht. Die gesamte Materie wird
expressiv. Der Affekt ist metallisch, kristallin, steinern ... und die
Empfindung ist nicht farbig, sie ist, wie Cézanne sagt, farbgebend.[26]
Gilles Deleuze/Felix Guattari

Hillers Ansatz, sich selbstorganisierende Naturstrukturen zum Thema der Malerei zu machen, setzte einen Erfindungsreichtum an technischen Innovationen in Gang, der immer wieder in Erstaunen versetzt. Eines der ungewöhnlichsten Beispiele ist seine Idee, Realreliefs aus Gips oder anderen modellierfähigen Substanzen zu bauen und diese dann mit einem geschlossenen „Sack" aus einer starken Kunststofffolie zu überziehen. Dieser wird danach durch Absaugen der Luft ganz dicht auf das Relief gepresst und schließlich in der Art einer Grattage oder Frottage mit Farbe bedeckt. Nach Trocknung der Farbschichten wird die Folie wieder glatt gestrichen und auf Leinwand gezogen. Auf diese Art entstanden Bilder von irreal wirkender Dreidimensionalität. Der Nachteil dieser Arbeiten ist ihre Verletzlichkeit. Die Kunststofffolie ist kein idealer Bildträger für ein wässriges Medium wie Acrylfarbe. Doch genau in ihrer spürbaren Fragilität und im Widerspruch zwischen der Leichtigkeit des transparenten Materials und dem massiven, plastischen Eindruck des Reliefmotivs liegt der außerordentliche ästhetische Reiz dieser Arbeiten.

26 Gilles Deleuze/Félix Guattari, *Was ist Philosophie?* Aus dem Französischen von Bernd Schwibs und Joseph Vogl, Frankfurt a. M. 1996, S. 195.

Painting as Process

The sensation does not become real in the material
without the material completely transforming into the sensation,
the perception or the affect. The matter becomes expressive
in its entirety. The affect is metallic, crystalline, stony ...
and the sensation is not colored; as Cézanne says, it is coloring.[26]
Gilles Deleuze/Félix Guattari

Hiller's approach of making natural structures that organize themselves the theme of painting triggered a wealth of inventions of technical innovations that astonish us over and over again. One of the most unusual examples is his idea of building real reliefs out of plaster or other substances suitable for modeling and then covering them with a closed "sack" made of heavy plastic foil. After sucking the air out, the foil clings very closely against the relief and is subsequently covered with paint in the form of a grattage or a frottage. After the layers of paint have dried the foil is then flattened out again and stretched on canvas. In this way, pictures came about with a three-dimensionality that seemed unreal. The disadvantage of these works is their vulnerability. The plastic foil is not an ideal picture carrier for a water-based medium such as acrylics. But it is their discernible fragility and the contradiction that prevails between the lightness of the transparent material and the massive plastic impression of the relief motif, which convey the exceptionally aesthetic attraction of these works.

26 Gilles Deleuze/Félix Guattari, *Was ist Philosophie?* Translated from the French into German by Bernd Schwibs and Joseph Vogl, Frankfurt am Main 1996, p. 195, (English quote translation: e.v.).

Acryl auf Papier/*Acrylics on paper*, 70 x 50 cm, 1988 (Ausschnitt/*Detail*)

Während manche Serien den Betrachter vor unlösbare Rätsel über ihre technische Realisation stellen, sind andere wiederum von einer bestechenden Klarheit und Einfachheit, die Hillers Fragestellungen in aller Anschaulichkeit zutage treten lassen. Eine solche Serie stellen die wenigen „Eisblumen"-Arbeiten von 1988 dar. Nach vielen Experimenten über das Verhalten von wässrig angerührter Acrylfarbe bei Minustemperaturen fand Joachim Hiller heraus, dass diese unter bestimmten Bedingungen zu hochkomplexen Formen gefriert, vergleichbar den Eisblumen, die sich an schlecht isolierten Fenstern aus dem Kondenswasser von Innenräumen bilden. Also strich er Papierbögen mit Farbe ein und ließ diese bei günstigen (und im Rhein-Main-Gebiet äußerst seltenen) winterlichen Temperaturen von minus 10 bis 12 Grad Celsius gefrieren. Es war notwendig, diese Temperatur konstant über mindestens 12 Stunden zu erhalten, damit die zu filigranen Formen geronnene Farbe nicht wieder verlief. Die Bilder waren erst dann sicher auf dem Papier fixiert, wenn alle Feuchtigkeit vollständig verdampft war und Gebilde von fremdartiger Schönheit zurückgelassen hatte. Wie kaum eine andere Serie verdeutlichen diese Blätter, worauf es Hiller bei seiner Arbeit ankommt: Bedingungen zu schaffen, unter denen das Material selbsttätig Formen kreiert; Formen, die man selbst nicht oder zumindest nicht in dieser Weise erfinden könnte; Formen, die nicht nur den außenstehenden Betrachter, sondern auch den Maler selbst überraschen.

While some series confront the viewer with insolvable mysteries as to their technical realization, others are captivatingly clear and simple, allowing Hiller's issues to come into the full light. One such series is the "Frost flowers" works of 1988, of which there are only a few in numbers. After much experimenting on how water-based acrylics react in sub-freezing temperatures, Joachim Hiller found out that they freeze to highly complex forms under certain conditions, similar to the frost flowers that form from water condensing on the insides of badly insulated windows. So he spread paint on sheets of paper and let them freeze at suitable winter temperatures (extremely rare for the Rhine-Main area) of minus 10° to 12° Celsius. It was necessary that the temperature remained constant for at least 12 hours so that the paint's gelling into delicate forms would not thaw and run again. The pictures were only securely fixed on the paper when all of the dampness had completely evaporated, leaving behind formations of strange enchanting beauty. As almost no other series, these pages manage to make it very clear what is important to Hiller in his work: namely, to create conditions where the material creates the forms itself; forms that we could not invent ourselves, at least not in this manner. Forms that not only surprise the viewer, but also the painter himself.

Acryl und Sand auf Leinwand/*Acrylics and quartz sand on canvas*

100 x 100 cm, 1990

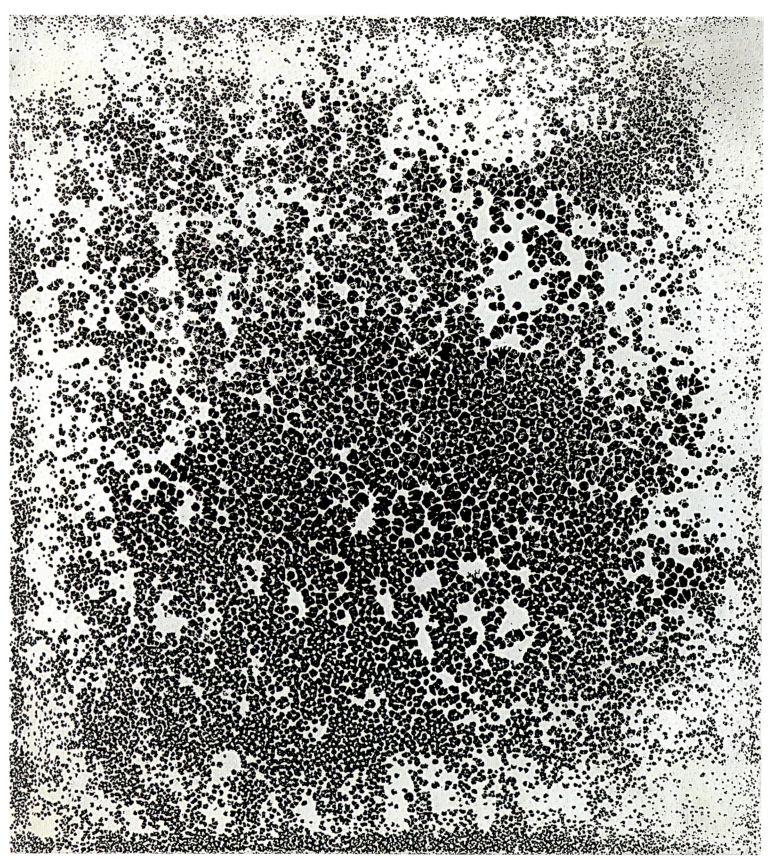

Acryl auf Leinwand/*Acrylics on canvas*
100 x 90 cm, 1991

Dasselbe gilt für eine Reihe von Arbeiten, die großenteils auf Papier, aber auch in mehreren Exemplaren auf Leinwand realisiert wurde. Es sind dies Gemälde, die ich als „Dispersionsbilder" bezeichnen möchte. Unter Dispersion (wörtlich: Verteilung, Zerstreuung) versteht man die Ausbreitung verschiedener Substanzen oder auch Populationen auf einem wie auch immer gearteten Feld. In der Chemie spricht man genauer von der Verteilung zweier (oder mehrerer) Substanzen, die chemisch nicht miteinander reagieren und sich nicht ineinander lösen. Genau das geschieht mit der Farbe der Dispersionsbilder. Das gemeinsame, im Grunde sehr einfache Prinzip dieser Arbeiten besteht darin, zwei Farbsubstanzen zusammenzubringen, die sich aufgrund ihrer chemischen Eigenschaften gegenseitig abstoßen. Hiller tut also ganz bewusst das, was jedes Anfängerbuch zur Malerei zu vermeiden empfiehlt, nämlich „mager auf fett" bzw. „fett auf mager" zu malen. Der Auftrag von wässriger Acrylfarbe auf dem Untergrund von Ölfarbe lässt erstere ausflocken und in Farbgerinnseln stocken. Hiller hat diesen Effekt über Jahre studiert und erforschte mit geradezu naturwissenschaftlicher Experimentierfreude, welche Wirkungen sich durch die Variation der Zusammensetzung, der Dichte und Konsistenz der Farbe sowie der Quantität ihres Auftrags ergeben. Auf manchen Blättern zeigt sich eine dichte Folge von Pünktchen, auf anderen netz- oder zellenartige Strukturen, die umso komplexer werden, je mehr Schichten übereinandergelegt werden. In anderen Arbeiten zog sich die Acrylfarbe soweit zusammen, dass Hunderte von isolierten Einzelformen übrig blieben, die sich wie Sterne am Nachthimmel oder – eher noch – wie Kleinstlebewesen unter dem Mikroskop über die Papierfläche verteilten. Dabei weist dann jede einzelne Form winzige Varianten auf – feinste Farbfädchen, -spitzen, Protuberanzen –, die sie alle individualisieren.

The same applies to a series of works which were mostly done on paper, but also in several instances on canvas. These are paintings I would like to call "dispersion pictures". By dispersion (literally: distribution, scattering) we understand the spreading of various substances or also populations across some kind of field. In chemistry we refer more precisely to the distribution of two (or more) substances, which do not react to one another chemically and do not dissolve into one another. Precisely this is what happens with the paint on the dispersion pictures. The common principle of these works, very simple actually, consists of bringing together two paint substances, which repel each other due to their chemical properties. Thus, Hiller consciously does exactly what every beginner's painting book recommends avoiding, namely to paint "thin onto fat" or "fat onto thin". The application of a water-based acrylic paint to a grounding of oil makes the former flake and gel into runs of color. Hiller studied this effect for years, researching it with a virtual scientific joy of experimentation concerning what effects came about by varying the mixture, the density and consistency of the paint as well as the quantity of its application. Some of the pages display a dense succession of dots, on others there are network or cell structures that become all the more complex the more layers are applied over each other. In yet other works the acrylics shrank to the extent that hundreds of isolated individual forms remained, distributing themselves over the paper's surface like stars in the night sky or—rather—like micro-organisms under the microscope. In doing so, each individual form displays minute variations—the finest threads of colors, tips, and protuberances, making each one unique.

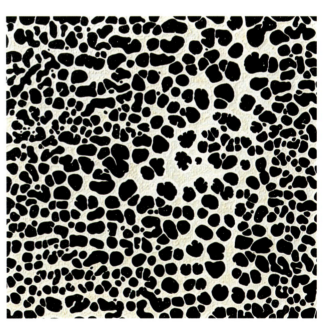

Acryl auf Leinwand/*Acrylics on canvas* (Ausschnitt/*Detail*)

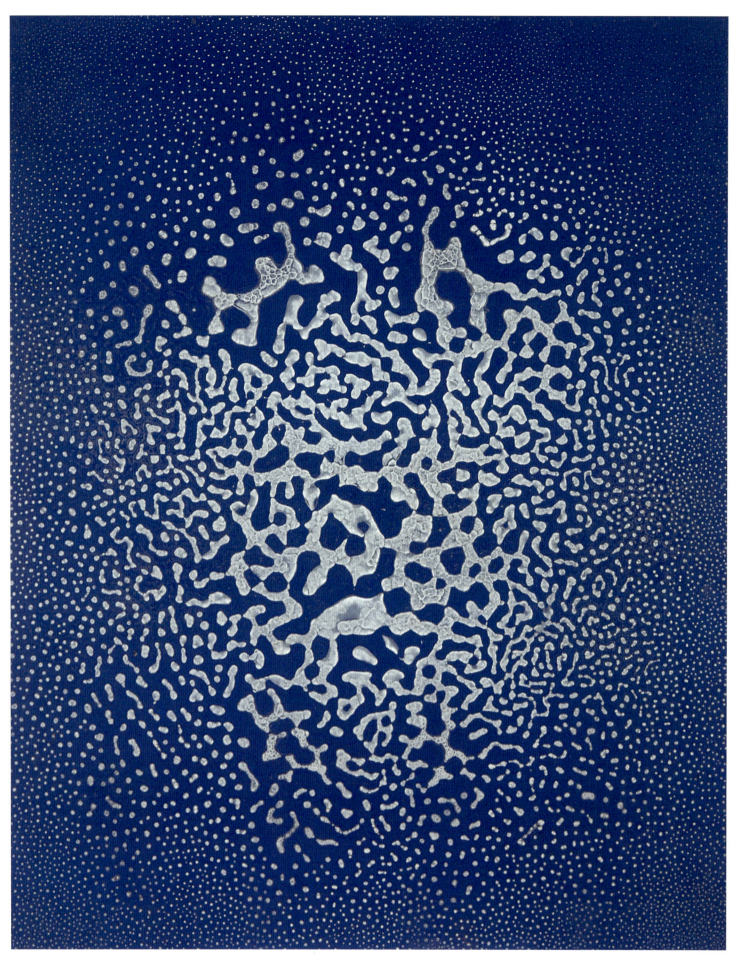

Öl auf Karton/*Oil on cardboard*, 75 x 50 cm, 1991

Öl auf Karton/*Oil on cardboard*, 75 x 50 cm, 1991

Der Künstler wird mit diesen Arbeiten zum Experimentator. Jede Änderung der „Laborbedingungen" bedeutet eine Änderung im Resultat der Dispersionsmuster. Wenn Hiller zum Beispiel die Leinwand bewegt oder schräg stellt, bevor die Farbe vollständig getrocknet ist, entstehen Verwischungen und Verlaufsmuster, die wieder einen ganz anderen Strukturzusammenhang und einen anderen ästhetischen Eindruck erzeugen als die Bearbeitung der Leinwand in horizontaler Lage. Was hier sichtbar wird, ist die verblüffende Fähigkeit der Farbsubstanzen zur „Selbstorganisation".

Es ist übrigens interessant, dass das Thema Selbstorganisation in den 70er-Jahren in den Mittelpunkt wissenschaftlicher Forschung rückte, zur selben Zeit also, als Hiller damit beschäftigt war, eine angemessene künstlerische Form der Naturdarstellung zu finden. Die Begriffe Selbstorganisation, Struktur und Prozess, die mir für eine Beschreibung der Kunst Joachim Hillers unerlässlich zu sein scheinen, sind in der systemtheoretischen Naturwissenschaft untrennbar miteinander verbunden. Ein kurzes Zitat des aus Wien stammenden Astrophysikers Erich Jantsch, der als einer der Ersten den neuen Forschungszweig umfassend dargestellt hat, kann dazu beitragen, dieses Begriffsfeld – gerade auch mit Blick auf Hillers „Dispersionsbilder" – anschaulicher zu machen. Jantsch geht von einem Alltagsphänomen aus. Wenn wir den Wasserhahn aufdrehen, zeigt sich ein glatter, runder Strahl. Drehen wir weiter auf und erhöhen den Wasserdruck übermäßig, springt der Strahl in eine neue, turbulente, „chaotische" Struktur: „Doch der Schein trügt. Gerade in der turbulenten Strömung herrscht ein höheres Maß an Ordnung. [...] In unserem Beispiel bewirkt die Erhöhung von Wasserdruck und Durchflussmenge, dass die laminare [glatte, ruhige] Strömung instabil wird und sich eine turbulente Struktur einstellt [...]. Dabei ist, was hier Struktur genannt wird, keineswegs etwas Solides, immer aus den gleichen Bestandteilen Zusammengesetztes, sondern ein dynamisches Regime, das immer neue Wassermoleküle in den gleichen Strähnen kraftvoll durchschleust. Es handelt sich um eine Struktur von *Prozessen*."[27]

The artist becomes an experimenter with these works. Each change in the "laboratory conditions" means a change in the result of the dispersion pattern. For example, when Hiller moves his canvases or places them at a slant before the paint has completely dried, blurs and runs come about that have yet another structural context and generate a different aesthetic impression than when the canvas remains in a horizontal position. What becomes visible here is the astonishing ability of the paint substances to "organize themselves".

Incidentally it is of interest that the theme of self-organization was the focus of scientific research in the 1970s, i.e. at the same time Hiller was trying to find an appropriate artistic form of natural portrayal. The concepts of self-organization, structure, and process, which for me seem vital to the description of Joachim Hiller's art, are inseparably linked to one another in the system theory of the natural sciences. A short quote by the Viennese astrophysicist Erich Jantsch, one of the first to comprehensively describe and define this new branch of research, can serve to illustrate this concept—especially with respect to Hiller's dispersion pictures". Jantsch departs from everyday occurrences. When we turn on the water faucet, the flow is smooth and round. But if we turn it on further, with too much pressure, the spray jumps into a new and turbulent "chaotic" structure: "However appearances are deceptive. Precisely in the turbulent flow there is a higher degree of order. [...] In our example the increase in water pressure and the volume of the water flow causes the laminar [smooth, quiet] flow to become instable and a turbulent structure occurs [...]. What we refer to here as structure is in no way something solid, always composed of the same components, but a dynamic regime, which energetically pushes ever new molecules of water through in the same jets. This is a structure of processes.*"*[27]

---

27 Erich Jantsch, *Die Selbstorganisation des Universums. Vom Urknall zum menschlichen Geist*. München ³1986, S. 51 f.

27 Erich Jantsch, *Die Selbstorganisation des Universums. Vom Urknall zum menschlichen Geist*. Munich ³1986, p. 51.

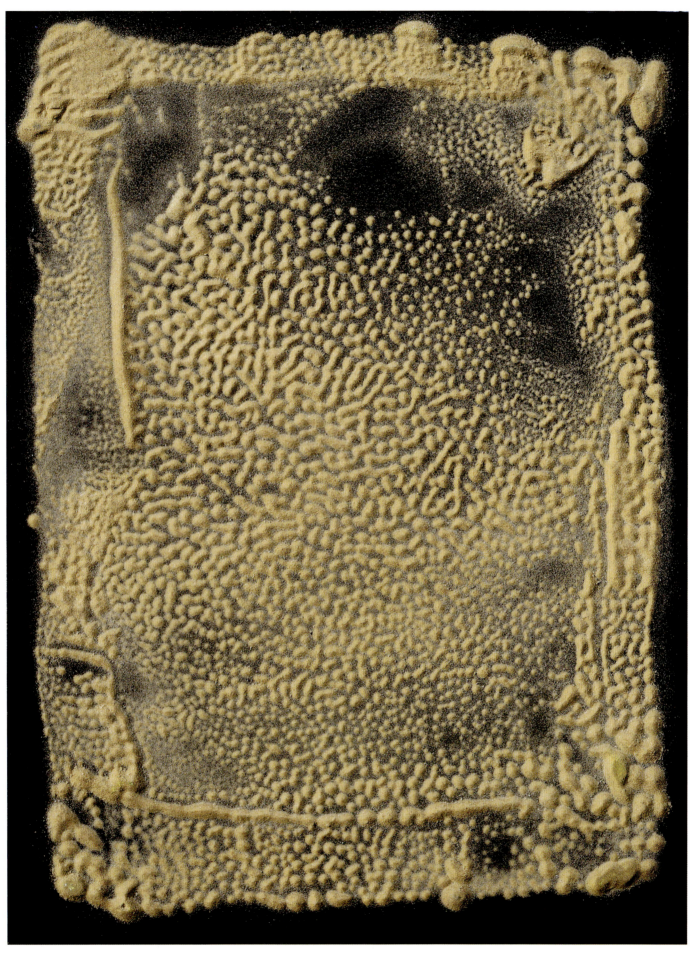

Acryl und Quarzsand auf Holz/*Acrylics and quartz sand on wood*, 60 x 80 cm, 1982

Acryl und Sand auf Leinwand/*Acrylics and sand on canvas*

100 x 100 cm, 1980

Eine im „Versuchsaufbau" noch einfachere Art der Bilderzeugung basiert auf dem, was man aus dem Physikunterricht als „Chladnische Klangfiguren" kennt. Es handelt sich dabei um ein einfaches Verfahren, Schwingungsphänomene anschaulich zu machen. Gewöhnlich wird dabei feiner Sand oder Metallstaub auf eine Metallplatte gestreut, die mit einem Geigenbogen gestrichen und dadurch in Schwingung versetzt wird. Der Sand ordnet sich durch die Schwingungen des Metalls zu verblüffend regelmäßigen, meist symmetrischen Mustern. Dieses Verfahren hat Hiller gelegentlich für seine Malerei genutzt, jedoch in einer stark vereinfachten und vergröberten Variante. So streute er Sand auf eine gerahmte Leinwand, die er dann durch rhythmisches Klopfen in Schwingung versetzte. Es entstanden selbsttätig „Buckel" und Linien, die ein wenig an Sandverwehungen oder Dünenbildung erinnern. Diese wurden mit einem Fixativ konserviert und – fertig war das Sandrelief. Es ist typisch für Hillers Auffassung der Naturformen, dass er nicht die fein ziselierten Formen des physikalischen Experiments erzeugte, die allzu sehr die künstliche Laborsituation erkennen lassen, sondern eine gröbere Anwendung desselben Prinzips, die im Ergebnis Landschaftsassoziationen zulässt, Vorstellungen von geologischen Strukturen, von Dünenbildung und Sandwüste.

An even simpler "experimental set-up" for generating pictures is based on what we know from physics as "chladni figures". This is a simple process for making the phenomena of vibrations visible. Normally fine sand or metal dust is spread across a sheet of metal, which is then stroked with a violin bow and thus set into vibration. Due to the vibration of the metal the sand arranges itself in astonishingly regular, mostly symmetric patterns. At times Hiller used this procedure for his painting, but in an extremely simplified and rudimentary variation. By scattering sand across a framed canvas, he then set this into vibration by tapping it in rhythm. "Bumps" and lines came about on their own that remind us a little of sand drifts and the formation of dunes. These were preserved with a fixative and—the sand relief was finished. It is typical for Hiller's notion of natural forms that he did not produce the finely chiseled forms of the physical experiment, which are all too reminiscent of the artistic laboratory situation, but chose a rougher treatment of the same principle, which allows for landscape associations in the results, notions of geological structures, dune formation, and sand deserts.

Acryl und Sand auf Leinwand/*Acrylics and sand on canvas*
100 x 100 cm, 1980

Excursus:
Hiller and Art Informel—A Few Art Historical Thoughts

Art does not fall from heaven, but develops its formal language and its aesthetic principles in a dialogue with art that already exists. "Art has to come from art,"[28] according to the artist himself, even when you are orienting yourself to the structures of nature. Joachim Hiller finds the popular notion repeatedly backed up in conjunction with van Gogh's statement that artists are "ahead of their time" silly and fundamentally wrong. You can only work with what is at your disposal in your own time and place this in new contexts at best, summarizing it more precisely. Applied to the painter himself, the question is thus raised concerning the sources he used and how his work shows itself in relationship to existing directions of art.

Hiller is an artist very conscious of the painting tradition and disposing over broad knowledge of art historical relationships. Incidentally, his exams at the master school were completed with a thesis on Pieter Brueghel the Elder and Max Beckmann, whereby the latter has remained for him a great master he reveres even today. Asked about the figure he did most identify with in his early years, Hiller does not hesitate to name Max Beckmann. This may seem surprising at first glance, since Beckmann's figurative painting does not appear to contain anything comparable in form with the non-objective structures of Hiller. What fascinates Hiller about Beckmann is above all his absolute will to painting, even under the most adverse circumstances after World War I and later during his emigration. Just as important is the sensual aspect of Beckmann's painting, the powerful expression of what Beckmann himself referred to as his "terribly vital sensuality".[29] But as much as Beckmann was a model as a type, there are no mutual correspondences concerning style.

---

28 Joachim Hiler in: Erik Buchheister, „*Wie kommt Farbe in die Form?*". Interview with Joachim Hiller, in: *Art Profil*, 4, 2008, p. 44 ff, quote p. 45.

29 "My form of expression is, after all, painting. Burdened or gifted with a terribly vital sensuality, I must search for wisdom with my eyes. I especially emphasize the eyes, since nothing would be more senseless and useless than a cerebrally-painted way of looking at the world without the terrible furore of the senses for each form of beauty and ugliness of the visible." Max Beckmann, Über meine Malerei [On My Painting], in: M. B., *Die Realität der Träume in den Bildern. Aufsätze und Vorträge. Aus Tagebüchern, Briefen, Gesprächen 1903–1950*, Leipzig 1987, p. 134–142, (quote: p. 137, translation: e.v.).

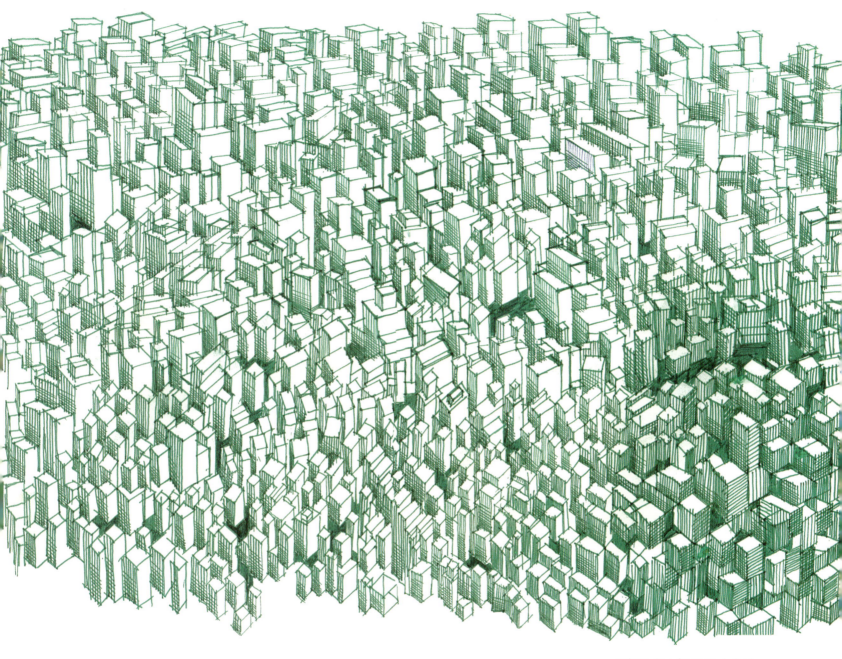

Frühe Studie auf Papier/*Early sketch on paper*

Frühe Studie auf Papier

Early sketch on paper

Die abstrakte Malerei der Nachkriegszeit, die sich grob in zwei Lager, das geometrisch-konstruktive und das informelle (oder tachistische, lyrisch abstrakte) einteilen lässt, war für ihn bestimmend. Dass Hiller nach anfänglicher Begeisterung für den russischen Konstruktivismus schnell die andere, „informelle" Richtung einschlug, ist evident. Doch reicht die visuelle Ähnlichkeit, um Hillers Werk unter dem Begriff „Informel" zu rubrizieren? Diese Frage ist keine akademische Spielerei, sondern ermöglicht es, anhand der kunsthistorisch vorgegebenen Begrifflichkeit Hillers künstlerischen Ansatz in seinem kunsthistorischen Umfeld zu sehen, zugleich aber seine Besonderheiten herauszuarbeiten.

Das Wort „Informel", wohl von dem französischen Maler Georges Mathieu geprägt, verweist auf die Auflösung einer definierten Form. Schon diese Basisbegrifflichkeit ist irreführend, wie zuletzt Rolf Wedewer in seiner ausführlichen Studie zur Malerei des Informel gezeigt hat: „Kategorial gesehen, ist Informel ein Sammelbegriff, der in groben Zügen umrissen zwei differente Ausdrucksweisen umschließt – das Gestische und die Texturologien. Beide sind charakterisiert durch eine jeweils eigentümliche Thematisierung des Prinzips der Formlosigkeit, das selbstverständlich nicht gleichgesetzt werden kann und darf mit Willkür und also Unbedachtheit der Bildformulierung. Diese zeichnet sich vielmehr aus durch eine zwar offene, aber zugleich präzise Strukturiertheit!"[30]

30 Rolf Wedewer, *Die Malerei des Informel. Weltverlust und Ich-Behauptung*, München/Berlin 2007, S. 10.

The abstract painting of the post-war era, which may be roughly divided into two camps, the geometrically-constructive and the Informel (or tachistic, lyrically abstract) was decisive for him. It is evident that Hiller, following initial enthusiasm for the Russian constructivists, quickly chose the other "Informel" direction. But does the visual similarity suffice to classify Hiller's works under the heading of "Informel"? This question is not one of academic musing, because it makes it possible for us to use the concepts art history has provided us with in order to view Hiller's artistic approach in its art historical environment, even as we work out its peculiarities at the same time.

The term "Informel", coined most likely by the French painter Georges Mathieu, indicates the dissolution of a defined form. This basic concept is already misleading, as Rolf Wedewer recently showed in a detailed study of Informel painting: "In terms of category, Informel is a collective term which, roughly outlined, encompasses two different manners of expression—the gestural and the "texturological". Characteristic of both is that they make respective themes of the principle of formlessness, which of course should not be confused with randomness or not thinking through the picture formulation. This is distinguished by a granted, open, but at the same time precise, structuring!"[30]

30 Rolf Wedewer, Die Malerei des Informel. Weltverlust und Ich-Behauptung, Munich/Berlin 2007, p. 10.

Frühe Studie auf Papier

Early sketch on paper

Um Hillers stilistische Gemeinsamkeiten mit dem Informel und zugleich seine im Kern doch völlig eigenständige Haltung herauszupräparieren, sei zunächst das gestische Informel näher betrachtet. Dies geschieht am einfachsten im Medium Zeichnung. Wedewer arbeitet in seiner Studie die Bedeutung der Kalligrafie für das Informel und die amerikanische Parallelbewegung des Abstrakten Expressionismus heraus. Er erwähnt die spontanen, aus inneren Impulsen gespeisten „Kritzeleien", die den „automatischen", d. h. nicht von Verstandeskontrolle zensierten Zeichnungen einiger Surrealisten (insbesondere André Massons) viel verdanken.[31] Fragwürdig wird es, wenn er nicht nur die Zeichnung des Informel, sondern das Medium Zeichnung überhaupt charakterisiert: „Die Linie der Zeichnung vereint mithin drei Funktionen: als Lebensausdruck, als Spur subjektiver Verhältnisse und Befunde sowie als Selbstausdruck."[32] Abgesehen von dem erläuterungsbedürftigen Begriff „Ausdruck": Dass jede Zeichnung eine Spur eines Lebendigen ist, mag man nicht ernsthaft bestreiten wollen; dass jede künstlerische Äußerung eine Selbständerung ist, wird man mit einigem interpretatorischem Aufwand wohl auch immer reklamieren können.

Aber wie sieht es mit den „subjektiven Verhältnissen und Befunden" aus? Hillers an der dalmatinischen Küste entstandene Zeichnungen sind gerade durch die Ausschaltung subjektiver Willensakte bestimmt, sie sind, soweit dies überhaupt möglich ist, reines Protokollieren. Die zahlreichen Strukturstudien, die Hiller immer wieder gezeichnet hat und von denen hier nur einige Beispiele gezeigt werden sollen, haben nichts mit subjektivem Selbstausdruck zu tun. Sie arbeiten vielmehr mit den Mitteln Repetition und Variation einfacher Basiselemente bestimmte Strukturmerkmale heraus. Aus Schrägstrichen, Schraffuren oder kleinen Kuben entstehen durch bloßes Aneinanderreihen in unterschiedlichen Dichtegraden Strukturen, die offen sind für gegenständliche Lesarten, im einen Fall etwa Dünen oder Stofffalten, auf dem anderen Blatt mineralische Substanzen oder auch Architekturen usw. Was für Hillers Zeichnungen gilt, lässt sich ebenso auf sein Gesamtwerk übertragen: Mit subjektivem Ausdruckswillen, mit informellen Gesten, die sich aus inneren, triebgesteuerten Impulsen, aus motorischen oder emotionalen Quellen speisen, haben seine Arbeiten wenig gemein. Sie sind, um meine Lieblingsformulierungen aus der Hoch-Zeit des Informel zu zitieren, weder „Drang zum Delikt" noch „Rückkehr zum Tier".[33]

31 Ebd., S. 60–73.
32 Ebd., S. 62.
33 *Junge Maler der Gegenwart*, Ausstellungskatalog Wien, Künstlerhaus, 24.7.–15.8.1959, hrsg. v. J. Alvard u. F. Benrath, Wien 1959, S. 82 u. 89, hier zitiert nach: Ekkehard Stärk, *Hermann Nitschs Orgien Mysterien Theater* und die „*Hysterie der Griechen*". *Quellen und Traditionen im Wiener Antikebild seit 1900*, München 1987, S. 25.

In order to distil what Hiller's style has in common with Informel and at the same time single out what is fundamentally his idiosyncratic attitude, we will first look closer at the gestural Informel. In his study Wedewer works out the meaning of calligraphy for Informel and its parallel movement in America, abstract expressionism. He mentions the spontaneous "scribbles" fed from inner impulses, which owe much to the "automatic" drawings, i.e. not controlled and censored by the mind, of several surrealists (especially André Masson).[31] But problems crop up when he not only characterizes Informel drawing, but also the medium of drawing per se as follows: "The line of drawing unites three things: it has the functions of an expression of life, the trace of subjective relationships and findings and of self-expression."[32] Apart from the term "expression", which needs defining, the contention that each drawing is a trace of something alive, is not something open to dispute: furthermore, that each artistic statement is a self-statement is something that can stand upright if enough of an interpretative effort is made.

But what is the situation with "subjective relationships and findings"? The drawings Hiller made on the Dalmatian coast are defined precisely by turning off any act of subjective will. They are, in as much as this is possible, a pure act of putting something on record. The numerous studies of structure, which Hiller drew over and over again and of which only a few examples shall be shown here, have nothing to do with subjective self-expression. Rather, by repeating and varying simple basic elements, they work out certain features of structure. From slanted marks, hatchings, and small cubes that are arranged in rows of varying degrees, structures come about that are open to interpretations as concrete objects, here maybe dunes or folds of cloth, on another page mineral substances or pieces of architecture, etc. What applies to Hiller's drawings also applies to his work in general: his works have little in common with a subjective will to expression, with Informal gestures driven by inner instinctive impulses fed from material and emotional sources. They are, to quote my favorite formulation from the heyday of Informel, neither the "urge towards the offense" nor the "return to the animal".[33]

31 Ibid., p. 60–73.
32 Ibid., p. 62.
33 *Junge Maler der Gegenwart*, Exhibition catalogue Vienna, Künstlerhaus, 24 July– 15 August 1959, edited by J. Alvard and F. Benrath, Vienna 1959, p. 82 and 89, quoted here after: Ekkehard Stärk, *Hermann Nitschs Orgien Mysterien Theater und die „Hysterie der Griechen". Quellen und Traditionen im Wiener Antikebild seit 1900*, Munich 1987, p. 25.

Acryl auf Hartschaum/*Acrylics on Styrofoam*

130 x 190 cm, 2007

Acryl, Zement und Spachtelmasse auf Holz/*Acrylics, cement and putty on wood*

90 x 90 cm, 1987

Acryl auf Leinwand/*Acrylics on canvas*, 100 x 100 cm, 1987

Wie steht es mit dem zweiten Zweig des Informel, den Wedewer, in Anspielung auf eine Werkserie Jean Dubuffets als „Texturologien" oder auch als „Materiales Informel" bezeichnet? Vergleicht man einige von Hillers Arbeiten, besonders die „Erosions"- und „Mauer"-Bilder mit bestimmten Arbeiten von Dubuffet oder Antoni Tàpies, fallen zweifellos Gemeinsamkeiten ins Auge. Insbesondere die an geologischen Formationen und Erdbodenstrukturen interessierten Arbeiten Dubuffets Anfang der 50er-Jahre sowie Tàpies' Obsession für mauerartige Bildträger fallen einem hier ein. Doch sollte man sich von gewissen visuellen Ähnlichkeiten nicht täuschen lassen.

Antoni Tàpies begann Mitte der 50er-Jahre, seinen Malmitteln Sand, Marmorstaub, Leim und Ähnliches unterzumischen. Diese Technik gab ihm die Möglichkeit, seine Bilder reliefhaft zu gestalten. In diese materielle Oberfläche konnten nun Zeichen eingeritzt oder als Spur eingedrückt werden. In seinen Bildern finden sich immer wieder Kreuze, Buchstaben (vor allem seine Initialen AT), Zahlen sowie Hand- und Fußabdrücke. Wie die Kunsthistorikerin Barbara Catoir erstmals aufgezeigt hat, gehen viele dieser Zeichen auf Tàpies' Beschäftigung mit mystischen Texten des Mittelalters zurück, insbesondere auf die symbolische Buchstabenkombinatorik des katalanischen Philosophen und Theologen Ramon Llull (lateinisch: Raimundus Lullus).[34] Ebenso finden sich in Tàpies' Arbeiten immer wieder politische Symbole wie etwa die vier roten Streifen der katalanischen Flagge, der Senyera. Sein katalanischer Lokalpatriotismus war Ausdruck seines Freiheitswillens und des Protests gegen die bis zum Tod des Generals Franco (1975) dauernde faschistische Diktatur in Spanien.

But how does the situation look with regard to the second branch of Informel, which Wedewer, alluding to a series of works by Jean Dubuffet, refers to as "texturologies" or also as "material Informel"? If we compare several of Hiller's works, especially the "Erosions" and the "wall" pictures with certain works by Dubuffet or Antoni Tàpies, we are doubtlessly struck by things they have in common. Especially Dubuffet's works that reveal an interest in the geological formations and earth structures, dating from the beginning of the 1950s, as well as Tàpies' obsession for wall-like picture carriers come to mind here. But we should not be misled by certain visual similarities.

In the middle of the 1950s, Antoni Tàpies began adding sand, marble dust, glue, and similar substances to his painting medium. This technique provided him with the possibility for creating his pictures like reliefs. In this material surface, signs could now be scratched in or imprinted as traces. In his pictures we repeatedly find crosses, letters (above all his initials AT), numbers, as well as hand- and footprints. Like the art historian Barbara Catoir first showed us, many of these signs go back to Tàpies' study of medieval mystic texts, especially to the symbolic combination of letters used by the Catalan philosopher and theologian Ramon Llull (Latin: Raimundus Lullus).[34] Likewise, in Tàpies works we repeatedly find political symbols such as the four red stripes of the Catalan flag, the Senyera. His local Catalan patriotism was the expression of his urge for freedom and the protest against the fascist dictatorship in Spain that lasted until the death of General Franco (1975).

---

34 Barbara Catoir, *Gespräche mit Antoni Tàpies*, München/New York 1987, S. 14–32.

34 Barbara Catoir, *Gespräche mit Antoni Tàpies*, Munich/New York 1987, p. 14–32.

Tàpies' Auffassung der Mauer kann man als eine doppelte Schnittstelle lesen. Zum einen treffen sich an ihr Individuum und Öffentlichkeit. Die Mauer ist für Tàpies ein Medium, das private oder subjektive Äußerungen aus ihrem Kontext heraushebt und zu geheimnisvollen Zeichen werden lässt. Diese Qualität der Mauer als Ort oder Träger rätselhafter Zeichen findet sich bereits in den Graffiti-Fotos von Brassaï, die für Tàpies eine wichtige Inspirationsquelle gewesen sind.[35] Diese Fotos lassen die alltäglichen Kritzeleien auf Hauswänden wie eine archaisch anmutende Formensprache erscheinen. Aus dem rein privaten Anlass ihrer Äußerung, ihrem Bekenntnischarakter, erwächst ein zeitenthobenes Vokabular. Zum anderen interessiert Tàpies die Mauer als Schnittstelle zwischen Materie und Geist. Die meist schwarzen oder erdhaft braunen Mauerstrukturen betonen den materiellen Charakter, sie symbolisieren nicht bloß, sondern verkörpern unmittelbar die hermetische Verschlossenheit der geistigen Welt. Tàpies' Mauerbilder offenbaren damit – folgt man den Analysen Wedewers – einen Grundzug dessen, was man als das „Materiale Informel" bezeichnen kann: „Schematisch vereinfacht lässt sich das thematisch Spezifische des materialen Informel auf die Formel vom umfassenden, mythisch bedeuteten Weltverständnis bringen, in dem das ICH konstitutiv eingebunden ist."[36] Tatsächlich lassen sich im Informel zahlreiche Beispiele für einen Versuch finden, sich an mythische Vorstellungswelten anzudocken. Wedewer zeigt das am Primitivismus Dubuffets, an der Malerei Gerhard Hoehmes und den schon mit den Bildtiteln signalisierten mythischen Anklängen bei Emil Schumacher, um nur einige wenige zu nennen.

All diese auf ursprüngliche, primitive oder archaische Seinszustände zurückgreifenden Haltungen finden sich nicht bei Joachim Hiller. Bei Tàpies, um bei diesem Beispiel zu bleiben, ist die Materie der Wände der Träger einfachster menschlicher Zeichen und Spuren. Es ist die Kontaktstelle, an der sich menschlicher Geist im Material konkretisiert. Bei Hiller jedoch sind die menschlichen Zeichen (die selten genug in seinem Werk auftauchen) lange vergessene Relikte, die von der Natur wieder eingeholt und in einem Erosionsprozess ausgelöscht werden. Remythisierung ist hier nicht zu sehen, eher die ernüchternde Vision einer Elementarnatur ohne Menschen, ja ohne Spuren von Lebensformen überhaupt.

35 Ebd., S. 42.
36 Wedewer [Anm. 30], S. 141.

We may regard Tàpies' understanding of the wall as a double interface. On the one hand this is where the individual meets the public. For Tàpies the wall is a medium, which selects private or subjective statements from out of their contexts and thus turns them into mysterious hermetic signs. This characteristic of the wall as the place or carrier of mysterious signs may already be found in the graffiti photos of Brassaï, which were an important source of inspiration for Tàpies.[35] These photos make the everyday scribblings on the facades of the houses look like an archaic language of forms. Released from the purely private reason of their utterance, their confessional character, a vocabulary has grown that stands apart from all time. On the other hand Tàpies is interested in the wall as the interface between matter and mind. The mostly black or earthy brown wall structures emphasize their material character. Not only do they symbolize, but also immediately embody the hermetic closedness of the spiritual world. Tàpies's wall pictures thus reveal—if we follow the analyses of Wedewer—a basic feature of what we call "material Informel": "Schematically simplified, we may reduce what is thematically specific in the material Informel to the formula of a comprehensive understanding of the world seen in myth in which the EGO has been constitutively included."[36] And indeed, in Informel art we find numerous examples of the attempt to dock onto mythic notions of the world. Wedewer demonstrates this in the primitivism of Dubuffet, in the painting of Gerhard Hoehmes, and with Emil Schumacher's picture titles, which already signalize mythical connotations to cite only a few here.

None of these attitudes based on primal, primitive, or archaic states of being do we find with Joachim Hiller. For Tàpies, just to stay with his example, the material of the walls is the carrier of the most simple human signs and traces. It is the contact point, where the human spirit becomes concrete in the material. For Hiller, however, the human signs (which occur in his works rarely enough) are long forgotten relics, repossessed again by nature and extinguished in a process of erosion. A remythification is not witnessed here, but rather the sobering vision of an elementary nature without human beings, indeed without any traces of forms of life at all.

35 Ibid., p. 42.
36 Wedewer [footnote 30], p. 141.

Acryl auf Leinwand/*Acrylics on canvas*
100 x 100 cm, 1987 (Ausschnitt/*Detail*)

Acryl auf Leinwand/*Acrylics on canvas*

100 x 100 cm, 1988

Doch damit bleibt Hiller selbstverständlich dem Problemhorizont verbunden, in den Rolf Wedewer das Informel stellt: „Weltverlust und Ich-Behauptung". Auch wenn jede Psychologisierung von Kunst stets fragwürdig und in ihren Ergebnissen unbefriedigend bleibt: Hillers Werk kann durchaus als eine Reaktion auf eine Art Weltverlust verstanden werden. Der Krieg zerstörte die Welt seiner Kindheit und Jugend, die ihm vertraut war, der Modernisierungsschub der Nachkriegszeit tat sein Übriges. Diese Erfahrung war generationsspezifisch. Der Abschied von der Arbeitswelt, der Rückzug in sein Atelier, in eine Gegenwelt aus Malerei, lässt sich durchaus ebenfalls in diesen Deutungsrahmen stellen. Dabei entwickelte sich jedoch ein Malereiverständnis, das bei aller gedanklichen und visuellen Nähe zum Informel doch viel von den aktuellen Debatten der 6oer-Jahre aufgenommen hat.

Als Hiller seine ernsthafte Künstlerlaufbahn begann, war das Informel bereits von der jüngeren Künstlergeneration infrage gestellt worden. Beispielhaft zeigte dies die *documenta III* in Kassel, bei der das europäische Informel und der Abstrakte Expressionismus aus den USA im Mittelpunkt standen und sozusagen auf dem Höhepunkt der öffentlichen Anerkennung angelangt waren. Zugleich aber waren dort auch schon die Gegenpositionen zu sehen. Dazu zählt etwa die ZERO-Bewegung, der auf der *documenta* ein eigener Raum zugestanden wurde. Hiller hatte die ZERO-Gruppe mit Interesse und Sympathie zur Kenntnis genommen, deren bekannteste Protagonisten Piene, Uecker und Mack nur wenige Jahre älter sind als er. Diese Künstler hatten sich mit Entschiedenheit vom Subjektivismus des Informel distanziert. Industrielle Strukturen, nüchterne Rasterkompositionen, moderne Materialien, Themen wie Licht und Material läuteten ein neues künstlerisches Zeitalter ein. Auch wenn Hiller weder den Fortschrittsoptimismus von ZERO teilte noch den Abschied von der Malerei vollziehen mochte – ein starker Einfluss war doch geblieben: Es ist das Signal des Aufbruchs aus einer subjektzentrierten Malerei hin zu der Suche nach Strukturen. Das Zauberwort der 6oer-Jahre – „Struktur" – es findet sich bei ZERO ebenso wie etwa in Max Bills konkreter Kunst, in der amerikanischen Minimal Art oder der experimentellen Fotografie jener Zeit und nicht zuletzt in den Wissenschaften: Die 6oer waren die Blütezeit des französischen Strukturalismus. „Struktur" ist auch das Hauptwort für Joachim Hiller – Strukturen der Natur sind es, die er veranschaulichen möchte, nicht Strukturen des Ich, des Unbewussten oder der Schnittstellen von Material und Menschengeist als Erinnerungsspuren und Ursprungsorte von Kultur (wie bei Tàpies und anderen).

In this respect Hiller remains, of course, tied to the problematic horizon, in which Rolf Wedewer places Informel: "The loss of the world and the maintenance of the Ego". Even if any psychologizing of art is always questionable and remains unsatisfactory in its results: Hiller's work can certainly be understood as a reaction to a kind of loss of the world. The war destroyed the world he was familiar with in his childhood and youth, and the thrust towards modernization in the postwar era did the rest. This experience was generation specific. Taking leave of the working world, the withdrawal to his studio to another world made of painting may indeed be placed in this framework of interpretation. But in doing so, an understanding of painting developed that for all its proximity to Informel in thought and visual aspects, nevertheless adapted much of the contemporary debates of the 1960s.

When Hiller began his serious career as an artist, Informel was already being questioned by the younger generation of artists. The documenta III in Kassel shows this in an exemplary manner, where the European Informel and the Abstract Expressionism in the USA were the central focus and had, so to speak, reached their zenith of public recognition. At the same time, however, there were also opposite positions being represented there already. Among these was, for example, the ZERO movement, which received its own room at the documenta. Hiller noted ZERO with interest and sympathy, the group's most known protagonists being Piene, Uecker, and Mack, all of them only a few years older than he was. These artists had decidedly distanced themselves from the subjectivism of the Informel. Industrial structures, sober grid compositions, modern materials, themes such as light and material heralded a new artistic age. Even though Hiller neither desired to share the progressive optimism of ZERO, nor to take leave from painting—the mov ement still exerted a strong influence on him: it signaled the change from a subject-focused painting to the search for structures. The magic word of the 1960s—"structure"—you can find it with ZERO as well as in Max Bill's concrete art, in American minimal art or in the experimental photography of those days and last, but not least, in science: the 1960s were the heyday of French structuralism. "Structure" is also a keyword for Joachim Hiller. It is the structures of nature he wants to make visible, not the structures of the ego, the unconscious, or the interfaces of matter, and the human spirit as traces of memory and primal places of culture (like with Tàpies and others).

Acryl auf Leinwand/*Acrylics on canvas*

100 x 100 cm, 1988

„Ich-Behauptung" ist das sicherlich auch – wie könnte ein ernst gemeintes künstlerisches Œuvre je etwas anderes sein als das? Doch bei Hiller geschieht die Ich-Behauptung paradoxerweise durch weitgehende Absehung vom Ich, von subjektiven Zuständen, vom Fokussieren auf die Relation von Welt und Mensch. Die Achtsamkeit auf nicht subjektiv hervorgebrachte Strukturen und auf den Strukturierungsprozess selbst ist es, was meines Erachtens Hillers Kunst vom Informel abhebt. Obwohl er den radikalen Strömungen wie der Analytischen Malerei oder der Prozesskunst sonst fernsteht, der Diskussionsstand der 60er-Jahre, die Kritik an der Malerei und der daraus resultierende Versuch, Malerei aus den Prozessen des Malens und aus den Materialien neu zu formulieren, fließen doch in seine Malerei ein.

It is certainly a case of "ego maintenance" as well—how could a seriously-meant artistic œuvre ever be anything else but that? But paradoxically, with Hiller ego maintenance takes place by largely foregoing the ego, dispensing with subjective circumstances and with focusing on the relation between world and man. The attention to non-subjectively produced structures and to the structuring process itself is what, in my opinion, sets Hiller's art apart from Informel. Although he is otherwise far from the radical movements such as analytic painting or process art, the state of the discussion in the 1960s, namely the criticism of painting and the resulting attempt to formulate painting anew out of painting processes and out of the materials used do indeed enter into his painting.

Acryl auf Leinwand/*Acrylics on canvas*
100 x 100 cm, 1988

Acryl auf Leinwand/*Acrylics on canvas*

100 x 100 cm, 1988

Acryl auf Leinwand/*Acrylics on canvas*

100 x 100 cm, 1987 *(Ausschnitt/Detail)*

Ein Cézanne-Intermezzo

Wer einmal das Vergnügen hatte, sich in Joachim Hillers Archivräumen umzuschauen, wird sich an die Überraschungen erinnern, die immer wieder eintreten, sobald der Künstler aus irgendeiner Ecke, aus irgendeinem Regal Arbeiten hervorzaubert, die dem, was man über ihn zu wissen glaubte, so gar nicht entsprechen. Hiller erlaubt sich Widersprüche in seinem Werk: Wenn es sein muss, greift er malend in die Prozesse der Formbildung ein; wenn das Bild es verlangt, verfügt er auch über illusionistische Kniffe oder den Rückgriff aufs Altmeisterliche. Das steht oft quer zum ästhetischen *Mainstream* und irritiert den Betrachter, doch Irritation ist ohnehin das Schlechteste nicht, was relevante Kunst zu bieten hat. Zu den unerwarteten und auf den ersten Blick am wenigsten in das Gesamtwerk passenden Arbeiten zählt eine Werkserie, die um 1987 entstand. Hier sind weder naturhafte Strukturen noch prozesshafte Materialexperimente zu sehen, sondern Agglomerationen von ineinander verkeilten stereometrischen Körpern. Doch obwohl diese Bilder ganz traditionell gemalt sind und weit von der übrigen Produktion der 80er-Jahre entfernt zu sein scheinen, loten sie dennoch, auf den ersten und zweiten Blick kaum ersichtlich, das Problem des Zusammenhangs zwischen Natur und Bild aus.

Diese Arbeiten sind nämlich nichts anderes als eine Anwendung des berühmten, für die Entwicklung des Kubismus so außerordentlich folgenreichen Satzes von Paul Cézanne, dass sich alles in der Natur wie Kugel, Kegel und Zylinder modelliere und dass man in der Malerei mit diesen einfachen, grundlegenden Elementen beginnen müsse, dann könne man machen, was man wolle. „Tout dans la nature se modèle selon la sphère, le cône et le cylindre. Il fut s'apprendre à peindre sur ces figures simples, on pourra ensuite faire tout ce qu'on voudra."[37] Man kann also in Joachim Hillers stereometrischen Etüden den Versuch sehen, diese Anweisung einmal ganz wörtlich zu nehmen. Mit einem Zusatz: Hiller bezieht auch den Kubus in die Reihe der elementaren Körper mit ein, während Cézanne, gemäß seiner Behauptung, dass alle Körper im Raum konvex erschienen („Les corps vus dans l'espace sont tous convexes"[38]), nur sphärische, im Raum gebogene Körper aufgezählt hat. Auf einigen der fraglichen Bilder von Hiller sind die stereometrischen Körper klar zu unterscheiden, auf anderen sind sie zu komplizierten Mischformen „verbacken".

A Cézanne Intermezzo

The person who has ever had the pleasure of being able to look at Joachim Hiller's archive rooms will recall being surprised over and over again as soon as the artist conjured up from some far corner or some shelf works that do not seem to correspond to what we know about him. Hiller allows for contradictions in his work. If need be, he intervenes in the processes of form creation through painting; if a picture calls for it, he also disposes over illusionist tricks or relies on the techniques of the old masters. This often stands in opposition to the aesthetic mainstream and thus confuses the viewer, but being confused is anyway not the worst thing relevant art has to offer. Among the unexpected works that, at first glance, seem to least fit into his work in general, is a series of works the artist made around 1987. We see neither nature-like structures nor processes of material experiments here, but rather agglomerations of entwined, stereometric bodies. Although these pictures have been very traditionally painted, and thus appear to be far distant from the rest of what he produced in the 1980s, they nevertheless probe the problem of the relationship between nature and picture, though we scarcely notice this at first or even second glance.

These works are namely nothing else than the implementation of the famous statement by Paul Cézanne, which was so exceptionally momentous for the development of Cubism that everything in nature may be modeled like a sphère, cone, and a cylinder, and that we must begin with these simple and fundamental elements in painting, and then we can do what we want: "Tout dans la nature se modèle selon la sphère, le cône et le cylindre. If fut s'apprendre à peindre sur ces figures simples, on pourra ensuite faire tout ce qu'on voudra."[37] Thus we may witness also in Joachim Hiller's stereometric etudes the attempt to take these instructions entirely literally. With one enlargment: Hiller also includes the cube in the series of elementary bodies while Cézanne, according to his claim that all bodies appear to be convex in space ("Les corps vus dans l'espace sont tous convexes")[38] has only listed spherical bodies, i.e., bodies curved in space. On several of Hiller's pictures in question, the stereometric bodies may be clearly differentiated, though on others they have been "baked together" with one another into complicated mixed forms.

---

37 Conversations avec Cézanne. Emile Bernard, Jules Borély, Maurice Denis, Joachim Gasquet, Gustave Geffroy, Francis Jourdain, Léo Larguier, Karl Ernst Osthaus, R. P. Rivière et J. F. Schnerb, Ambroise Vollard. Edition critique présentée par P. M. Doran. Paris 1978, S. 36.
38 Ebd., S. 16.

37 *Conversations avec Cézanne.* Emile Bernard, Jules Borély, Maurice Denic, Joachim Gasquet, Gustave Geffroy, Francis Jourdain, Léo Larguier, Karl Ernst Osthaus, R. P. Rivière et J. F. Schnerb, Ambroise Vollard. Edition critique, présentée par P. M. Doran, Paris 1978, p. 36.
38 Ibid., p. 16.

Aquarell auf Karton/*Watercolor on cardboard*

30 x 40 cm, 1988

Acryl auf Leinwand/*Acrylics on canvas*

100 x 100 cm, 1987

Die Agglomeration von Körpern verliert ihren Bezug zu jeglicher beobachtbaren Naturwirklichkeit.
The agglomeration of bodies loses its context to any observable reality of nature.

Dass sich Joachim Hiller gedanklich und malerisch mit Cézanne auseinandersetzte, ist nicht weiter verwunderlich, ist Cézanne doch einer der ersten und wichtigsten Künstler der Moderne gewesen, die sich die Frage gestellt haben, wie man Natur malen könne, ohne sie zu kopieren. Bei Cézanne geht es freilich immer um die *betrachtete* Natur und um die Frage, wie man das, was vor Augen liegt, als Malerei „realisieren" könne. Die Frage nach dem strukturellen Aufbau des Bildes wird bei ihm entscheidend. Diese Frage beschäftigt auch Hiller permanent; daher sein Versuch, in einem typisch Cézanne'schen Medium, nämlich dem „trockenen" Aquarell, mehr oder minder stark abstrahierte Felslandschaften oder mineralische Strukturen zu erfassen. Auf sie trifft zu, was Gottfried Böhm über Cézannes Aquarelle schreibt: „Mit der Zeichnung teilt das Aquarell das Papier, vor allem aber das Arbeiten mit der Leere des offenen Grundes. […] Es ist mehr als eine Auskunft zur Technik, wenn wir beachten, dass der Künstler [Cézanne] nicht Naß-in-Naß malte, sondern den gesetzten Fleck abtrocknen lässt, er dadurch Formwerte und Farbklarheit behält. Flüssige Übergänge, bei denen eine Farbe in der anderen verschwimmt, beobachten wir höchst selten."[39]

In den Aquarellstudien, die zum Teil sehr stark mit Leerstellen und daher mit der Vorstellungskraft des Betrachters arbeiten, ist der Ausgangspunkt der betrachteten Naturformen noch deutlich zu spüren. In diesen Studien geht es gewissermaßen um den Punkt der Umsetzung von Naturbeobachtung ins gemalte Bild. Doch bei den gemalten stereometrischen Körpern tritt der phänomenologische Aspekt ganz zurück. Die Agglomeration von Körpern verliert ihren Bezug zu jeglicher beobachtbaren Naturwirklichkeit. Hiller versucht stattdessen, durch Abstraktion eine ganz modellhafte, plastische Situation für die Substanz der Naturdinge zu konstruieren. Nicht viel anderes tun wir, wenn wir uns im Chemieunterricht die Materie auf atomarer Ebene mit plastischen Modellen, mit Klötzchen und Kugeln anschaulich machen.

That fact that Joachim Hiller has studied the thoughts and painting of Cézanne is not surprising, since Cézanne is one of the first and most important artists of the modern movement to pose the question as to how nature could be painted without copying it. Cézanne's concern was always for the nature he viewed and the question of how what you have before your eyes may be "realized" as painting. The issue of the structural set-up of the picture becomes decisive for him. This is a question that consistently accompanies Hiller as well. Therefore, his attempt using a medium typical for Cézanne, namely the "dry" watercolor to capture more or less abstracted rocky landscapes or mineral structures. What Gottfried Böhm writes about Cézanne's watercolors applies to these works as well: "The watercolor shares the paper with the drawing, but above all the working with the empty space of the open ground. […] It is more than an information about technique when we observe that the artist [Cézanne] does not paint wet in wet, but allows the area he has placed to dry in order to preserve the form value and the clarity of the color. Fluid transitions with one color bleeding into the next are something we only very rarely witness."[39]

In the watercolor studies, which sometimes work extensively with empty space, and thus with the imagination of the viewer, the departure point of the nature forms viewed may still be clearly traced. To a certain extent the concern in these studies is—so to speak—for the point where the observation of nature is transformed into the painted picture. But with the painted stereometric bodies the phenomenological aspect diminishes altogether. The agglomeration of bodies loses its context to any observable reality of nature. Instead, Hiller by using abstraction tries to construct an entirely model-like plastic situation for the substance of natural things. We ourselves do not do otherwise when in chemistry class we demonstrate matter on the atomic level by using plastic models of blocks and spheres.

---

39 Gottfried Boehm, *Paul Cézanne. Montagne Sainte-Victoire*, Frankfurt a. M. 1988, S. 80, 81.

39 Gottfried Boehm, *Paul Cézanne. Montagne Sainte-Victoire*, Frankfurt am Main 1988, p. 80, 81, (Translation: e.v.).

Aquarell auf Karton / *Watercolor on cardboard*
30 x 40 cm, 1980

So sind diese Arbeiten konzeptuell wichtig als Versuch, sich malend mit einem Strukturmodell der malerischen Umsetzung von Naturgebilden zu vergewissern. Ästhetisch waren diese Versuche auf Dauer aus zwei Gründen unbefriedigend: Erstes erschöpfte sich das geometrisch-abstrakte Verfahren sehr schnell, zweitens ergab sich das unabweisbare Problem der Perspektive. Sobald man sich auf die Bildsprache stereometrischer Abstraktion einlässt, erhebt sich die Frage der korrekten perspektivischen Darstellung. Je komplexer die Verzahnung unterschiedlicher Basiselemente, desto anspruchsvoller wird diese Anforderung. Dies ist der Grund, warum Hiller der Meinung ist, dass eine Komposition dieser Art eigentlich mit einem Computerprogramm entworfen werden sollte. Andererseits beziehen diese Bilder gerade aus der inhomogenen und teils unklaren perspektivischen Anlage ihren besonderen Reiz. Je länger man sich die kompakte Ansammlung der dreidimensionalen Körper anschaut, desto unheimlicher wird die räumliche Situation: Der Raum beginnt zu pulsieren, wird ungreifbar, irreal und zeigt die Tendenz, in der Betrachtung in wechselnde Deutungen zu „springen".

And so these works are conceptually important as an attempt by the artist to ascertain the painterly transformation of natural forms by using a structural model. Aesthetically, in the long run these attempts did not prove satisfactory for two reasons: first, the geometric-abstract process exhausted itself very quickly; second, problems came up concerning perspective, which could not be denied. As soon as one enters into the pictorial language of stereometric abstraction, the issue arises as to the correct portrayal of perspective. The more complex the meshing of the various basic elements, the more demanding this requirement becomes. This is the reason why Hiller is of the opinion that a composition of this type should actually be developed using a computer program. On the other hand these pictures derive their special attraction precisely from the non-homogenous and partially unclear state of the perspective. The longer we gaze at the compact assemblage of three-dimensional bodies, the more mysterious the spatial situation becomes: the space begins to pulsate, becomes intangible, unreal, and tends to "become volatile" in the various ways the viewer looks at it.

Acryl auf Leinwand/*Acrylics on canvas*

100 x 100 cm, 1987

Acryl auf Leinwand/*Acrylics on canvas*

100 x 100 cm, 1987

Die Ausarbeitung dieser stereometrischen Bilder ist jedoch keineswegs eine folgenlose Erscheinung im Gesamtwerk Hillers. Als Etüden mit dem Zweck, die Schichtung von dreidimensionalen Elementen zu studieren, waren sie zweifellos wichtige Schritte hin zu dem größten Objekt, das der Künstler je ausgeführt hat. Es handelt sich um das große Wandrelief, das 1989 als Auftragswerk für den Konferenzraum einer amerikanischen Agentur für Pharma- und Gesundheitswerbung in Frankfurt entstand. Obwohl er abseits der Öffentlichkeit arbeitete, hat Hiller zweimal große Auftragsarbeiten angenommen. Das erste Mal geschah dies 1969 in Amsterdam, wo er, noch ganz unter dem Eindruck der Felsen an der dalmatinischen Küste, das Treppenhaus einer Werbeagentur mit „künstlichen" Felsformationen ausstattete. Den Auftrag dazu hatte ihm ein in Wiesbaden ansässiger Galerist aus den Niederlanden vermittelt. In der großen Arbeit Ende der 80er-Jahre verwendete er jedoch eine ganz andere, viel stärker vom Naturvorbild abstrahierende Formensprache. Doch im Vergleich zu den Acrylbildern von 1987 entfernte sich Hiller insofern wieder weit von Cézanne, als er nur komplexe, kantig geschnittene Formen verwendete und auf sphärische Formen ganz verzichtete.

Das mittlerweile nicht mehr existierende Relief war aus mehrschichtig aufgetürmten Einzelelementen aufgebaut. Aus Hartschaum geschnitten und bemalt, gaben diese Elemente eine eindeutige Leserichtung von links nach rechts vor. Während sich auf der äußersten linken Seite noch ein horizontal-vertikales Raster erahnen lässt, geraten die Elemente im zweiten Abschnitt in eine Bewegung nach rechts unten. Diese Abwärtsbewegung wird in der rechten Hälfte durch eine mehrstufige kurvige Bewegung ausgeglichen und am äußersten rechten Bildrand in einer wiederum horizontal-vertikal beruhigten Spalte zum Stillstand gebracht. Was das Relief mit den stereometrischen Bildern von 1987 verbindet, ist der überraschende Verzicht auf naturhafte Anmutung. Die Formensprache, die sich aus Hillers Beschäftigung mit Felsformationen herleitet, ist so weit abstrahiert, dass sich eine Beziehung zu dieser Referenz nicht mehr aus der bloßen Betrachtung des Reliefs herleiten lässt, sondern sich allenfalls aus Kenntnis des Gesamtwerks erschließt.

Hiller's development of these stereometric pictures is, however, in no way a phenomenon that does not have ramifications for his work in general. Designed as ètudes for the purpose of studying the layering of three-dimensional elements, they were undoubtedly important steps towards the largest object the artist has ever made. I refer here to the large wall relief done in 1989 as a piece commissioned for the conference room of an American public relations company for pharmaceutical and health advertising in Frankfurt. Although he had been working outside of public view, Hiller nevertheless twice took on large commissioned works. The first time was in Amsterdam in 1969, where, still under the influence of the rocks on the Dalmatian coast, he outfitted a stairwell of an advertising agency with "artificial" rock formations. He received the contract for this via a gallery owner in Wiesbaden who originally came from the Netherlands. But in the large work at the end of the 1980s he was to use a very different language of forms, much more heavily abstracted from its natural model. However, in comparison to the acrylics pictures of 1987 Hiller distanced himself again from Cézanne in as much as he only used complex, sharp-edged forms, dispensing with spherical forms entirely.

The relief, which meanwhile no longer exists, was built up from multiple layers of individual elements. Cut from rigid foam and then painted, these elements clearly signaled the direction they were to be read in, i.e., from left to right. While on the extreme left side a horizontal-vertical grid may yet suspected, the elements in the second part display a movement towards the lower right. This downward movement is then compensated for in the right half by a multistage, curving movement, brought to a standstill at the extreme left corner in what is again a horizontally and vertically balanced fissure. What the relief has in common with the stereometric pictures of 1987 is the surprising renunciation of nature-like appearance. The language of forms, certainly going back to Hiller's grappling with the rock formations, has been abstracted so much that a relationship to this connection may no longer be inferred by just looking at this relief; it may at best be deduced from the knowledge of the overall work.

Wandrelief, Auftragsarbeit / *Wall relief, commissioned work*
Acryl auf Hartschaum / *Acrylics on hard foam*
Arbeit ist zerstört / *Work destroyed*
290 x 620 cm, 1989

Exkurs: Gedanken zum Quadrat

Hillers mit großem Abstand am häufigsten verwendetes Format für seine Arbeiten ist das Quadrat. Geschätzte 80, eher noch 90 Prozent seiner Gemälde und Reliefs haben einen quadratischen Bildträger. Hillers Vorliebe für das quadratische Bildformat ist sicher nicht zufällig und rechtfertigt einen kurzen Exkurs zur kulturell überdeterminierten Figur des Quadrats. Da es Hiller vor allem um das Erzeugen von Strukturen geht, die sich gleichförmig, als „Allover", d. h. ohne bevorzugte Richtung ausbreiten, ist ein quadratischer Bildträger für ihn ein ideales Format. Breitformate haben immer die Tendenz, landschaftliche Assoziationen wachzurufen. So wundert es nicht, dass sich dieser Formattypus am ehesten bei den Arbeiten findet, die sich wie Faltengebirge oder aber wie Wasserflächen panoramaartig vor dem Betrachter erstrecken. Hochformate sind in Hillers Malerei und Reliefs besonders selten und vorwiegend bei seinen Arbeiten auf Papier zu finden.

Über seine ästhetischen Eigenschaften hinaus ist das Quadrat kulturell mit gewissen historisch nachweisbaren Bedeutungen aufgeladen, die in die Interpretation der Hiller'schen Werke mit einfließen können. Die geometrische Grundform des Quadrats begegnet uns Tag für Tag in unspektakulärsten Zusammenhängen, von den Betonplatten unserer städtischen Gehwege bis zum Schachbrett, von den Badezimmerkacheln bis zur CD-Hülle oder einer gewissen Schokoladensorte, die damit wirbt, „quadratisch, praktisch, gut" zu sein. Seine massenhafte industrielle Produktion lässt leicht vergessen, dass es sich beim Quadrat um eine geistige Form handelt. „Geistig" bedeutet hier zunächst, dass das Quadrat nicht aus der Natur genommen oder durch Nachahmung einer Naturform in die Kunst und in das formale Repertoire des Gebrauchs- und Produktdesigns gelangt ist. Reine Quadrate kommen, mit Ausnahme gewisser seltener Salzkristalle, in der unendlichen Vielfalt natürlicher Formbildungen erstaunlicherweise überhaupt nicht vor. Das Quadrat ist nicht nachgeahmte oder imitierte, sondern wesentlich *gedachte*, also konstruierte Form.

Excursus: Thoughts on The Square

The format Hiller uses by far the most for his works is the square. Around 80, but probably closer to 90 percent of his paintings and reliefs have a square picture carrier. This frequency is certainly no coincidence and justifies a short diversion to the culturally over determined figure of the square. Since Hiller is mainly concerned with producing structures that spread uniformly, as "allovers" so to speak, without favoring any particular direction, a square picture carrier is an ideal format for him. Wide formats always have the tendency of evoking landscape associations. Thus it is no surprise that he uses this type of format for the works that spread out before the viewer as panoramas resembling anticline mountain ranges or surfaces of water. Upright formats are particularly rare in Hiller's paintings and reliefs, mostly found in his works on paper.

Beyond its aesthetic characteristics, from a cultural standpoint, the square is associated with certain historically proven meanings, which may be used for the interpretation of Hiller's works. The basic geometric form of the square is something we encounter every day under the most unspectacular circumstances ranging from concrete slabs on the sidewalks of our cities to the chessboard to bathroom tiles to the CD-case or a certain type of chocolate advertised as "square, practical, and good". Its mass production tends to make us forget that the square is a particular spiritual form. "Spiritual" initially means here that the square has not been taken from nature or found its way into art and the formal repertory of commercial product design by imitating a natural form. It is astonishing that, with the exception of certain rare salt crystals, the pure form of the square practically does not occur anywhere in the endless diversity of natural form developments at all. The square is not copied or imitated, but is essentially a thought-up, *i.e. constructed form.*

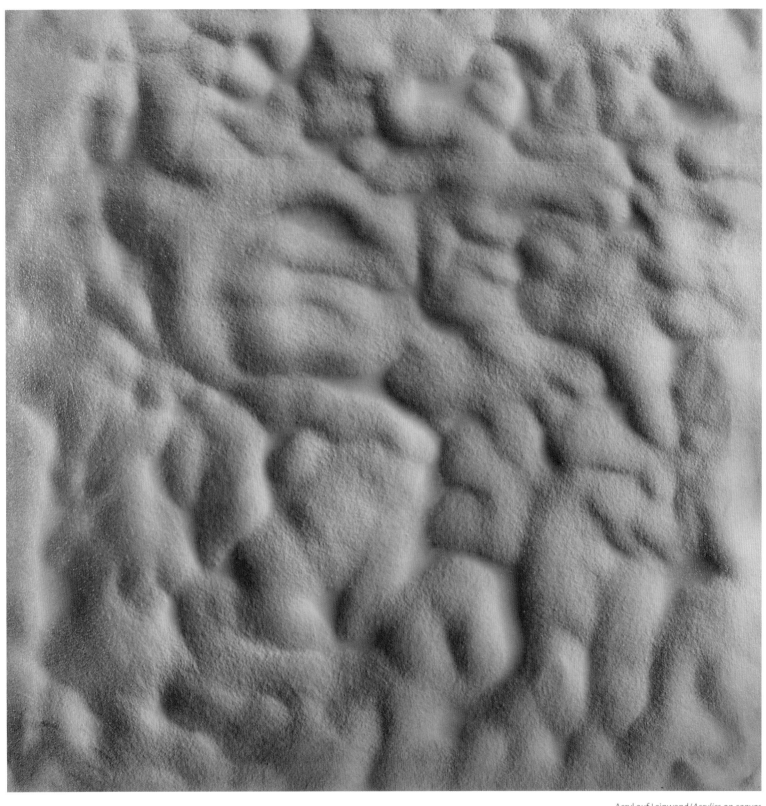

Acryl auf Leinwand/*Acrylics on canvas*

100 x 100 cm, 1998

Acryl auf Leinwand/*Acrylics on canvas*

100 x 100 cm, 1984

Acryl und Zement auf Leinwand/*Acrylics and cement on canvas*

100 x 100 cm, 2007

Acryl und Zement auf Leinwand/*Acrylics and cement on canvas*

100 x 100 cm, 1982

Eine geistige Form ist das Quadrat darüber hinaus auch insofern, als ihm im symbolischen Formenschatz der verschiedensten Kulturkreise ein hoher Stellenwert zugeschrieben wurde. Als geometrische Figur mit vier Ecken, vier gleich langen Seiten und vier gleich großen Winkeln verweist es in potenzierter Form auf die Zahl vier und ihre reiche Symbolik. Es würde zu weit führen, hier der überbordenden spekulativen Zeichenhaftigkeit der Vier in den unterschiedlichen Kulturen auch bloß im Ansatz nachgehen zu wollen. Es mag genügen, daran zu erinnern, dass die Vier in unserem europäischen Kulturkreis von alters her vielfach als Weltzahl verstanden wurde. Dies bedeutet, dass die Welt mit ihren Eigenschaften immer wieder als eine vierfach gegliederte Ganzheit vorgestellt wurde. Man muss nur die vier Elemente der antiken Philosophie (Erde, Wasser, Luft und Feuer) nennen, die vier Himmelsrichtungen, die vier Tages- und Jahreszeiten, die von Homer erstmals beschriebenen vier Winde der antiken Erdkunde und die vier Paradiesflüsse der biblischen Schöpfungsgeschichte, um anzudeuten, was mit der Zahl vier als *Weltzahl* gemeint ist. Es ist nicht verwunderlich, dass das Quadrat, die sinnfälligste Veranschaulichung der Weltzahl vier, immer wieder als Kosmogramm, d. h. als grafisches Symbol für die Welt schlechthin, verwendet wurde. Noch Kasimir Malewitschs berühmtes „Schwarzes Quadrat" (um 1914/15), das längst zu einer Art „Ikone der Moderne" geworden ist, lässt sich überzeugend als Weltsymbol in offensichtlicher Anspielung auf die traditionelle religiöse Symbolik der östlichen Ikonenmalerei interpretieren.[40] Im christlichen Denken wurde die antike Vorstellung der „viereckigen", d. h. viergeteilten Welt, des sogenannten „mundus tetragonus", dann mit der Vierzahl der Evangelien wie mit der Gestalt des Kreuzes als Zeichen der Erlösung in Verbindung gebracht.[41]

Gleichgütig, ob sich Hiller der symbolischen Auflading der Quadratform bewusst bedient oder nicht, sein erklärtes Ziel, mit seiner Malerei die Welt abzubilden, bzw. eine Welt zu schaffen, lässt sich zwanglos mit der tief in der abendländischen Kultur verankerten Bedeutung dieser geometrischen Figur verbinden. Das Quadrat erweist sich somit sowohl formal als auch inhaltlich als stimmige Rahmenform für Joachim Hillers Anspruch, zu malen „wie die Natur".

In addition, the square is a spiritual form in as much as it is highly esteemed in the most varying cultures. As a geometric figure with four corners, four equally long sides, and four equal angles it connotes in an intensified manner the number four and its rich symbolism. It would be too much to enter here into even the basics of the excessive speculative symbolism of the figure four in the various cultures. May it suffice to recall that the number four in our European cultural context has for a long time been understood as a world number. *This means that the world with its characteristics has repeatedly been imagined as a unity which may be divided into four parts. We need only think of the four elements in antique philosophy (earth, water, air, and fire), the four geographical directions, the four times of the day and the four seasons, the four winds of antique geography described by Homer for the first time and the four rivers of Paradise from the Story of the Creation in the Bible, just to indicate what is meant by the number four being a world number. It does not come as a surprise that the square, the most evident illustration of the world number four, was used as a cosmogram, i.e. as a graphic symbol of the world in general. Even Kazimir Malevich's famous "Black Square" (around 1914/15), long since a sort of "icon of modern art," may be convincingly interpreted as a symbol of the world in plain reference to the traditional religious symbolism of Eastern icon painting.[40] In Christian thought, the antique notion of the "square" world, i.e. a world divided into four, the so-called "mundus tetragonus", was then brought into connection with the four Evangelists as well as with the shape of the cross as a sign of salvation.[41]*

No matter if Hiller makes conscious use of the symbolic content of the square form or not, his declared goal of portraying the world in his painting, or respectively, of creating a world, may easily be associated with the meaning of this geometric figure deeply rooted in western culture. The square thus turns out to be a harmonious frame concerning both form and content in accordance with Joachim Hiller's claim of painting "like nature".

---

40 Jeannot Simmen, *Kasimir Malewitsch. Das Schwarze Quadrat. Vom Anti-Bild zur Ikone der Moderne*, Frankfurt am Main 1988. „Malewitsch malt ein schwarzes und ein rotes Quadrat und behauptet, dies seien die zeitgenössischen Ikonen, welche die Welt bedeuten. Dann malt er noch einen schwarzen Kreis und ein Kreuz und sagt, zusammen mit dem Quadrat seien sie die drei Grundformen, welche das Universum bedeuten – und er hat recht. Es sind die drei Grundformen der Ikone des Pantokrators, die schon immer für den Kosmos standen." (Noemi Smolik, „Malewitsch – der erste postmoderne Künstler", in: *Kasimir Malewitsch. Werk und Wirkung*. Herausgegeben von Evelyn Weiss, Köln 1995, S. 18–27, Zitat S. 26.).

41 Zur Symbolik des Quadrats und der Vierzahl: Angelo Lipinsky, Quadrat, in: *Lexikon der christlichen Ikonographie* [LCI], Bd. 3, Sp. 485; Hans Holländer, Vier, Vierzahl, in: LCI, Bd. 4, Sp. 459 f.; ders.: Weltall, Weltbild, in: ebd., Sp. 498–509, bes. Sp. 500–504; Paul von Naredi-Rainer, *Architektur und Harmonie. Zahl, Maß und Proportion in der abendländischen Baukunst*, 5., überarbeitete Auflage, Köln 1995, S. 65 ff.

40 Jeannot Simmen, *Kasimir Malewitsch. Das Schwarze Quadrat. Vom Anti-Bild zur Ikone der Moderne*, Frankfurt am Main. 1998."Malevich paints a black and a red square, claiming these to be the contemporary icons that designate the world. Then he paints yet a black circle and a cross and says, together with the square, these are the three basic forms that signify the universe—and he is right. These are the three basic forms of the icon of the Pantocrator, which always stood for the cosmos." (Noemi Smolik, "Malewitsch – der erste postmoderne Künstler", in: *Kasimir Malewitsch. Werk und Wirkung*. Edited by Evelyn Weiss, Cologne 1995, p. 18–27, quote p. 26 (translated by e.v.).

41 On the symbolism of the square and the Number Four see: Angelo Lipinsky, Quadrat, in: *Lexikon der christlichen Ikonographie* [LCI], vol. 3, column 485; Hans Holländer, Vier, Vierzahl, in: LCI, vol. 4, column 459 f; Ibid: Weltall, Weltbild, in Ibid, columns 498–509, especially column 500–504; Paul von Naredi-Rainer, *Architektur und Harmonie. Zahl, Maß und Proportion in der abendländischen Baukunst*, 5, revised edition, Cologne 1995, p. 65 ff.

Acryl auf Leinwand/*Acrylics on canvas*, 100 x 100 cm, 1987

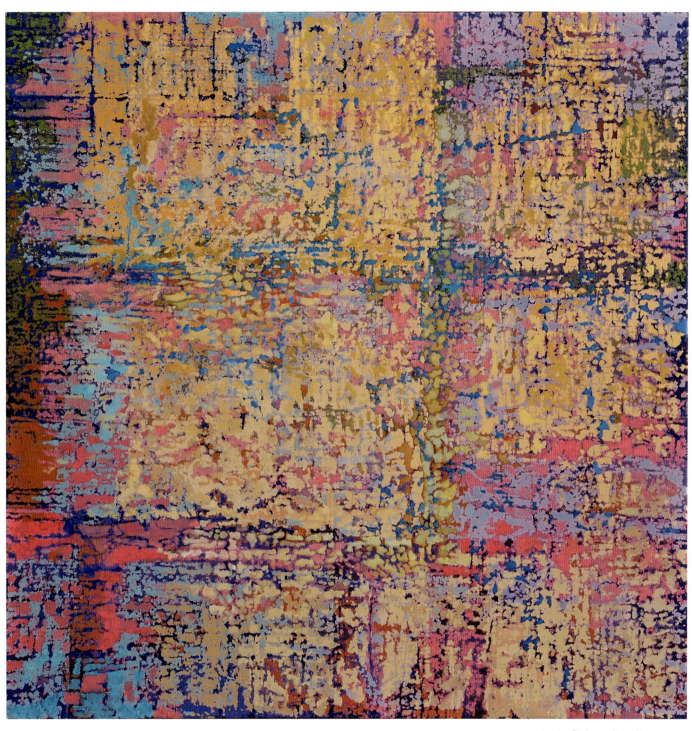

Acryl auf Leinwand/*Acrylics on canvas*

100 x 100 cm, 1988

Das Quadrat erweist sich somit sowohl formal als auch inhaltlich als stimmige Rahmenform für Joachim Hillers Anspruch, zu malen „wie die Natur".

The square thus turns out to be a harmonious frame concerning both form and content in accordance with Joachim Hiller's claim of painting "like nature".

Acryl auf Leinwand/*Acrylics on canvas*

100 x 100 cm, 1987

Acryl auf Leinwand/*Acrylics on canvas*

100 x 100 cm, 1997

Acryl auf Leinwand/*Acrylics on canvas*

100 x 100 cm, 1985

Acryl auf Leinwand/*Acrylics on canvas*

100 x 100 cm, 1987 *(Ausschnitt/Detail)*

Gemalte Reliefs

*Dem Eindruck nach ist der Berg von oben,
aus der fast gleichfarbenen Atmosphäre, nach unten geflossen
und hat sich hier zu einem kleinen Weltraummassiv verdichtet.*[42]
Peter Handke

Hillers Kunst steht von Beginn an im Spannungsfeld zwischen Malerei und Relief. Bereits in seinen frühen eigenständigen Bildern ist Farbe ganz wesentlich Material. Sie ist schrundig, tastbar, weist ein zartes Relief auf. Oft stehen in Hillers Werk Relief und Malerei in schroffem Gegensatz. Wuchtige Konstruktionen, zerklüftet wie verwitterte Felsen, entstanden in den 70er-Jahren neben seiner Malerei. Doch immer wieder gab es Ansätze, die beiden Genres miteinander in Einklang zu bringen. Reliefarbeiten werden bemalt, Folie wird auf Reliefs aufgebracht und nach dem Bemalen wieder glattgezogen usw. Erst um 1990 gelingt es dem Künstler, eine Technik zu entwickeln, Fläche und Räumlichkeit, Relief und Malerei in einer bis dato nicht dagewesenen Weise zu einer Einheit zu verschmelzen. Diese „gemalten Reliefs" gehen – wieder einmal – von der Frage aus, wie man zu einer notwendigen und stimmigen Flächenteilung kommen kann, die nicht konstruiert ist und bei der alle Einzelelemente verschieden sind. Die Lösung war ebenso genial einfach wie die der zerbrochenen Glasplatten in den 70er-Jahren und zudem aus der Alltagserfahrung sogar noch vertrauter. Die Lösung des Problems kann sich jeder deutlich machen, der ein Blatt Papier zerknüllt und danach wieder glattzieht. Das Papier bewahrt die Faltungen als Liniennetz. Keine der von den Linien begrenzten Drei-, Vier-, Fünfecke usw. hat ein gleiches Ebenbild. Was uns aus alltäglichem Umgang vertraut und normalerweise keines weiteren Gedankens wert ist, übertrug Hiller aufs große Format: Er entdeckte eine Methode, präparierte Leinwände zu zerknüllen und das dadurch entstandene Relief der Faltungen erst mit der Spritzpistole zu fixieren und danach farbig auszuarbeiten.

42 Handke [Anm. 18], S. 37.

Painted Reliefs

Our impression is that the mountain has flowed down
from the atmosphere of nearly the same color,
condensing here to a small massif of outer space.[42]
Peter Handke

From its very start Hiller's art has been located somewhere in the field of tension between painting and relief. Paint has been a vital component of his materials since his earliest independent pictures. It is fissured, tangible and displays a delicate relief. Often in Hiller's works, relief and painting stand in stark contrast to one another. In the 1970s he was carrying out huge constructions, jagged like weathered cliffs, in addition to his painting. But there were repeated approaches to bring both genres into mutual harmony. Relief works are painted; foils are attached to reliefs, and then, after painting, stretched smooth again. Only around 1990 did the artist manage to develop a technique of melding surface and space, relief and painting into a hitherto unknown unity. Once again, these "painted reliefs" depart from the question of how a necessary and harmonious division of the surface may be reached that is not construed and yet harmonious and in which all of the individual elements are different from one another. The solution was as congenially simple as the broken sheets of glass of the 1970s. Moreover, from our everyday experience it was even more familiar to us than the latter. Anyone can understand the solution of the problem if he or she crumples up a piece of paper and then smoothes it out again. The paper maintains the folds as a network of lines. None of the triangles, quadrangles, pentagons, etc. defined by the lines has an exact look alike. Something we know from everyday experience and would normally attribute no further importance to has been transferred by Hiller to a large format: he discovered a method of wadding up prepared canvases and then fixing the relief of folds that has come about like this with a spray gun and then coloring it.

42 Handke [footnote 18], p. 37.

Acryl auf Leinwand/*Acrylics on canvas*
100 x 100 cm, 1987 (Ausschnitt/*Detail*)

Acryl auf Leinwand/*Acrylics on canvas*

150 x 150 cm, 2007

Hiller ist mit Goethes Farbenlehre ebenso vertraut wie mit der Farbkugel von Philipp Otto Runge.
Hiller is just as familiar with Goethe's theory of color as with Philipp Otto Runge's color sphere.

Acryl auf Leinwand/*Acrylics on canvas*, 100 x 100 cm, 2000

Diese Methode unterscheidet sich strukturell von den bisherigen Versuchen, Malerei und Relief zusammenzubringen. Was nun entstand, waren keine *be*malten Reliefs, auch keine auf die Leinwand übertragene Reliefstrukturen. Es waren *gemalte* Reliefs. Die Leinwand, also die Malfläche selbst, ist in die dritte Dimension erweitert und die dabei entstandenen Strukturen werden anschließend wieder auf zwei Dimensionen zurückprojiziert. Ein Foto von 2007, das den Künstler während der Arbeit an einem noch nicht wieder völlig glattgezogenen gemalten Relief zeigt, gibt eine Vorstellung von diesem eigenwilligen Verfahren.

Das aus dem Zerknüllen hervorgegangene „Faltengebirge" der Leinwand mit der Spritzpistole aus einer Richtung hell, aus der Gegenrichtung dunkel zu spritzen, ist ein erster Schritt, das Relief malerisch umzusetzen. Bei vielen der auf diese Weise entstandenen Werke fällt dabei ein sehr bewusster Einsatz der Farbigkeit auf. Hiller mag die Vorstellung, die Gebirgsmassive gleichsam mit einem Farbkreis zu umgeben, will heißen aus unterschiedlichen Richtungen mit einer abgestuften Reihe von Farben zu akzentuieren. Hiller ist mit Goethes Farbenlehre ebenso vertraut wie mit der Farbkugel von Philipp Otto Runge, die ihn fasziniert (wenn auch nicht die farbmystischen Spekulationen, die der Romantiker damit verknüpfte). Dessen Vorstellung, gleichsam einen Raum aus Farbe zu konstruieren, hatte Einfluss auf die Farbgebung der gemalten Reliefs. Wenn kühle Farben (wie Graublau) gegen warme (wie Rotorange) gesetzt und von Zwischentönen getrennt werden, ergibt sich eine suggestive räumliche Wirkung. Diese Bilder entfalten atmosphärische Stimmungen, die überaus stark auf die Wahrnehmung der Bilder als Landschaften einwirken.

This method differs structurally from the former attempts to bring together painting and relief. What now came about were not reliefs covered with paint *and neither were they reliefs with structures transferred to canvas. These were* painted *reliefs. The canvas, i.e., the surface to be painted, has been extended into the third dimension; the resulting structures then being projected again back to two dimensions. A photograph from 2007, showing the artist working on a not yet completely smoothed, painted relief, gives us an idea of this particular procedure.*

Using a spray gun on the "anticline fold mountains" that resulted from the procedure of wadding up the canvas, light from one direction and dark from the opposite direction, is a first step in transforming the relief in a painterly manner. In many of the works that were made in this manner, we notice a very conscious use of color. Hiller likes the notion of surrounding his mountain massifs with a circle of color; that is, accenting them from different directions with a graduated series of colors. Hiller is just as familiar with Goethe's theory of color as with Philipp Otto Runge's color sphere, which fascinates him (though not the mystic color speculations the Romanticist connected with it). The latter's notion of constructing a space from color so to speak influenced the coloration of the painted reliefs. When cool colors (such as blue-gray) are placed against warm colors such as (red-orange) and separated by intermediate tones, the result is a suggestive effect of space. These pictures unfold atmospheric moods that do have an effect on the perception of the pictures as landscapes.

Acryl auf Leinwand/*Acrylics on canvas*

120 x 190 cm, 1990

Seite/*Page* 132/133

Acryl auf Leinwand/*Acrylics on canvas*

120 x 190 cm, 1990

Das für die Reihe der gemalten Reliefs häufiger gewählte Breitformat von 120 x 190 Zentimeter erleichtert es zusätzlich, in vielen dieser Arbeiten – zumindest auf den ersten Blick – wild aufgeworfene, durch tiefe Schatten zusätzlich zerklüftete Erdfaltungen einer von einer externen Lichtquelle erhellten Gebirgslandschaft aus der Vogelperspektive zu sehen. Sonnenaufgänge über alpinem Panorama, lichte Gebirgsmassive jenseits der Baumgrenze, von Satelliten aufgenommene und in Farbcodes umgesetzte Höhenmessungen – solche gegenständlichen Interpretationen stellen sich wohl unvermeidlich ein. Zu den interessantesten und aufschlussreichsten Seh-Erfahrungen, die man mit Hillers Bildern machen kann, gehören diejenigen beim Betrachten der gemalten Reliefs, wenn diese Vorstellungen langsam oder auch schockhaft schnell von den Bildern selbst wieder dementiert werden. Dies geschieht, wenn einem bewusst wird, dass die Perspektive dieser Bilder keineswegs lückenlos konsistent ist, sondern merkwürdige Brüche aufweist. Oder wenn man plötzlich wahrnimmt, dass die Faltenbildung nicht naturwüchsig sein kann, weil sie zu regelmäßige Linien aufweist (offenbar Quer- und Längsfaltungen der Leinwand). Dann bekommen die anscheinend bekannten und leicht zu interpretierenden Formen eine Fremdheit (Handkes „Weltraummassiv") und Rätselhaftigkeit, die unser Bedürfnis nach Wiedererkennen düpiert.

The wide format of 120 x 190 cm, often chosen for the series of painted reliefs, also makes it easier to see in many of these works—at least at first glance—a wildly upthrust mountain landscape from a bird's eye perspective, lit by an external source of light that because of the deep shadows it casts, makes the folds of the earth appear even more rugged. Sunrises above an alpine panorama, light mountain massifs above the timberline, their heights recorded by satellites and transformed into color codes—such concrete and objective ways of reading the pictures inevitably occur to us. Among the most interesting and informative visual experiences you can have with Hiller's pictures are those that come about when viewing the painted reliefs, when these notions are slowly, but sometimes also shockingly quickly rectified again by the pictures themselves. This happens when it becomes clear to us that the perspective of these pictures is in no way entirely consistent, but displays odd breaks. Or when we suddenly perceive that the creation of the folds cannot be a natural one, because the lines it reveals are too regular (evidently the upright and horizontal folds of the canvas). Then the apparently known and easily readable forms take on a foreignness (Handke's "massif of space") and mysteriousness, which dupes our need for recognition.

Acryl auf Leinwand/*Acrylics on canvas*

100 x 100 cm, 1987

Acryl und Quarzsand auf Leinwand/*Acrylics and quartz sand on canvas*

150 x 150 cm, 2007

Sommer/*Summer*, 2007

Unserer Wahrnehmung wird weiter verunsichert, wenn man sich vor den Arbeiten bewegt, sie schräg anschaut oder so nahe an sie herantritt, dass die illusionistische Reliefwirkung kollabiert und man sich bewusst wird, dass die Gemälde, entgegen ihrem Anschein, flach sind. Fläche und Raum, Malerei und Relief, Wiedererkennen und Fremdheit sind in dieser Werkreihe so sehr zu einer Einheit verschmolzen, dass gerade diese Bilder in der kurzen Zeit von Hillers neuer Öffentlichkeit zu einer Art „Klassiker" geworden sind, als Arbeiten mit dem größten Wiedererkennungswert. Dass sie für den Künstler einen äußerst fruchtbaren Ansatz darstellten, ein wahres Forschungsfeld im Grenzbereich von Malerei und Relief eröffneten, das eine Fülle von Varianten ermöglichte, kann hier nur behauptet, nicht aber ausführlich dargelegt werden. Dieser Teil von Hillers Werk ist so weit verzweigt, dass eine angemessene Darstellung den Rahmen dieses Überblicks sprengen würde.

Further complicating our perception is the discovery that when we move before the canvas, look at it from an angle or from so close-up that the illusionist relief effect collapses and we become aware that the paintings, against all appearances, are still flat. Surface and space, painting and relief, recognition and strangeness are melded in this series into such a unity that it is not surprising that precisely these pictures have become a kind of "classic" in the short time of Hiller's new presence in the public area as these works possess the highest degree of being recognizable. The fact that they afforded the artist an extremely fruitful approach, opening a veritable field of research in the border area between painting and relief, that offered an abundance of variations, is something I can only state here, but am unable to dwell on any further. This part of Hiller's work branches out so diversely that a fitting description would go beyond the scope of this survey.

Acryl auf Leinwand/*Acrylics on canvas*

120 x 190 cm, 1990

Acryl auf Leinwand/*Acrylics on canvas*

100 x 100 cm, 1987

Acryl auf Leinwand/*Acrylics on canvas*

120 x 180 cm, 2007

Acryl auf Leinwand/*Acrylics on canvas*

100 x 100 cm, 1987 *(Ausschnitt/Detail)*

Öl auf Leinwand/*Oil on canvas*

100 x 100 cm, 2000

Öl auf Leinwand/*Oil on canvas*

100 x 100 cm, 2000

Wasser und Wellen

Das Beste aber ist das Wasser …[43]
Pindar

Mit der perfekten Amalgamierung von Gemälde und Relief war Hiller eine konsequente Formulierung seiner künstlerischen Idee gelungen, die in der Folge fast zwangsläufig einen neuen Ansatz notwendig machte, denn nichts steht seinem künstlerischen Denken ferner als die Idee der Wiederholung. Nicht, dass das Thema der Dreidimensionalität aufgehört hätte, ihn länger zu beschäftigen – bis heute arbeitet Hiller immer wieder sowohl an Realreliefs wie an gemalten Reliefs –, aber im Verlauf und verstärkt gegen Ende der 90er-Jahre fällt die zunehmende Beschäftigung mit dem ganz anderen Thema Fläche auf. Betrachtet man die betreffenden Werke unmittelbar nach den gemalten Reliefs, ist man frappiert über die Heftigkeit des Umschwungs. Auf die Tastbarkeit der Reliefformen, die geradezu körperlich erlebbaren Schluchten und Aufwerfungen der Faltengebirge aus Malerei, folgen rein visuelle, farbstarke, in der Malfläche verharrende Bilder. Wie bei Hiller üblich, sind jedoch auch diese so anders gearteten Bilder auf seine Beschäftigung mit Naturstrukturen zurückzuführen.

Der plötzliche Wechsel des malerischen Stils geht mit einem Wechsel der Aufmerksamkeit auf die Naturmaterialien einher. Waren bisher Felsen, Erde, Sand und Stein, also das Tellurische, Erdenschwere als Paradigma in seiner Malerei vorherrschend, wurde nun Wasser mit all seinen faszinierenden Eigenschaften zum Material. Wasser hatte Hiller bezeichnenderweise bis dato nur in seiner erstarrten, mineralischen Form als Eis interessiert. Nun entdeckte er die „Wässrigkeit" des Wassers, seine Fähigkeit, sich in ganz spezifischer Weise in der Fläche auszubreiten, als ästhetisches Faszinosum. Wasser ist selbstverständlich weit mehr als ein Material. Wasser ist in der antiken Philosophie eines der vier Elemente, für den Vorsokratiker Thales sogar der Urstoff, aus dem „alles" entstanden sei. Dass diese Idee, Wasser als Grundstoff aufzufassen – als ein Grundstoff der Kunst, wenn schon nicht der Natur – Joachim Hiller faszinierte, liegt auf der Hand. Eine Äußerung des Künstlers in einem Interview anlässlich seiner ersten Retrospektive im Sommer 2008 macht dies deutlich: „Im Grunde genommen ist […] alles ähnlich oder es kommt alles zusammen. Wenn man beispielsweise Wasser nimmt: Wasser ist flüssig, Wasser ist als Wolke luftig und Wasser ist als Eis fest. Und wenn man nun feste Körper hat und flüssige Körper und flüchtige, gasförmige Körper, dann hat man die ganze Welt eigentlich beisammen. Und wenn man das kann, wenn man diese drei Elemente richtig darstellen kann, dann müsste man die ganze Welt darstellen können, oder besser gesagt: eine neue Welt daraus machen. Und das ist natürlich so eine Idee dabei …"[44]

43 Olympische Oden I,1
44 Hiller Interview [Anm. 17].

Water and Waves

Water is the best of all things …[43]
Pindar

Hiller managed to accomplish a logical formulation of his artistic idea with the perfect amalgamation of painting and relief. As a consequence, however, it made it necessary to develop a new approach, since nothing was further from his artistic thinking than repetition. Not that the theme of three-dimensionality would have ceased to occupy him any longer—even today Hiller works from time to time both on real and painted reliefs—but over time, and particularly at the end of the 1990s, we notice an increasing occupation with the wholly different theme of surface. If we look at the corresponding works immediately after the painted reliefs we are amazed by the severity of the change. After the tangibility of the relief forms, the ravines and upward thrusts of the anticline mountains in painting that we can almost experience physically, follow the purely visual, vibrantly colorful pictures that remain on the painted surface. With Hiller everything is traceable to the occupation with natural structures, and these pictures are no exception.

The sudden change in painterly style is in accordance with a change in the attentiveness to natural materials. Where previously cliffs, earth, sand, and stone, i.e. the telluric, the heaviness of the earth, prevailed as a paradigm of his painting, now water as material emerges to the forefront with all its fascinating characteristics. Up to that point, Hiller had only been interested in water in its solidified, mineral form as ice. Now he discovered its "aqueous" traits, its capacity to spread over a surface in an entirely specific way, as aesthetically fascinating. Water is, of course, much more than a material. In antique philosophy, it is one of the four elements. For the precursor to Socrates, Thales, it was even the primal stuff from which "everything" was made. It goes without saying that this notion declaring water to be a basic material of art—a basic material of art, if not of nature—would fascinate Joachim Hiller. A statement by the artist made in an interview on the occasion of his first retrospective in the summer of 2008 makes this clear: "Basically everything is […] similar or it all comes together. Take water as an example. Water is fluid. Water as a cloud is airy, and water as ice is solid. And if you have solid bodies and fluid bodies, and volatile, gaseous bodies, then you have the entire world together, really. And if you can do this, if you can portray these three elements correctly, than you should be able to portray the whole world, or better said, make a new world out of this. And this is, of course, just an idea for doing so …"[44]

43 Olympic Odes I,1.
44 Hiller Interview [footnote 17].

Acryl auf Leinwand/*Acrylics on canvas*
100 x 100 cm, 1997 (Ausschnitt/*Detail*)

Acryl auf Leinwand/*Acrylics on canvas*

100 x 100 cm, 1997

Diese Aussage ist in zweifacher Weise aufschlussreich. Zum einen ist es bemerkenswert, dass Hiller die drei Aggregatzustände fest, flüssig, gasförmig als „Elemente" bezeichnet. Dies zeigt, dass sie für ihn die eigentlichen Elementarthemen seiner Kunst sind – und nicht etwa die etwas konstruiert wirkende Idee, die vier antiken Elemente Wasser, Erde, Luft und Feuer darzustellen, selbst wenn dies gelegentlich vom Künstler selbst behauptet wurde.[45] Feuer nämlich kommt bei ihm als gestaltende Kraft kaum vor, auf die Ausnahme des verkohlten Holzstücks wurde bereits hingewiesen. Sonst wird auf Feuer allenfalls als hinzugedachte Größe angespielt, so etwa in den neueren, auf die Farben Schwarz, Weiß und Rot gestimmten Arbeiten, die offenbar von den Aufenthalten auf der Vulkaninsel Lanzarote inspiriert sind. Dasselbe gilt für die wie Lava auf die Leinwand geschleuderte Farbmaterie in einigen 2008 entstandenen Bildern. Solche Arbeiten evozieren zwar die feurigen Kräfte der Natur, ihre Strukturen sind aber aus anderen Prozessen hervorgegangen.

Zum anderen verdeutlicht das Zitat in aller wünschenswerten Klarheit die Intention des Künstlers, mit den Naturstrukturen eine „neue Welt" zu schaffen, d. h. eine Welt, die allein in der Kunst Bestand hat. Wie eingeschränkt die Möglichkeiten der Kunst im Vergleich zu dem schier grenzenlosen Formbildungsvermögen der Natur auch immer sein mögen: Es muss in den Kunstwerken etwas vorhanden sein, was der Natur zur Seite steht, etwas, was durch Naturbetrachtung allein nicht zu erreichen ist. Die Äußerung Hillers, er habe es als Kränkung empfunden, dass er keine neue Farbe hat erfinden können[46], zielt in eine ähnliche Richtung: Hillers Kunst lebt aus der Dialektik zwischen dem maßlosen Anspruch, eine neue Welt zu erfinden und der bescheidenen Einsicht in die unüberbietbaren Formkräfte der Natur.

Eine erste Annäherung an die Idee, durch die Wandlungsfähigkeit von Wasser zu neuen Bildlösungen zu gelangen, erfolgte durch die Beobachtung, die jeder Aquarellist kennt, dass sich nämlich Papier wellt, wenn es befeuchtet wird. Abhängig von den Papiereigenschaften, der Stärke, Dicke usw. sowie von der Wassermenge fallen die Wölbungen und Aufwerfungen unterschiedlich aus. Wie sich das Papier jeweils verformen wird, ist prinzipiell unvorhersehbar. Dass sich dieser Vorgang unendlich variieren lässt und dabei immer neue Formen hervorbringt, war Grund genug für Hiller, diesen Vorgang in Malerei zu umzusetzen.

This statement is informative in two ways. For one, it is remarkable that Hiller designates the three states of aggregation, solid, fluid, gaseous as "elements". This shows that they are for him the actual elementary themes of his art—and not, for example, the idea that seems somewhat contrived to us of portraying the four antique elements water, earth, air, and fire, even though the artist himself occasionally maintained this.[45] Fire namely scarcely figures in his works as a creative force and we pointed out above the rare exception of the charred piece of wood. Otherwise fire is only hinted at as an entity, such as in the newer works characterized by the colors of black, white and red, and apparently inspired by trips made to the volcanic island of Lanzarote. The same applies to the paint matter spewed like lava onto the canvas in some of his pictures of 2008. Such works evoke, granted, the fiery forces of nature, but their structures have come about as the result of other processes.

The other thing that the quote makes unmistakably clear is the artist's intention of creating a "new world" with the aid of natural structures, that is a world which exists alone in art. However limited the possibilities of art may be in comparison to the sheer boundless morphogenetic possibilities of nature: There has to be something in the art works that stands at nature's side, something which may not be obtained alone from our contemplation of nature. Hiller's statement that he found it hurtful that he was never able to invent a new color,[46] goes in the same direction: Hiller's art lives from the dialectics between the inordinate claim of inventing a new world and of the modest insight into the unsurpassable formative powers of nature.

A first approximation to the idea of using the water's capacity for transformation to reach new picture results, came about because of an observation known to every watercolorist, namely that paper buckles when it is made wet. Depending on the properties of the paper, the strength, thickness, etc. and the amount of water used, these bumps and buckles will vary. In principle we may not predict beforehand how the paper will well up. That this process may be endlessly varied and produces ever new forms was enough reason for Hiller to transfer this process into painting.

---

45 Held [Anm. 8], S. 12 f.
46 Interview mit Erik Buchheister [Anm. 28], S. 45.

45 Held [footnote 8], p. 12 f.
46 Interview with Erik Buchheister [footnote 28], p. 45.

Die Idee bestand darin, simultan mehrere Wellenbildungen von Papier zu fixieren, auf Leinwand zu übertragen und dabei übereinanderzublenden. Das Resultat sind hochkomplexe, flirrende Überlagerungen von sich verfasernden, sich in der Grundrichtung horizontal erstreckende Liniengebilden. Durch die Beschränkung der Palette auf Blau-, Gelb- und Grüntöne ist die Assoziation von im Licht funkelnden Wasserflächen nahe liegend, obwohl – und das ist das Frappierende – hier keinerlei Abbildung oder Imitation vorliegt. Die grobe strukturelle Verwandtschaft zwischen den Wellengebilden, die das Wasser im Papier bewirkt, und den Oberflächen, wie sie große Wasseransammlungen selbst hervorbringen, genügt der Vorstellungskraft, hier eine Identifikation herzustellen. Ebenfalls interessant ist die merkwürdige Dialektik dieser Vorstellung, das ständige Umkippen zwischen einer vor uns liegenden (also sich horizontal erstreckenden) Wasserfläche und der reinen Faktizität der vor uns ausgebreiteten (vertikal an der Wand hängenden) Bildfläche. Hillers „Wasser"-Bilder aktivieren und dementieren zugleich die Illusion, die sie mit der gegenständlichen Deutung („Lichtreflexionen auf Wasserfläche") erzeugen.

Sehr schön lässt sich das an einigen Bildern zeigen, bei denen Hiller die Wellenmuster nicht bis an die Bildränder herangeführt hat, sodass an den oberen und unteren Bildgrenzen die Grundierung sichtbar bleibt. Wenn der Blick des Betrachters sich auf diese Zonen richtet, bricht die Illusion sofort ab. Aus den Wellenmustern wird ein Bild an der Wand. Sobald der Blick jedoch zurück in Richtung Bildmitte gleitet, wird es wieder zu einer horizontal vor uns liegenden Wasserfläche, auf dem sich das Spiel von Licht und Wellen abspielt. Dies ist ein hervorragendes Beispiel für unsere natürliche Neigung, stets etwas „als etwas" wahrzunehmen. Der ständige Rückbesinnung auf die in unserer Erfahrung gespeicherten Kenntnisse („Das sieht aus wie …") ist unsere Weise, zu sehen. Dass Hiller diese Neigung mit seinen Bildern zugleich bedient und enttäuscht, macht ihre besondere Qualität aus. So werden die Bilder zu Auslösern einer geschärften Aufmerksamkeit auf unsere eigene Wahrnehmung.

Nur beiläufig sei hier darauf hingewiesen, dass mit diesen Arbeiten ein Thema wieder aufgenommen und intensiviert wird, das Hiller in der Folge immer öfter beschäftigen wird. Es ist das Thema des Bildlichts, d. h., einer scheinbar aus dem Bild herausstrahlenden Lichtquelle. In seinen früheren Arbeiten gab es kaum ein Bildlicht in diesem Sinne. Es taucht zum ersten Mal in einigen der gemalten Reliefs auf, die an Gebirgsmassive denken lassen, die von der Sonne überstrahlt werden. In den verschiedenen „Wasser"-Serien und den sich daraus entwickelnden „Wolken"-Bildern werden Licht und Farbe zunehmend zu wichtigen Parametern der Bildwirkung.[47]

The idea consisted of fixing several wave-like formations of paper simultaneously, transferring them to canvas while layering them in the process. The results are highly complex, vibrating layers of horizontal, frayed linear formations. By limiting the color to blue, yellow, and green tones the association of light shining on water surfaces is undeniable, although—and this is what is amazing—here the pictures have nothing to do with the reproduction or imitation of models. The rough structural relationship between the wave formations caused by the water in the paper and the surfaces caused by large collections of water itself suffices for our power of imagination to produce an identification here. Likewise interesting is the strange dialectics of this notion, the constant alternation between the interpretation of it as a surface of water lying before us (i.e. spreading out horizontally) and the pure fact of the picture surface extending in front of us (hanging vertically on the wall). Hiller's "water" pictures activate and cancel at the same time the illusionism they produce in connection with an objectively concrete interpretation ("light reflexes on a surface of water").

This is nicely shown in several pictures where Hiller has not continued the wave patterns to the edges of the picture, so that the ground remains visible at the upper and lower borders of the pictures. When the viewer's gaze meets these zones, the illusionism ceases immediately. The wave patterns turn into a picture on the wall. As soon as the gaze returns towards the center of the picture, it once again becomes a horizontal surface of water spread out before us, upon which the play between light and waves takes place. This is a magnificent example of the natural tendency to always perceive something "as something". The constant recourse to the knowledge stored in our experience ("that looks like …") is our way of seeing. The fact that Hiller at the same time serves and frustrates this inclination in his pictures is what defines their special quality. In this way the pictures become triggers for a heightened attentiveness to our own perception.

In passing, it should be mentioned here that with these works a theme has been taken up again and intensified, which Hiller will subsequently deal with more and more often. It is the theme that relates to the light of the picture, i.e., a source of light that seemingly radiates from out of the picture. In his earlier works light in this sense was hardly traceable in the pictures. It occurs for the first time in several of the painted reliefs recalling mountain massifs, with the sun shining over them. In the various "water" series and the "cloud" pictures developing from out of them, light and color increasingly become important parameters of the picture effect.[47]

---

[47] Zurzeit bereitet die Kölner Kunsthistorikerin Dr. Marta Cencillo Ramírez eine Studie zum Thema Farbe, Licht und Helldunkel bei Joachim Hiller vor.

[47] At present the Cologne art historian Dr. Marta Cencillo Ramírez is preparing a study on the topic of color, light, and dark in Joachim Hiller's works.

Acryl auf Leinwand/*Acrylics on canvas*

100 x 100 cm, 1997

Acryl auf Leinwand/*Acrylics on canvas*

100 x 100 cm, 1999

Acryl auf Leinwand/*Acrylics on canvas*, 100 x 150 cm, 1999

Die indirekte Methode, die Wirkung von Wasser auf Papierbögen auf die Malerei zu übertragen, verlangte geradezu danach, eine direktere Methode zu entwickeln, die Wellenbewegung des Wassers zu verbildlichen. Hiller suchte also nach einer Möglichkeit, mit der Wässrigkeit des Wassers, mit seinen Fließeigenschaften selbst zu arbeiten. Wasser ist schließlich ein wichtiger Bestandteil der Acrylfarbe – und so lag es nahe, eine Strukturen bildende Methodik aus den Bewegungen der Farbe selbst zu entwickeln. Interessant ist, dass diese Idee sich zugleich mit Kindheits- und Jugenderinnerungen verbindet. Das heißt, sie basiert im sinnlichen Erleben von Wasser. Gemeint sind die schon im ersten Kapitel angedeuteten Erinnerungen an die Tage, die Joachim Hiller in seiner Jugend in Berlin am Wannsee verbrachte, an das Beobachten der sich verändernden Wasseroberfläche und ihrer Reflexionen, an die schaukelnden Bootsfahrten über den See. Diese Schaukelbewegungen nun, die so typisch sind für das körperliche Erfahren von Wasser, wird zur Basis einer Serie von Bildern, die nun die Strukturbildung des Farbmaterials direkt thematisieren.

Das verblüffend einfache Prinzip dieser Bilder besteht darin, dass verschiedene Farbpfützen auf dem flach ausgebreiteten Bildträger verteilt werden und diese sich dann durch leichte Schaukelbewegungen „selbsttätig" auf der Bildfläche verteilen. Was so einfach klingt, ist in der Praxis vertrackt und im visuellen Ergebnis komplex. Hiller reaktivierte in diesen Bildern eine Technik, die er Anfang der 90er-Jahre bereits mit von Sand und sich wolkenartig ausbreitenden Acrylstrukturen ausprobiert hatte. Damals ging es noch nicht darum, das Thema Wasser zu veranschaulichen, sondern um Experimente mit Strukturen, die sich aus dem Bewegen des Bildträgers ergeben. Eine der Schwierigkeiten bei diesem Verfahren liegt darin, dass die Konsistenz der Farbsubstanzen ganz genau abgestimmt sein muss. Die Farbe darf nicht zu dünnflüssig, aber auch nicht zu zäh sein. Sie darf nicht zu schnell trocknen, vor allem aber dürfen die unterschiedlichen Farben sich nicht zu einem grauen Einerlei mischen. Wie bei vielen anderen Werkreihen Hillers gehen diese „Wasser"-Bilder mit akribischer Materialforschung und einem stetigen Prozess des Perfektionierens der Resultate einher.

The indirect method of transferring to painting the effect water has on paper virtually called for the development of a more direct method of depicting the wave movements of the water. Thus, Hiller was searching for a method of working with the liquid nature of water, its flow properties themselves. Water is, after all, an important component of acrylic paint—and so it seemed logical to develop methods for forming structures from the movement of the paint itself. It is interesting that the artist connects this idea at the same time with memories of his childhood and youth. The idea is based on the sensual experience of water. What I refer to here are the memories of the days Joachim Hiller spent in his youth at Lake Wannsee in Berlin, hinted at above, watching the changing surface and reflections of the water, making trips across the lake with a boat that rocked back and forth. These rocking movements, so typical for the physical experience of water, now become the basis of a series of pictures that make the development of structure of the paint materials a direct theme.

The surprisingly simple principle behind these pictures consists of distributing various puddles of paint across the stretched picture carrier and then by rocking the canvas back and forth the paint puddles spreading over the picture surface "on their own". This sounds simple, but it has its pitfalls in practice and the visual result is complex. In these pictures Hiller reactivated a technique, which he had tried out at the beginning of the 1990s already, using sand and acrylic structures that spread like clouds. At the time he was not yet concerned with treating water as a theme, but rather experimenting with structures that resulted from moving the picture carrier. One of the difficulties in this process is that the consistency of the paint substances must be exactly proportioned. The paint must not be too thin, but also not too thick. It should not dry too quickly and above all the various colors should not mix to form a muddy gray. As with many of Hiller's other work series these "water" pictures are in keeping with his meticulous research of the material and an ongoing process of improving the results.

Da die Farbpfützen beim „Schaukeln" des Bildträgers derselben Bewegungsfolge ausgesetzt sind, bilden sie ganz ähnliche Verlaufsformen aus. Bei einigen der auf diese Weise entstandenen Bilder schließen sich die einzelnen Farbflächen zu einem übergreifenden System zusammen, das auf den ersten Blick wie ein geschlossenes Muster erscheint. Aber bei genauerem Hinsehen zeigt sich schnell, dass es keinen durchgehenden Rapport gibt, dass die einzelnen Farbflächen jeweils individuelle, mehr oder minder abweichende Eigenheiten aufweisen. Wieder einmal wird Hillers Zentralthema von der Unwiederholbarkeit der Naturformen anschaulich. Vergleicht man die ästhetische Wirkung dieser Arbeiten mit denen der früheren „Wasser"-Serie, dann fällt auf, dass die Farbmuster hier noch eindeutiger in die Fläche drängen. Die gegenständliche Vorstellung von Wasseroberfläche tritt deutlich zurück, was auch auf die Verwendung von Farben wie Orange, Violett, Lindgrün usw. zurückzuführen ist.

Die „Versuchsanordnung" dieser „Wasser"-Bilder ist so sehr vereinfacht, dass selbst geringfügige Änderungen der Ausgangsbedingungen beträchtliche Unterschiede im Ergebnis zeitigen. Zum Beispiel sind Art und Heftigkeit der Bewegungen entscheidend, mit der die Farbpfützen zum Fließen gebracht werden, ebenso die Konsistenz der Farbsubstanzen und ihre Fähigkeit, mehr oder weniger stark aufeinander zu reagieren. Ein aufschlussreiches Werk in diesem Zusammenhang ist ein Gemälde von 1995, das zwar das zugrunde liegende Muster deutlich erkennen lässt, sich aber an einzelnen Stellen in reich detaillierten Binnenformen auflöst. Die Farben fließen auf eine „chaotische" Weise ineinander, bilden Verwirbelungen, Schlieren, einzelne, sich weit in benachbarte Farbregionen schlängelnde Linien. Dieses Bild steht an der Grenze, an der sich die gegenständliche Vorstellung einer Wasseroberfläche aufzulösen beginnt. Wenn die Farbpfützen nicht mehr regelmäßig über die Bildfläche verteilt und die Bewegungen nicht mehr gleichmäßig und repetitiv erfolgen, werden die Formen freier. Der Maßstab der Assoziationen springt um. Erinnerungen an Satellitenfotos, an Küstenlinien, an Aufnahmen von Großwetterlagen stellen sich ein. Diese Vorstellungen verfolgte Hiller systematisch weiter, indem er sich die Frage stellte: Was ist – strukturell gesehen – eine Wolke?

Since the puddles of paint are subject to the same successions of movement when the picture carrier is "rocked", their runs form very similar shapes. With several works that came about using this technique, individual surfaces of paint combine to an overarching system that appears at first glance to be a closed pattern. But when we look closer, we quickly recognize that there is no consistent pattern, that the individual surfaces of paint display individual properties that deviate sometimes less, sometimes more. If we compare the aesthetic effect of these works with those of the earlier "water" series it is striking that the spread of the color patterns across the surface is even more pronounced here. Any attempt to interpret this as the objective surface of the water clearly recedes, owing to the use of colors such as orange, violet, lime-green, etc.

The "test arrangement" of these "water" pictures has been so greatly simplified that even slight changes in the initial conditions cause considerable differences in the result. For example the type and amount of energy exerted in the movement are decisive for the way the paint puddles flow. Likewise the consistency of the paint substances and their ability to more or less react to each other play a role. A key work in this context is a painting from 1995 which, although we clearly recognize a basic pattern, dissolves it in places into richly detailed interior forms. The colors run into one another in a "chaotic" way, forming swirls, smears, and individual lines that undulate far into the adjacent regions of color. This picture is close to dissolving our notion of a water surface. When the puddles of paint are no longer regularly spread across the picture surface and the movements are no longer carried out in an even and repetitive fashion, the forms become freer. The scale of associative measures changes. Memories of satellite photographs, coastlines, and photographs of large weather fronts come to mind. Hiller systematically pursued these notions by asking the question: From a structural standpoint, what is a cloud?

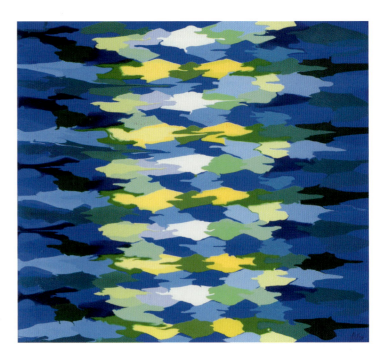

Acryl auf Leinwand/*Acrylics on canvas*

100 x 110 cm, 1999

Acryl auf Leinwand/*Acrylics on canvas*

100 x 100 cm, 1999

Acryl auf Leinwand/*Acrylics on canvas*

105 x 105 cm, 2006

Wolken

Hamlet: Seht Ihr die Wolke dort, beinah in Gestalt eines Kamels?
Polonius: Beim Himmel, sie sieht auch wirklich aus wie ein Kamel.
Hamlet: Mich dünkt, sie sieht aus wie ein Wiesel.
Polonius: Sie hat einen Rücken wie ein Wiesel.
Hamlet: Oder wie ein Walfisch?
Polonius: Ganz wie ein Walfisch.[48]
William Shakespeare

Von allen Naturerscheinungen, mit denen wir vertraut sind, ist kaum eine so wandelbar wie die Wolke. Sie ist geradezu ein klassisches Symbol für die Unbeständigkeit der Zeit. Entsprechend stark wirken Wolkenerscheinungen auf unsere vergleichende Vorstellungskraft. Aus wissenschaftlicher Perspektive sind Wolken ein geeignetes Objekt, um anhand ihrer Eigenschaften die Fragen von Determinismus und Indeterminismus zu diskutieren. Der Philosoph Karl Popper hat sich in einem berühmten Aufsatz von 1971 mit dem Titel „Wolken und Uhren" dieses Themas angenommen. In einem späteren Gespräch erläuterte er noch einmal die dort geäußerten Grundgedanken: „P: [D]as Gegenteil der Uhr ist die Wolke, die wir offenbar nicht vorausbestimmen können wie die Uhr. Natürlich ist das ein Symbol. Die eine Theorie sagt: Würden wir nur die Wolken besser kennen, so gut wie die Uhren, so könnten wir sie komplett vorausbestimmen. Die andere Theorie sagt: Würden wir die Uhren näher und näher untersuchen, so würden wir entdecken, dass sie eigentlich Elektronenwolken sind oder Wolken von Elementarteilchen, die nicht voll vorausbestimmt sind und in denen auch alle möglichen Dinge geschehen, die nicht vorauszusehen sind; dass also nur die makroskopische Größe der Uhr uns dazu verhilft, eine Uhr als einigermaßen vorausbestimmbar anzusehen. K: Also alle Uhren sind Wolken? P: Ja."[49] Dieses längere Zitat ist hier nicht nur deswegen wiedergegeben, weil sich Joachim Hiller auch mit Karl Popper beschäftigt hat, sondern vor allem deshalb, weil die Beschäftigung mit der inneren Struktur von Wolken zu elementaren Fragen unseres Natur- und Weltverständnisses führt und damit mitten in die Kernzone von Hillers künstlerischen Fragestellungen.

48 Hamlet, 3. Akt, Zweite Szene [Übersetzung: August Wilhelm von Schlegel].
49 Karl R. Popper/Franz Kreuzer, *Offene Gesellschaft – offenes Universum. Ein Gespräch über das Lebenswerk des Philosophen*, München/Zürich 1986.

Clouds

Hamlet: Do you see that cloud, that's almost in shape like a camel?
Polonius: By the mass, and 't is like a camel, indeed.
Hamlet: Methinks, it is like a weasel.
Polonius: It is backed like a weasel.
Hamlet: Or, like a whale?
Polonius: Very like a whale.[48]
William Shakespeare

Of all the natural appearances we are familiar with, hardly any is as changeable as clouds. They are virtually a classical symbol for the volatility of time. Likewise they have a strong effect on our comparative imagination. From a scientific perspective, due to their properties, clouds are thus a suitable object for discussing questions of determinism and indeterminateness. In his famous article of 1971 entitled "Wolken und Uhren" (Clouds and Clocks), the philosopher Karl Popper took on this theme. In a later interview he explained once again the basic thoughts of his article: "P: The opposite of the clock is the cloud, which we obviously cannot predict as we can the clock. This is, of course, a symbol. The one theory says: if we only knew clouds better, as well as we know clocks, we could predict them completely. The other theory states: if we examined clocks more and more closely, we would discover that they are actually clouds of electrons or clouds of elementary particles that are not completely predictable and in which all kinds of things happen that are unpredictable; that thus, only the macroscopic size of the clock helps us to view a clock as somewhat predictable. K: So all clocks are clouds? P: Yes."[49] This lengthy quotation has not been included here only because Joachim Hiller also studied Karl Popper, but mainly because studying the inner structure of clouds leads to elementary questions of our understanding of nature and the world and is thus, central to Hiller's issues as an artist.

48 Hamlet, Act 3, Scene II.
49 Karl R. Popper/Franz Kreuzer, *Offene Gesellschaft – offenes Universum. Ein Gespräch über das Lebenswerks des Philosophen*. Munich/Zurich 1986.

Acryl auf Leinwand/*Acrylics on canvas*

100 x 100 cm, 2005

Die Struktur von Wolken ist denkbar weit entfernt von der Struktur geologischer Formationen, von Steinen und Erdschichten, mit denen sich Hiller über viele Jahre beschäftigt hat. Während Felsen in Jahrmillionen ihre Form erhalten, wandeln sich Wolken als komplexe, dynamische Systeme permanent. Dafür eine angemessene künstlerische Umsetzung zu finden, war für Hiller eine besondere Herausforderung, umso mehr, als es in der Kunstgeschichte viele Beispiele für exzellente Wolkenmaler gibt – man denke nur an William Turner, Gustave Courbet und in unserer Gegenwart Gerhard Richter. Es ist an dieser Stelle wohl überflüssig, darauf hinzuweisen, dass es Hiller nicht darum ging, sichtbare Wolkenerscheinungen zu malen. Auch hier wieder war seine Frage, wie das Farbmaterial aufgrund seiner ihm immanenten physikalischen Eigenschaften aus sich selbst heraus Wolkenstrukturen hervorbringen kann. Wie bereits erwähnt, hatte er bereits Anfang der 90er-Jahre mit Bildern experimentiert, die optisch den Strukturen von Wolkenbildern sehr nahekommen. Durch das Bewegen der Leinwand verteilte sich die wässrige Farbe, erzeugte Verwirbelungen und Schlieren. Doch das war eine rein visuelle Ähnlichkeit. Strukturell fehlte noch ein entscheidendes Element: Luft.

The structure of clouds is considerably far removed from the structure of geological formations, stones, and layers of earth that Hiller has been dealing with for years. While cliffs and rocks have received their forms over a period of millions of years, clouds constantly change, being complex, dynamic systems. Finding an appropriate artistic expression of this, was a particular challenge for Hiller, the more so because art history knows many examples of excellent cloud painters—we need only think of William Turner, Gustave Courbet and in our time Gerhard Richter. It goes without saying that Hiller was not concerned with painting the visible appearances of clouds. Here again it was his question as to how the paint material, due to its immanent physical properties, could produce cloud structures all by itself? As mentioned above, already at the beginning of the 1990s he had been experimenting with pictures that, from a visual standpoint, come very close to the structures of cloud pictures. By moving the canvas the watery paint spread, produced swirls and smears. But this was purely a visual similarity. Structurally a decisive element had still been lacking: air.

Acryl auf Leinwand/*Acrylics on canvas*

105 x 105 cm, 2006

Acryl auf Leinwand/*Acrylics on canvas*

100 x 100 cm, 2005

Wolken sind nichts anderes als Ansammlungen feinster Wassertröpfchen (in kälteren Luftschichten auch kleinster Eiskristalle) in der Atmosphäre. Ihre Formenvielfalt ist in hohem Maße von den jeweils herrschenden Windverhältnissen und Luftströmungen abhängig. Über diese Grundstruktur der Wolkenformen nachdenkend, erinnerte sich Hiller an den alten Akademietrick, Farbe mit Tapetenkleister anzurühren. Was zu Studienzeiten zur Herstellung eines billigen Malmittels diente, erwies sich nun als ideales Medium zur Erzeugung von Wolken aus Farbe. Hillers Idee besteht darin, eine dicke Schicht Kleister auf die Leinwand zu packen, Farbpigmente darauf zu verteilen und diese mit einem Kompressor in Bewegung zu versetzen. Der Luftstrom, der die Farbe durch das zähflüssige Medium treibt, entspricht dem Wind, der in der Natur die Verteilung der Wassertröpfchen und damit die Form der Wolken bestimmt. Obwohl Richtung und Stärke des Luftstroms von Hiller willentlich beeinflusst werden können, lässt sich die Verteilung der Farbpigmente doch nur grob steuern. Die Feinverteilung erfolgt nach eigengesetzlichen Regeln, es entstehen unvermutete Formen, Ballungen, Aufwirbelungen, wolkige, bis in kleinste Verästelungen sich verzweigende Materieverteilungen, die so zart sind, dass sie sich einer fotografischen Abbildung entziehen.

Was bei den meisten der auf diese Weise geschaffenen Gemälden ins Auge sticht, ist die gegenüber den „Wasser"-Serien wiederum gesteigerte Thematisierung des Bildlichts. Weiße Pigmente spielen dabei eine wichtige Rolle. Auf vielen Bildern scheinen die Wolkenstrukturen von einer aus der Raumtiefe leuchtenden, sehr hellen Lichtquelle zu stammen. Wie so oft bei Hiller werden die räumlichen Maßstäbe unklar. Lassen einige der Bilder unmittelbar an Nebelschwaden oder ferne Wolkenballungen denken, wirken andere eher wie aus großer Höhe durch eine Satellitenkamera beobachtete Großwetterlagen, während wiederum andere Arbeiten aufgrund der enormen Strahlkraft der Wolke und der Dunkelheit des Umgebungsraums eher an kosmische Wolken, an interstellare, von fernen Sonnen erleuchtete Gase denken lassen.

Clouds are nothing else than collections of the finest drops of water (in colder strata, also of the most minute ice crystals) in the atmosphere. Their diversity of form is highly dependent upon the respective prevailing wind conditions and airstreams. While reflecting upon this basic structure of cloud forms, Hiller remembered the old academy trick of mixing paint with wallpaper paste. What served as a cheap paint medium during his days as a student, now turned out to be an ideal medium for producing clouds out of paint. Hiller's idea consists of packing thick layers of paste upon the canvas, distributing color pigments on it and then placing them into motion by using a compressor. The stream of air that drives the paint through the sluggish medium corresponds to the wind, which determines the distribution of the drops of water and thus, the form of the clouds in nature. Although the direction and strength of the airstream can be varied by Hiller at will, the distribution of the color pigments may only be roughly influenced. The fine distribution takes place according to intrinsic rules; unsuspected forms come about in balls, swirls, cloudy distributions of matter that branch out into the tiniest ramifications, so delicate that they do not avail themselves to photographic reproduction.

What strikes us with most of the paintings created in this manner is how the theme of light in the picture has been treated here more intensively than in the "water series" works. White pigments play an important role in this. On many paintings the cloud structures appear to come from a very bright source of light in the depth of the picture. As so often with Hiller, the spatial proportions become unclear. Some of the pictures remind us of patches of fog or distant piles of clouds, others seem rather as if they had been taken of a large weather front from a great height with a satellite camera and yet other works are more reminiscent of cosmic clouds, interstellar gases lit by distant suns, due to the enormous radiance of the cloud and the darkness of the surrounding space.

Wasser – Farbe

„Radikale Kunst heute heißt soviel wie finstere, von der Grundfarbe schwarz. Viel zeitgenössische Produktion disqualifiziert sich dadurch, daß sie davon keine Notiz nimmt, etwa kindlich der Farben sich freut."[50] Dieser Satz aus Theodor W. Adornos „Ästhetischer Theorie", erstmals erschienen 1970, macht in aller Kürze deutlich, welchen Stellenwert die Farbe Ende der 60er-, Anfang der 70er-Jahre in Avantgardekreisen hatte. Die avancierteste Malerei jener Jahre weist einen gewissen „chromophoben" Charakter auf.[51] Wo das gemalte Bild veranschaulichte Idee zu sein hatte, konnte Farbe als Buntwert bloß als sinnlich, anekdotisch, subjektivistisch, kurz als naiv gelten. Malerei jener Jahre – wenn Malerei überhaupt noch stattfand – hatte gefälligst unbunt zu sein. Beispiele sind etwa die meist schwarzen oder dunkelbraunen Zumalungen eines Arnulf Rainer, Gerhard Richters Serie von grauen Bildern, die schiefergrauen Leinwände eines Cy Twombly oder die grauen Monochromien Alan Charltons.

Auch Hiller stellt in der farbfeindlichen Stimmung jener Jahre keine Ausnahme dar. Im Escheinungsjahr von Adornos wichtigem Buch war er mit Spritzpistolenbildern in seltsam düsteren olivgrünbraunen Tönen beschäftigt. In den „tellurischen" Bildern der folgenden Jahre herrschen Erdtöne vor: Braun, Grau, Ocker, Schwarz. Buntfarben sind in vielen seiner Werke dasjenige, was gerade in Auflösung begriffen ist: bröckelnder Anstrich, zerbröselnder Rauputz, von den Naturkräften ausgewischter Zivilisationsrest, während schwarzer Sand sich wie Ruß in den Mauerritzen sammelt. Es ist überaus spannend zu verfolgen, wie sich in Hillers Werk im Laufe der Jahre die Farbe mehr und mehr emanzipiert. Wenn auch meist gebrochen, kommen nach und nach immer mehr Buntwerte in Hillers Malerei zum Vorschein.

50 Theodor W. Adorno, *Ästhetische Theorie*. Frankfurt am Main 1970, S. 65.
51 Zur Thematik der Diffamierung und Vermeidung von Farbe vgl. den Essay von David Batchelor, *Chromophobia*, London 2001 (deutsch: *Chromophobie. Angst vor der Farbe*, 2., veränderte Neuauflage, Wien 2004).

Water—Color

"Radical art today is synonymous with dark art; its primary color is black. Much contemporary production is irrelevant because it takes no note of this and childishly delights in color."[50] This statement from Theodor W. Adorno's "Aesthetic Theory", which first appeared in 1970, clearly and succinctly states how color was valued in avant-garde circles at the end of the 1960s and beginning of the 1970s. The most progressive painting in those years was somewhat "chromophobic" in character.[51] Where the painted pictures were supposed to be the illustration of an idea, color could only be understood as sensual, anecdotal, subjective, and in short: naïve. The painting of those years—if painting was still even taking place at all—was supposed to be as non-colorful as possible. Examples of this are the pictures painted mostly black or dark-brown by Arnulf Rainer, Gerhard Richter's series of gray pictures, the slate-gray canvases of people like Cy Twombly or the gray monochrome pictures of Alan Charlton.

Hiller was also no exception in his hostile view towards color in those years. The same year Adorno's important book was published, he was using strangely-dark, olive-brown tones in his pictures, applied with a spray gun. In the "telluric" pictures of the subsequent years earth tones prevailed: brown, gray, ochre, and black. In many of his works, bright colors are the only things that are in a process of disintegration: crumbling paint, disintegrating roughcast plaster, remains of civilization washed out by natural forces, while black sand collects like soot in the cracks of the wall. It is exciting to see how color emancipates itself more and more in Hiller's works over the years. Even though mostly fragmented, gradually more and more color values emerge in Hiller's painting.

50 Theodor W. Adorno, Gretel Adorno, Rolf Tiedemann, Robert Hullot-Kentor, *Aesthetic Theory* (Translated by Robert Hullot-Kentor), Continuum International Publishing Group 2004, no place given 2004, p. 50.
51 On the theme of the defamation and avoidance of color, see the essay by David Batchelor, *Chromophobia*. London 2001

Acryl auf Leinwand/*Acrylics on canvas*

100 x 100 cm, 2008

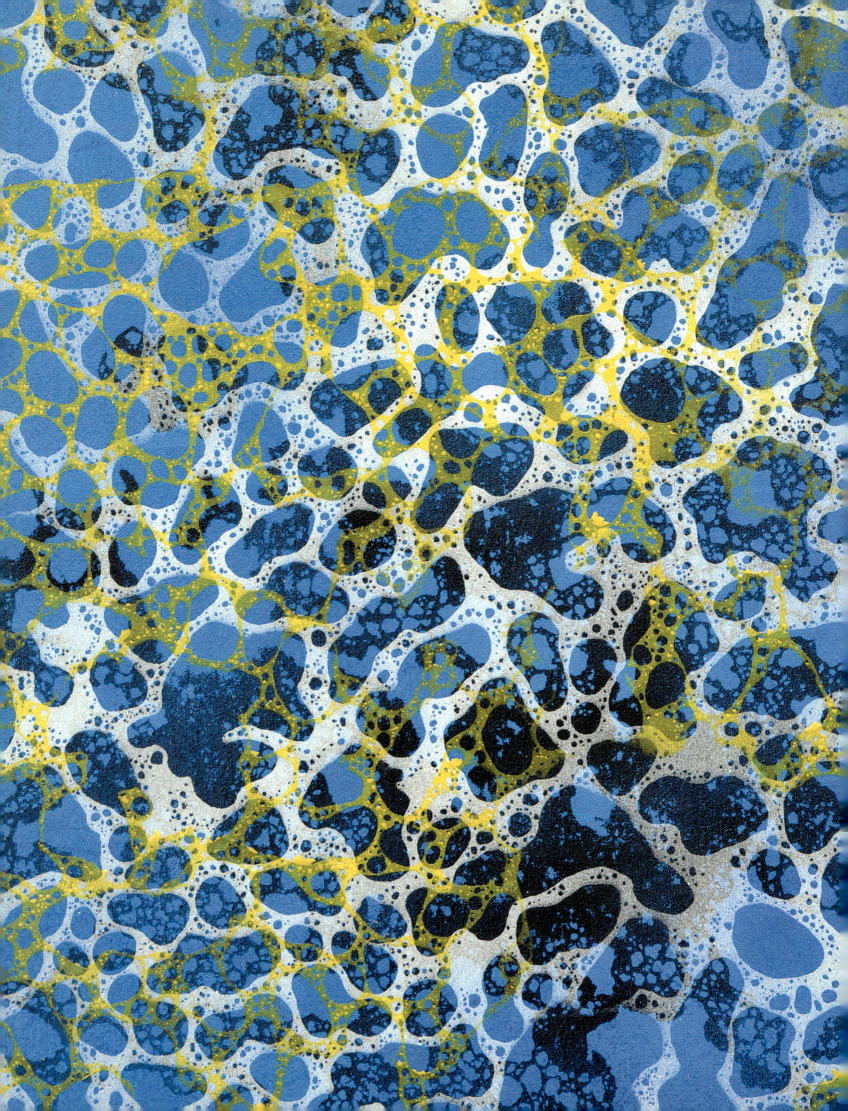

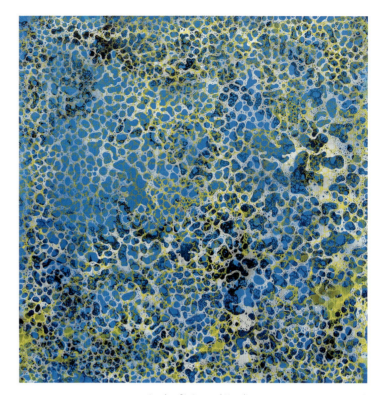

Acryl auf Leinwand/*Acrylics on canvas*, 110 x 110 cm, 2008

Seite/*Page* 163: Ausschnitt/*Detail*

„Wenn man Gegenstände malt", so Hiller, „dann hat der Gegenstand eine Lokalfarbe, wie der Maler sagt, die Ursprungsfarbe. Wenn man aber eine Kunstfarbe nimmt, dann muss der Körper keine feste Farbe haben, er kann irisierend, hell oder dunkel sein – das ist völlig gleichgültig."[52] Hillers frühe Arbeiten aus der zweiten Hälfte der 60er- und den frühen 70er-Jahre mit ihrer Quasi-Gegenständlichkeit sind noch immer mit dem Thema Lokalfarbe befasst. Und da die späteren Serien, die Mauerbilder, die Erosionsbilder usw. sehr stark von ihrer Materialität und plastischen Qualität bestimmt sind, ist Farbe noch längst nicht als Eigenwert thematisiert. Einige der gemalten Reliefs brachten ein Gleichgewicht aus Form und Farbe mit sich, doch erst die „Wasser"-Serien mit ihrer Reduktion des Plastischen und der Betonung der Fläche brachten die Farbe als Farbe zur Geltung. In einer Reihe von Arbeiten, die jeweils in den Sommermonaten 2007 und 2008 entstanden – wieder dem Thema Wasser verpflichtet –, kommt nun Farbe endgültig als primäres, ja eigentlich einziges Gestaltungsmittel zum Durchbruch. Es sind Bilder, die offensichtlich „sich der Farbe freuen" (ob „kindlich", im Sinne Adornos, sei dahingestellt): Farben spritzen und schäumen auf, überlagern einander in komplexer Vielschichtigkeit, bilden dichte Gewebe aus Flecken und Flächen, manchmal auf einen Grundton, manchmal auf kräftige Kontraste gestimmt. Keine Frage, dass diese Bilder Hillers malerischste Arbeiten sind. Dabei sind sie in einer Weise auf die Leinwand gebracht, die mit Malerei im klassischen Sinne nichts mehr gemein hat.

"If you paint objects," says Hiller, "then the object has a local coloration, as the painter says, the original color. But if you take an artificial color, then the body need not have a definite color; it can be iridescent, light or dark—it is all the same."[52] Hiller's early works from the second half of the 1960s and early 1970s with their semi-concrete objectivity still concern themselves with the theme of local color. And since the later series, the wall pictures, the erosion pictures, etc., are largely defined by their materiality and plastic quality, color is by no means an intrinsic value yet. Some of the painted reliefs had an inherent balance of form and color, but it was not until the "water" series, with their reduction of the plastic features and the emphasis on the surface, that color came into its own as color. In a series of works, done in the summer months of the respective years 2007 and 2008—dedicated again to the theme of water—color now finally makes the breakthrough once and for all as a primary, indeed as the only means of creation. These are pictures which apparently take a "delight in color" (though it is moot concerning whether or not it is "childish" in Adorno's sense of the term): paint and colors spatter and bubble up, overlap in complex multi-layeredness, form dense weaves of spots and surfaces, sometimes harmonizing with one ground shade, sometimes geared towards strong contrasts. There is no question that these pictures are Hiller's most painterly. But despite this, they have been transferred to the canvas in a manner no longer having anything in common with painting in a classical sense.

52 Interview mit Erik Buchheister [Anm. 28], S. 45.

52 Interview with Erik Buchheister [footnote 28], p. 45.

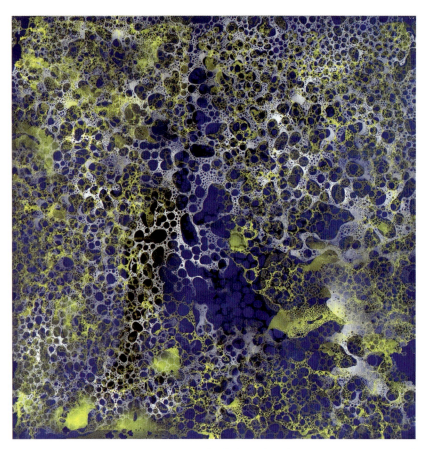

Acryl auf Leinwand/*Acrylics on canvas*, 100 x 100 cm, 2008

Joachim Hiller betont, dass 20 Jahre der Beschäftigung mit den Malmaterialien, den Acrylfarben, den Grundierungsmitteln und Fixativen notwendig waren, um diese Bilder möglich zu machen. Die Machart ist – wieder einmal – denkbar schlicht und denkbar raffiniert zugleich. Präparierte Leinwände werden mit Wasser benetzt, das auf dem trockenen Untergrund abperlt, Spritzer, Pfützen und Gerinnsel bildet. Anschließend wird die Malfläche mit Acrylfarbe eingespritzt. An den trockenen Leinwandstellen trocknet sie bei hohen Temperaturen und intensiver Sonneneinstrahlung sehr rasch (weshalb sie nur in den Sommermonaten 2007 und 2008 entstanden). Die im Wasser verbleibende Farbe wird heruntergespült, die Wasserflächen bilden Aussparungen im Farbfeld. Nun wird dieser Vorgang Mal um Mal mit anderen Farben wiederholt. Auf diese Weise bildet sich ein beinahe impressionistisches Flimmern aus Farbwerten. Die Wässrigkeit des Wassers und die Farbigkeit der Farbe sind die einzigen Gestaltungsfaktoren, die hier zum Einsatz kommen. Farbe und Form verschmelzen, werden eins und bilden das Allover des Bildes. Wie viele andere Werke Hillers auch, wirken diese Gemälde wie Ausschnitte aus unabsehbar großen Zusammenhängen. Die Farbfleckenlandschaften könnten nach allen Seiten hin unbegrenzt weitergehen. Wie Einblicke in Unterwasserwelten, Großaufnahmen von schäumender Gischt oder auch wie Einsichten in Mikrowelten oder Wiedergaben von Strahlungsfeldern können diese Bilder wirken, abhängig von den gewählten Farben und den subjektiven Assoziationen des Betrachters.

Joachim Hiller emphasizes that it took 20 years of studying the paint materials, the acrylics, the groundings and fixatives for these pictures to come about. The way they are made is—once again—incredibly simple yet refined at the same time. Prepared canvases are sprayed with water that the dry ground repels to run off again in pearl-drops, or the water forms spatters, puddles, and runs. Then the surface to be painted is sprayed with acrylic paint. On the dry places of the canvas and under conditions of high temperatures and intense sunlight, these dry very quickly (which is why they were only done in the summer months of 2007 and 2008). The color that remains in the water washes off, the water surfaces thus forming blank spaces in the field of color. This process is now repeated with various colors. In this way an almost impressionistic glimmer of color values comes about. The fluidity of the water and the colorfulness of the paint are the only creative factors at work here. Color and form melt into one and form the allover of the picture. Like many other of Hiller's works, these paintings also seem like excerpts taken from immeasurably large contexts. The landscapes of puddles of color could be endlessly continued in all directions. These pictures seem like we are looking into underwater worlds, close-up photographs of frothy spume or like insights into microworlds or reproductions of fields of radiation, depending on the colors chosen and the subjective associations of the viewer.

Acryl auf Leinwand/*Acrylics on canvas*

100 x 100 cm, 2008

Acryl auf Leinwand/*Acrylics on canvas*

100 x 100 cm, 2008

Acryl auf Leinwand/*Acrylics on canvas*

100 x 100 cm, 2008

Acryl auf Leinwand/*Acrylics on canvas*

110 x 110 cm, 2008

Acryl auf Leinwand/*Acrylics on canvas*
100 x 100 cm, 2008

Acryl auf Leinwand/*Acrylics on canvas*

150 x 150 cm, 2008

Nature, Freedom, Individuality

The individuality in nature is completely endless.[53]
Novalis

The phenomenon is not detached from the observer, but intertwined and involved with him.[54]
Johann Wolfgang von Goethe

After going through several of the most important stations of Hiller's work in general, how do we now evaluate his claim to paint "like nature"? Above all, if we take the works presented here as our measure, what is meant by the word "nature", this general concept under which the most varying, even the most contrary notions may be gathered? Pablo Picasso once said that he also wanted to paint like nature. But apparently his notion of nature was different than Hiller's. Otherwise the artistic results would not be so far apart from each other. In order to illustrate more clearly what Hiller's understanding of nature is and why for him it is inseparable from the concept of freedom, it may be helpful to first illustrate what nature does not *mean for him.*

The Renaissance notion that artists are in competition with nature is completely foreign to Hiller. The opinion held by Giorgio Vasari and others of his contemporaries that Michelangelo surpassed nature stands in diametrical contrast to Hiller's concept of nature. For Joachim Hiller nature's wealth of formal inventions, its sheer inexhaustible ability to produce ever new form variations on both a large and a small scale may in no way be surpassed by human ability. When he said in an interview: "It was hurtful that I was not able to invent a new color, but that I was also unable to invent a new form that had never existed before—that nearly killed me as an artist,"[55] *then this was not just an exaggeration. Hiller's initial enthusiasm for Malevich and the Russian constructivists changed over the course of the years he was learning as an artist to the insight that the human capacity for invention is extremely limited when compared with the morphogenetic tendency of nature. He once told me when we were talking: "Actually, I wanted to work against nature, like the Russian constructivists. And where did I land?"*

---

53 Novalis, Die Lehrlinge zu Sais. Gedichte. Fragmente. With an afterword by Martin Kiessig. Stuttgart 1979, p. 118, (translation: e.v.).
54 [From the legacy], quoted after Goethe. *Anschauendes Denken. Goethes Schriften zur Naturwissenschaft.* In a selection edited by Horst Günther. Frankfurt a. M. 1981, p. 300.
55 Interview with Erik Buchheister [footnote 28], p. 45.

Natur erscheint in diesem Werk nie als erholsames Rückzugsgebiet.
Nature never appears in this work as a place to pull back and relax.

Betrachtet man die Arbeiten Hillers ganz unbefangen und unabhängig von allen Aussagen des Künstlers, wird zumindest schnell deutlich, welche mit dem Begriff „Natur" verbundenen Vorstellungen von ihnen keineswegs bedient werden. Natur erscheint in diesem Werk nie als erholsames Rückzugsgebiet. Ein „retour à la nature" als ländliche Idylle, als domestiziertes Rokoko-Ambiente, als Naherholungsgebiet und Freizeitpark ist bei ihm bestimmt nicht zu finden. Hillers Natur ist auch nicht die Natur etwa von Franz Marc, hier gibt es keine „Tierschicksale", ja überhaupt keine Spuren tierischen oder pflanzlichen Lebens. Und sieht man einmal von den erotischen Allusionen der frühen 70er-Jahre, den „archäologischen" Mauerfugen und den ganz seltenen Kratz- und Kritzelspuren auf den Mauern ab, auch keine Hinweise auf menschliches Leben. Hillers Natur ist die Natur des Elementarreichs. Hier sind Felsen und Sand, Wasser und Eis, Wolken und Licht zu sehen. Möglicherweise gibt es hier komplexe Molekülketten, Vorformen organischen Lebens. Auf jeden Fall aber gibt es schäumendes Wasser, gebirgsartige Höhenzüge, viel Irdisches, Atmosphärisches, manchmal Kosmisches – aber abgesehen vielleicht von den Glasplattenreliefs keine dramatischen Effekte von Naturgewalten und ihrer zerstörerischen Kraft. Natur ist bei Hiller weder Sinnbild des Göttlichen noch das des Erhabenen. Sie ist nicht, was „gelassen verschmäht, uns zu zerstören", wie es in Rilkes berühmter erster Duineser Elegie heißt, sondern verhält sich merkwürdig gleichgültig gegen unseren Blick als Betrachter. Sie ist nicht die Gesundheits- und Muttergöttin der Ökofraktion, schon gar nicht das Reich der Esoteriker mit ihren dubiosen „Energieströmen" und Elementargeistern. Hillers Naturwelt ist auch nicht romantisch, weder im geläufigen Sinn sentimentaler Verklärung noch im Sinne der künstlerischen Romantik des 19. Jahrhunderts. Er projiziert kein Ich in seiner Einsamkeit in die Natur hinein, weder das eigene noch das des Betrachters. Diese bleibt in seinem Werk mit sich allein, unbekümmert um unseren Blick.

If we take a look at Hiller's work, wholly unbiased and independent of all statements made by the artist, it at least becomes clear very quickly what notions in no way comply with his concept of "nature". Nature never appears in this work as a place to pull back and relax. A "retour à la nature" as a pastoral scene, as a domesticated rococo ambience or as a recreation area and leisure park is certainly nowhere to be found in his work. Hiller's nature is not the nature of a Franz Marc; here there are no "fates of animals", nor even any traces of plant or animal life. And apart from the early erotic allusions of the early 1970s, the "archaeological" wall joints and the very rare traces of scratches and scribbles on the walls, neither are there any hints of human life. Hiller's nature is the realm of elementary nature. Here we see cliffs and sand, water and ice, clouds and light. Possibly there are complex chains of molecules here, pre-forms of organic life. At any rate there is foaming water, mountain-like ranges, much that is earthen and atmospheric, sometimes cosmic—but perhaps with the exception of the sheet-glass reliefs, there are no dramatic effects of natural forces and their destructive power. Nature for Hiller is neither a symbol of the divine nor of the sublime. It is not what "serenely disdains to annihilate us," as Rilke refers to it in his famous First Duino Elegy, but rather it behaves oddly indifferently vis-à-vis our gaze as viewers. It is not the goddess of health and nurturing of the ecological movement and certainly not the realm of the esoterics with their dubious "energy flows" and elementary spirits. Hiller's realm of nature is also not romantic, neither in the customary sense of sentimental transfiguration, nor in the sense of artistic romanticism of the 19th century. It does not project a lone ego, its own or that of the viewer, into nature. In his work nature remains alone, oblivious to our gaze.

Acryl auf Leinwand/*Acrylics on canvas*
150 x 150 cm, 2008 (Ausschnitt/*Detail*)

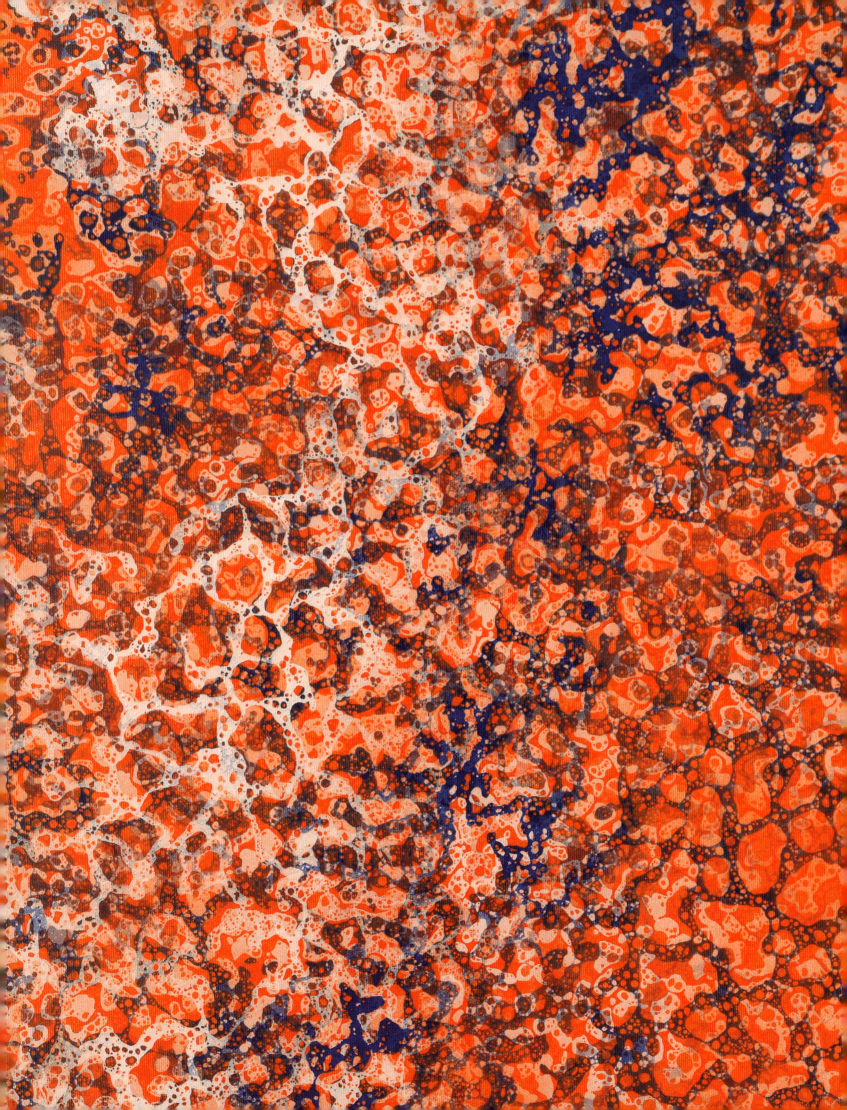

Und dennoch – oder genau deshalb – gibt es einen wichtigen Punkt, an dem sich Hillers Auffassung von Natur durchaus mit jener der idealistischen Philosophie der Frühromantik vergleichen lässt. Gemeint ist der auf die Natur bezogene Begriff der Freiheit. Das ist erklärungsbedürftig, denn wir sind es gewöhnt, Natur als das Gegenteil von Freiheit zu begreifen. Die Naturwissenschaften operieren mit der Annahme von konstanten Naturgesetzen. Alles Naturgeschehen wird in wissenschaftlicher Perspektive als naturgesetzlich determiniert begriffen und schließt somit das Postulat der Freiheit aus. Hillers Blickrichtung auf die Natur ist, trotz seines Interesses für naturwissenschaftliche Forschung und die Resultate neuester bildgebender Verfahren in den Wissenschaften, dem des Wissenschaftlers diametral entgegengesetzt. Die Wissenschaft ist am Herausarbeiten von Gesetzmäßigkeiten interessiert, sie richtet sich daher auf das Allgemeine. Hillers Interesse jedoch gilt dem, was für die Naturforschung, ja für Wissenschaft überhaupt am wenigsten interessant ist: das Individuelle.

And yet—or perhaps precisely because of this—there is an important point where Hiller's notion of nature does coincide with that of the idealistic philosophy of early romanticism. What I mean here is the concept of freedom with respect to nature. This needs explanation, since we are accustomed to understanding nature as the opposite of freedom. The natural sciences operate under the assumption of constant natural laws. Everything that happens in nature is conceived in scientific perspective as being determined by natural laws, and thus, excludes the postulation of freedom. Hiller's outlook on nature is virtually the opposite of that of a scientist, despite his interest in natural scientific research and the results of the newest processes of picture making in the sciences. Science is interested in working out laws and therefore looks to universal tendencies. Hiller's interest, however, focuses on what is least interesting for natural research and for science in general: on the individual thing.

Acryl auf Leinwand/*Acrylics on canvas*
100 x 100 cm, 2008

Acryl auf Leinwand/*Acrylics on canvas*

110 x 110 cm, 2008

Acryl auf Leinwand/*Acrylics on canvas*

100 x 100 cm, 2008

Jede Art von Wiederholung und Gleichförmigkeit empfindet er als ein Indiz von Unfreiheit.

Any type of repetition and uniformity he feels to be an indication of not being free.

Wissenschaft will das Wiederholbare. Ein Experiment, das nicht wiederholbar ist, erfüllt nicht die Kriterien von Wissenschaftlichkeit. Genau daran aber, am Unwiederholbaren, ist Joachim Hiller interessiert. Die Wissenschaft will wissen, welchen Naturgesetzen die Formenbildung von Steinen gehorcht. Hiller interessiert viel mehr die Vorstellung, dass unter den Milliarden von Sandkörnern auf Erden keine zwei absolut identisch beschaffen sind. Wenn Hiller Glasplatten zerbricht, dann in dem Wissen, dass die Art der Brüche nicht vorhersehbar ist. Wenn er Hunderte von gleichen Papierblättern befeuchtet, werden sich alle in unterschiedlicher Weise wellen. Wenn er Leinwände zerknittert, dann allein aus dem Grund, dass es bei diesem Vorgang keine Wiederholung gibt und jede Form einzigartig ist, die sich durch diesen mechanischen Akt bildet. Das ist es, was Hiller unter Freiheit versteht. Freiheit ist für ihn das Gegenteil von Einförmigkeit. Deshalb war er auch so sehr von der Nachkriegsarchitektur enttäuscht, von ihrer Uniformität, ihrer latenten Gewalt: „Aber Uniformität und Militarismus, Stichwort ‚Neue Heimat' – grauenvoll."[56]

Hier kommen unsere Überlegungen auf den Anfang unserer Darstellung, auf die Biografie zurück. Hillers Entscheidung gegen Beruf und für Kunst war eine Entscheidung für Freiheit. Im Gespräch sagt Hiller im Rückblick auf seinen Werdegang als Künstler: „Freiheit war das Wichtigste für mich." Und diese Freiheit als Voraussetzung seiner Kunst fand er im Blick auf die Natur: „Die Freiheit wird immer größer, je näher man die Naturformen studiert." Das Vielförmige, Unwiederholbare, die unendlichen Formvariationen, die nicht aus Willkür, sondern aus einem gesetzmäßigen Zusammenhang entspringen, sind für Hiller Freiheitsmomente. Das erklärt übrigens auch, warum Hiller, obwohl er von seiner Ausbildung her Grafiker ist und auch jahrelang als solcher gearbeitet hat, als freier Künstler stets auf die Anwendung druckgrafischer Techniken verzichtete. Seine Verweigerung gegenüber der Reproduktionsgrafik hat ohne Zweifel mit seinem generellen Interesse an Formenvielfalt zu tun. Jede Art von Wiederholung und Gleichförmigkeit empfindet er als ein Indiz von Unfreiheit (dazu zählt auch jede Art der Festlegung – daher rührt auch sein Bedürfnis nach Vielfalt, ja sogar Widersprüchen in seiner Malerei).

Science looks for the repeatable. An experiment you cannot repeat does not fulfill the criteria of science. But precisely this, the non-repeatable, is what interests Joachim Hiller. Science wants to know what natural laws the development of stone forms adhere to. Hiller is rather interested in the notion that among billions of sand grains on the earth no two are absolutely identical. When Hiller breaks sheets of glass, then he knows that the way they break is not predictable. If he wets down hundreds of the same sheets of paper, they will all bend and buckle and wave differently. If he crumples canvases, then only for the reason that there will be no repetition in this process and each form arising from this mechanical act is individual. This is what Hiller understands by freedom. Freedom for him is the opposite of uniformity. This is also why he was so very disappointed by post-war architecture, by its uniformity, its latent violence: "But uniformity and militarism and as a key word 'Neue Heimat' (former house building association)—horrible."[56]

At this point our deliberations go back to the beginning of this text, the biography. Hiller's opting against his career and in favor of art was a decision for freedom. In a conversation Hiller says in looking back at his becoming an artist: "Freedom was the most important thing for me." And this freedom as a prerequisite of his art he found when looking at nature: "Freedom becomes greater the more we study the forms of nature." The multi-form, non-repeatable, the endless variations of forms which did not arise from randomness but from a context governed by natural laws are moments of freedom for Hiller. Incidentally, this also explains why Hiller, although he trained in graphics design and for years also made a career out of it, always dispensed with using graphics techniques as a freelance artist. His refusal to work with graphics reproduction techniques doubtlessly has to do with his general interest in the diversity of forms. Any type of repetition and uniformity he feels to be an indication of not being free (to this he also reckons any type of predetermination—thus, also his need for diversity, even contradictions in his painting).

---

56 Interview mit Erik Buchheister [Anm. 28], S. 45.

56 Interview with Erik Buchheister [footnote 28], p. 45.

Ein Zitat des in Tübingen lehrenden Literaturwissenschaftlers und Philosophen Manfred Frank, eines bedeutenden Interpreten des Deutschen Idealismus', sei an dieser Stelle zitiert. Frank sagt mit Blick auf die Philosophie im Nachgang Kants und Fichtes: „Auch wenn ich ästhetisch nicht produziere, sondern genieße, muß ich mich meiner Freiheit bedienen. Denn nichts sinnlich Sichtbares und gedanklich Rekonstruierbares reicht hin, um einem Gegenstand der Natur den Charakter des Ästhetischen aufzuprägen. Ich muß, um die dargestellte *Freiheit* darin zu gewahren, meine eigene Freiheit gebrauchen, d. h., ich muß den im Kunstprodukt sinnlich-theoretisch erstarrten Appell wieder verflüssigen, ich muß ihn durch Gebrauch meiner eigenen Freiheit befreien. Kurzum: nicht jedes Sichtbare ist schön, und das für schön Befundene wird eben damit als Symbol der Freiheit angeschaut."[57]

Diese Aussage kann ohne Weiteres auf die Arbeiten von Hiller angewandt werden. Doch was ist der „sinnlich-theoretisch erstarrte Appell" in diesen Arbeiten, der sich in der Betrachtung wieder „verflüssigt"? Es ist, so meine ich, genau der Sinn für den Wert des Individuellen, des Unwiederholbaren, der sich in Hillers Arbeiten zeigt. Nichts zwingt mich als Betrachter, Sprünge im Glas, Risse im Zement, Strukturen der gegenseitigen Abstoßung zweier Farbsubstanzen als „schön" oder auch nur „ästhetisch interessant" zu empfinden. Es ist ein Akt der Freiheit, diesen von Joachim Hiller vorgeführten Strukturmomenten einen Wert zuzusprechen. Voraussetzung dafür ist, dass man nicht am Gängelband der „tieferen Bedeutung" geführt wird. Hillers Arbeiten tragen allesamt keine Titel, auch nicht den in der modernen Kunst beliebtesten Titel „Ohne Titel". Titel kommen bei ihm einfach nicht vor. Mithin gibt es auch keinerlei Interpretationshilfen oder -zwänge für den Betrachter. Symbolischen oder metaphorischen Bedeutungsgehalt auf seine Werke zu laden, ist Hiller suspekt. Der Übergang vom rein Faktischen des Werks zum Imaginären, der sich allein in der Vorstellung des Betrachters vollzieht, wird auch nicht mit subjektiven Vorgaben gebahnt, auch nicht mit irgendwelchen Zeichen oder Spuren der emotionalen Verfassung des Künstlers.

Selbstverständlich gibt es eine Art Perspektive in diesen Bildern. Ihre Faktizität, also die Proportionen, die Maße, die Farben usw., sind Rezeptionsvorgaben, die man nicht ignorieren kann. Jedoch gibt es, wie schon mehrfach erwähnt wurde, fast immer eine Offenheit oder Ambivalenz der Perspektive, die dem Betrachter die Freiheit lässt, seine eigenen Assoziationen daran zu knüpfen. Ist es ein Blick aus der Erdumlaufbahn oder durch das Mikroskop, Fernsicht oder Nahsicht, Makro- oder Mikrokosmos? Nichts ist hier festgelegt, verpflichtend oder fordernd.

A statement by Manfred Frank the literary critic and philosopher, who teaches in Tübingen and is one of the most important experts on German idealism, should be cited here. With a view to philosophy after Kant and Fichte, Frank says: "Even if I do not produce aesthetically, but [merely] enjoy, I still have to make use of my freedom. For nothing perceivable with our senses and reconstructable in thought will suffice to impress aesthetic character on an object of nature. I must, in order to perceive the freedom demonstrated therein, make use of my own freedom, i.e., I must liquefy again the sensory and theoretical appeal solidified in the art product. I must free it by using my own freedom. In short: not everything that is visible is beautiful, and what is found beautiful becomes thus regarded as a symbol of freedom."[57]

We may certainly apply this statement to Hiller's works. But what is the "solidified sensory and theoretical appeal" in these works, which becomes "liquid" again in contemplation? It is, I think, precisely the sense for the value of the individual, the non-repeatable, which reveals itself in Hiller's works. Nothing forces me as a viewer to find "beautiful" or even "aesthetically interesting" cracks in glass or concrete or the resulting structures from two mutually repellent paint substances. It is an act of freedom to attribute a value to the moments of structure brought about Hiller. The prerequisite for this is not to be tied to the leash of "deeper meaning". None of Hiller's works bears a title, also not the most favored title in modern art "Untitled". Titles simply do not occur with him. This means there are no interpretative aids or restrictions for the viewer. Burdening his works with semantic import, be it symbolic or metaphoric, is suspicious to Hiller. The transition from the purely factual of the work to the imaginary, which takes place only in the mind of the viewer, is also not predetermined by subjective rules, by any signs or traces of the artist's emotional state.

Of course, there is a type of perspective in these pictures. Their factuality, i.e., the proportions, the dimensions, the colors, etc. are given facts for the reception that we may not ignore. However, there is, as we have mentioned several times before, almost always an openness or ambivalence of the perspective which allows the viewer the freedom to make his own associations. Is it a view from the earth's orbit or through the microscope, a distant or close-up view, macrocosm or microcosm? Nothing is predetermined, obligatory, or demanding here.

---

57 Manfred Frank, *Der kommende Gott. Vorlesungen über die Neue Mythologie*. I. Teil, Frankfurt a. M., 1982, S. 184.

57 Manfred Frank, *Der kommende Gott. Vorlesungen über die Neue Mythologie*. Part 1, Frankfurt a. M. 1982; p. 184.

Acryl auf Leinwand/*Acrylics on canvas*, 100 x 100 cm, 2008

Was hier zählt, ist die individuelle Anerkenntnis des Werts von Individualität.
What counts here is the individual recognition of the value of individuality.

Wenn wir uns als Betrachter zu diesen Arbeiten verhalten, d. h. also den Materialstrukturen, die sie präsentieren, einen ästhetischen Wert zusprechen, verhalten wir uns als freie Individuen. Hillers Werke arbeiten nicht mit narrativen Mitteln, mit rhetorischen oder anderen Überwältigungsstrategien, mit Wirkungsästhetiken, denen man hilflos ausgeliefert wäre, solange man in die Betrachtung vertieft ist. Was hier zählt, ist die individuelle Anerkenntnis des Werts von Individualität. Als solche kann man die Hiller'schen Werke nur dann ästhetisch würdigen, solange man sich selbst als Individuum in seiner Freiheit schätzt. Individualität wird damit zu einem nicht nur ästhetischen, sondern auch zu einem ethischen Wert. Nicht zufällig schätzt Hiller das auf das Individuum und seine Freiheit gegründete Demokratieverständnis von Karl Popper. Für diesen ist Demokratie nicht einfach die Herrschaft des Volkes, also der Mehrheit, sondern sie verdient ihren Namen nur, wenn sie die Freiheit des Individuums als ihren höchsten Wert anerkennt.[58] Unsere Würde haben wir dadurch, dass wir individuelle Wesen sind. Das ist, wiederum laut Popper, die Voraussetzung für das Entstehen von Denken und Kultur. Zugleich verbindet uns das mit den elementaren Naturstrukturen: Die Natur wiederholt sich nicht. Hillers Kunst zeigt uns, was uns dies bedeuten kann.

Thus, when we as viewers of these works, i.e., of the material structures they present, attribute an aesthetic value to them, we are acting as free individuals. Hiller's works do not work with narrative means, nor do they use rhetorical or other strategies for overwhelming us or aesthetic effects, which we would invariably be unable to escape as long as we are immersed in the process of our viewing. What counts here is the individual recognition of the value of individuality. We can only esteem Hiller's works aesthetically as long as we value ourselves as an individual with our freedom. Thus, individuality becomes not only an aesthetic, but also an ethical value. It is no coincidence that Hiller highly regards Karl Popper's understanding of democracy that is based on the individual and his freedom. For him, democracy is not merely the rule by the people, i.e., by the majority; it earns its name only when it recognizes the freedom of the individual as its highest value.[58] We take our dignity from the fact that we are individual beings. This is, again according to Popper, the prerequisite for development of thought and culture. At the same time it connects us with the elementary structures of nature: nature does not repeat itself. Hiller's art shows us what significance this can have for us.

---

58 Poppers Demokratieverständnis ist am ausführlichsten dargelegt in seinem Buch: *Die offene Gesellschaft und ihre Feinde* [1945], 2 Bände, Stuttgart 1992.

58 Popper's understanding of democracy is most extensively portrayed in his book: *The Open Society and its Enemies*, London 1945.

Acryl auf Leinwand/*Acrylics on canvas*

110 x 110 cm, 2008

Acryl auf Leinwand/*Acrylics on canvas*

110 x 110 cm, 2008

Acryl auf Karton/*Acrylics on cardboard*, 30 x 40 cm, 2008

Zum Schluss

Meine Überlegungen enden, womit sie begannen: mit spekulativen Fragen. Joachim Hiller hat fast vier Jahrzehnte lang nur für sich selbst gemalt. Was wäre gewesen, wenn er seine Bilder frühzeitig der Öffentlichkeit präsentiert hätte? Wie hätte deren Reaktion auf seine Arbeit zurückgewirkt, welchen Einfluss hätte er in der deutschen oder gar internationalen Kunstszene haben können? Hätte Hiller Karriere gemacht oder hätte das „Betriebssystem Kunst"[59] seinen originellen Ansatz markttauglich abgeschliffen und zum bloßen Markenzeichen heruntergestuft? Wer auf dem Kunstmarkt reüssiert und wer nicht, hängt ohnehin von vielen Unwägbarkeiten ab. Qualität – was immer man im Einzelnen darunter verstehen mag – ist nur *ein* Faktor; nicht weniger entscheidend ist es, zur richtigen Zeit am richtigen Ort zu sein, die richtigen Leute im Betrieb zu kennen, die gerade „angesagten" Themen zu treffen usw., usf. Hillers Kunst war nur möglich, weil er sich um all das nicht gekümmert hat.

„Schade, dass die Bilder ein paar Jahrzehnte zu spät kommen", meinte eine Kunsthistorikerin beim Betrachten von Hillers Arbeiten. Tun sie das? Ich denke ganz im Gegenteil, dass sie genau zum richtigen Zeitpunkt kommen. Sie haben ihr eigenes Zeitmaß und genau deshalb sind sie jetzt an der Zeit. Unzeitgemäßheit ist Teil des Eigensinns dieses Malers und seiner Arbeit. Den meisten seiner Bilder sieht man den Zeitpunkt ihres Entstehens überhaupt nicht an, viele von ihnen wirken vom Konzept her so neu, vom Erscheinungsbild her so frisch, als seien sie eben erst erdacht und gemalt worden, auch wenn sie schon 20 oder 30 Jahre alt sind. Die *ups* und *downs* des launischen Kunstmarkts haben mit den großen Fragen der Kunst sowieso nicht viel zu tun. Wir leben in einer Zeit, in der wir besser als je zuvor begreifen, dass unser Überleben als menschliche Spezies ganz entscheidend davon abhängt, dass wir die Prozesse der Natur verstehen und respektieren. Wie wir die Natur aus den Blickwinkeln der Philosophie, der Wissenschaft, der Ökologie und Ökonomie betrachten, wird zunehmend zu einer existenziellen Frage. Die Kunst kann hier ebenfalls ihren Beitrag leisten. Der Ernst von Hillers Arbeit besteht darin, dass sie uns bewusst machen kann, dass die Schönheit der Natur nur dann existiert, wenn es menschliche Augen gibt, die sie in aller Freiheit betrachten. Der Natur selbst ist es gleichgültig, wie wir uns zu ihr stellen. Sie geht notfalls über uns und unsere kulturellen Erzeugnisse hinweg. Dass wir uns dieser Einsicht stellen und ein Verhältnis dazu entwickeln, das unter anderem auch eine Frage der Kunst und Ästhetik ist, ist kein Thema von gestern. Es ist zeitgemäßer denn je.

59 Zum „Betriebssystem Kunst" und seinen strukturellen Regeln und Zwängen vgl. Anne-Marie Bonnet, *Kunst der Moderne. Kunst der Gegenwart. Herausforderung und Chance,* Köln 2004, S. 86–97.

At Last

My thoughts end where they began: with speculative questions. For nearly four decades Joachim Hiller painted only for himself. What would have happened if he had presented his pictures to the public early on? How would their reactions have influenced his work? What influence would he have had on the German or even the international art scene? Would Hiller have made a career or would the "Art Operating System"[59] have slashed his original approach down to market size, downgrading him to a mere label? Success on the art market anyway depends on a lot of unknown quantities. Quality—whatever that means—is only one *factor; no less decisive is the timing, being in the right place at the right time, knowing the right people in the business, hitting the "in" topics, etc. Hiller's art was only possible because he did not bother with any of this.*

"Too bad the pictures have shown up a few decades too late," commented one art historian while looking at Hiller's works. Are they too late? Far from it! I think that they have shown up at precisely the right time. They have their own measure of time and precisely for this reason they are on time now. Being out of sync with time is part of the idiosyncrasy of this painter and his work. With most of his pictures, it is impossible to tell when they were made. In terms of concept and appearance, many of them seem so new and look so fresh, as if they had just been thought up and painted, even though they are twenty or thirty years old. Anyway, the ups *and* downs *of the volatile art market do not have much to do with the big issues of art. We live in a time when we understand better than ever before that our survival as a human species largely depends on understanding and respecting processes of nature. How we look at nature from the perspectives of philosophy, science, ecology, and economy is becoming an increasingly existential question. Art can make its contribution here as well. The seriousness of Hiller's works consists in making us aware that the beauty of nature only exists if there are human eyes that may view it in all freedom. As far as nature is concerned, it is all the same how we choose to regard it. If necessary it will pass over us and ignore the things our culture produces. Living up to this realization and developing a relationship to it—a question of art and aesthetics, among other things, as well—is not a topic of yesteryear. It is more contemporary than ever.*

59 Concerning „Betriebssystem Kunst" (The Art Operating System) and its structural rules and stipulations, see Anne-Marie Bonnet, *Kunst der Moderne. Kunst der Gegenwart. Herausforderung und Chance,* Cologne 2004, p. 86–97.

Acryl auf Leinwand/*Acrylics on canvas*

150 x 150 cm, 2008 (Ausschnitt/*Detail*)

Acryl auf Karton/*Acrylics on cardboard*, 30 x 40 cm, 2008

Acryl auf Leinwand/*Acrylics on canvas*

150 x 150 cm, 2008

Acryl auf Leinwand/*Acrylics on canvas*

150 x 150 cm, 2008

Acryl auf Karton/*Acrylics on cardboard*

30 x 40 cm, 2008 (Ausschnitt/*Detail*)

Acryl auf Karton/*Acrylics on cardboard*, 30 x 40 cm, 2008

Impressum *Imprint*

Joachim Hiller,
geb. 1933 in Berlin
1949–53 Studium, „Meisterschule für Kunsthandwerk", Berlin
1954–58 Grafiker in Berlin
1958–62 Werbegrafiker in Frankfurt
1963–68 Artdirector in Hamburg und Frankfurt am Main
seit 1969 Freier Maler in Frankfurt am Main
seit 1990 Freier Maler in Wiesbaden und Mainz, jetzt Nierstein
seit 2006 Vertreten durch die Galerie Nero, Wiesbaden

Autoren

Dr. Peter Lodermeyer,
geb. 1962 in Ottweiler, studierte Kunstgeschichte, Philosophie und Germanistik in Bonn. 1997 Promotion in Kunstgeschichte mit einer Dissertation über die Stillleben Picassos. Seit 1999 freiberufliche Tätigkeit als Kunsthistoriker, Kunstkritiker, freier Autor und gelegentlich als Kurator. Seit 2003 konzeptionelle Betreuung der internationalen Künstlerprojekte *Personal Structures* und *Personal Structures: Time – Space – Existence* (Publikationen, Symposien, Vorträge). Seit 2005 regelmäßige Beiträge für *Sculpture* (USA), seit 2007 für *Junge_Kunst*. Lebt und arbeitet in Bonn.
www.lodermeyer.com

Prof. Klaus Honnef,
geb. 1939 in Tilsit. Studierte Soziologie und Geschichte in Köln. Ab 1960 freier Journalist. 1965–1970 Redakteur und Ressortleiter Kultur der *Aachener Nachrichten*. Mehrjährige Tätigkeit als künstlerischer Leiter, Geschäftsführer, Ausstellungschef in Aachen, Münster und Bonn. 1972 und 1977 Mitorganisator der documenta V und VI in Kassel. 1979–1987 Deutscher Kommissar für die Biennale trigon, Steirischer Herbst, Graz. 1980 Honorarprofessor Kunsthochschule Kassel, seit 1986 Vertretungsprofessuren/Lehraufträge an den Universitäten/Fachhochschulen Trier, Köln, Hannover, Braunschweig und Wuppertal. Seit 2000 freier Ausstellungsmacher und Autor. Lebt in Bonn. www.klaushonnef.de

---

Joachim Hiller,
born in 1933 in Berlin
1949–53 Studies at the "Master School for Arts and Crafts", Berlin
1954–58 Commercial artist in Berlin
1958–62 Advertising artist in Frankfurt
1963–68 Art director in Hamburg and Frankfurt on Main
Beginning in 1969 freelance painter in Frankfurt on Main
Since 1990 freelance painter in Wiesbaden and Mainz, today in Nierstein
Since 2006 gallery representation by Galerie Nero, Wiesbaden

Authors

Dr. Peter Lodermeyer,
born in 1962 in Ottweiler. Studies of art history, philosophy, and German literature in Bonn. 1997 doctoral thesis in art history, the dissertation being on the still lifes of Picasso. Since 1999 he has been working as a freelance art historian, art critic, author, and occasionally, as curator. Since 2003, in charge of the concept of the international artists projects Personal Structures *and* Personal Structures: Time–Space–Existence *(Publications, symposiums, lectures). Since 2005, regular contributor to* Sculpture *(USA), since 2007, contributor to* Junge_Kunst. *Lives and works in Bonn.*
www.lodermeyer.com

Professor Klaus Honnef,
born in 1939 in Tilsit. Studies of sociology and history in Cologne. Beginning in 1960, freelance journalist. 1965—1970. Editor and Division Chief for Culture for Aachener Nachrichten. *Worked several years as artistic director, executive director, head of exhibitions in Aachen, Muenster, and Bonn. 1972 and 1977 Coorganizer of the documenta V and VI in Kassel. 1979—1987 German Commissioner for the Biennale trigon, Steirischer Herbst, Graz. 1980 Honorary professor at the Kunsthochschule Kassel, beginning in 1986 substitute professor and lecturer at universities and higher technical colleges in Trier, Cologne, Hanover, Braunschweig and Wuppertal. Beginning in 2000, freelance exhibition organizer and author. Lives in Bonn. www.klaushonnef.de*

Worte des Danks

Peter Lodermeyer hat Person und Werk des Künstlers detailliert nachgezeichnet. Entstanden ist eine erste kunstkritische und kunsthistorische Würdigung, die Hillers Kunstauffassung und Herstellungstechniken dem Leser nahe bringt, Verweisungen zur zeitgenössischen Kunst anführt und sie mit Hillers Auffassungen und Ausformungen in Bezug setzt.

Klaus Honnef zeichnet in seinem Vorwort ein pointiertes Bild von Joachim Hiller.

Elizabeth Volk übernahm die nicht leichte Aufgabe, den gesamten deutschen Text in amerikanisches Englisch zu übersetzen, was sie mit profunder Sprach- und Sachkenntnis elegant meisterte.

Der Berliner Galerist Walter Bischoff hat im vergangenen Jahr seine Räume in Berlin für eine erste Ausstellung und im Museum Villa Haiss Zell a. H. für eine Werkschau zur Verfügung gestellt, Hillers Arbeiten erstmals der Szene präsentiert und wichtige Arbeiten des Künstlers auf der *art KARLSRUHE* vorgestellt.

Susanne Kiessling richtet Hiller bereits seit 2006 in ihrer Wiesbadener Galerie Nero jährlich eine Ausstellung aus – ein Raum der Galerie ist sogar ganzjährig für Hiller exklusiv reserviert.

Der Verlag dankt ihnen und allen anderen herzlich, die am Zustandekommen dieser ersten Werksübersicht mitgewirkt haben und kündigt an, dass dies nicht die letzte Publikation über den Künstler Joachim Hiller sein wird. Da er nach wie vor täglich arbeitet, bleibt Raum für weitere Entdeckungen und Deutungen, denn sein künstlerisches Konvolut ist noch nicht gesichtet und katalogisiert.

Wir wünschen uns, dass diese Publikation mit dazu beitragen möge, das bereits vorhandene Interesse an dem vielfältigen und breit angelegten Werk von Joachim Hiller zu vergrößern.

Peter Feder und Robère Scholz
Soest, Februar 2009

Words of Thanks

Peter Lodermeyer has portrayed both the person and the work of the artist Joachim Hiller in great detail. This book is a first acknowledgement of art criticism and art history, introducing Hiller's understanding of art and his working process to the reader. Lodermeyer cross-references contemporary art and places it in relationship to Hiller's views and the shapes his art has taken.

Klaus Honnef draws a pointed picture in his foreword for Joachim Hiller.

Elizabeth Volk has completed the difficult task of translating the German text into American English—showing her profound knowledge and competence both in subject and in language.

Walter Bischoff, the Berlin gallerist, made space available last year for a first exhibition in Berlin and at the Villa Haiss in Zell a. H. in Baden-Württemberg. It was Bischoff who introduced Hiller's work to the art scene for the first time and presented important pieces at the art KARLSRUHE *fair.*

Susanne Kiessling has been organizing annual exhibitions of Hiller's works at her Wiesbaden Galerie Nero since 2006—one room at the gallery has even been exclusively reserved for Hiller's work throughout the entire year.

The publisher expresses his sincere gratitude to these people and to all of those involved in this first survey, announcing at the same time that this will not remain the last publication concerning the artist Joachim Hiller. Since the artist still works daily, there is much room left for further discovery and interpretation, especially since the scope of his entire artistic output has not yet been viewed and catalogued.

We do hope that this publication will serve as a further contribution towards increasing the interest which already exists in Joachim Hiller's diverse and comprehensive oeuvre.

Peter Feder und Robère Scholz
Soest, February 2009

Übersetzung/*Translation*
Elizabeth Volk, Sinzig
Korrektorat/*Proofreading*
B. Thomas Huber, Redaktions-Service K+I, Hannover
Fotos/*Photos*
Heiko Marcher, atelier weitblick, Beckum
Peter Quirin, Wiesbaden
Umschlag/*Cover*
Acryl auf Leinwand/*Acrylics on canvas*
1985, 70 x 90 cm (Ausschnitt/*Detail*)

Herausgeber/*Publisher*
arthellweg verlag+agentur

Erschienen März 2009 bei/*Published March 2009 by*
arthellweg verlag+agentur, Peter Feder und Robère Scholz GbR
Metzer Weg 16a, 59494 Soest
E-Mail post@arthellweg.de
www.arthellweg.de
ISBN 978-3-938966-13-6
ISBN 978-3-938966-14-3 (Vorzugsausgabe/*Special edition*)